# NO
# ESCAPE
# ZONE

# NO
# ESCAPE
# ZONE

## Nick Richardson

LITTLE, BROWN AND COMPANY

A *Little, Brown* Book

First published in Great Britain in 2000
by Little, Brown and Company

Copyright © 2000 by Nick Richardson

The moral right of the author has been asserted.

A CIP catalogue record for this book is available from the British Library.

ISBN 0 316 85314 3

Typeset in Goudy by M Rules
Printed and bound in Great Britain by Biddles Ltd, *www.biddles.co.uk*

Little, Brown and Company (UK)
Brettenham House
Lancaster Place
London WC2E 7E

# ACKNOWLEDGEMENTS

I owe so much to so many people, but special thanks go to the following.

Oz Phillips, for his support and confidence throughout the Bosnia operation and afterwards as a dear friend. BAe for making the Sea Harrier capable of surviving a missile strike. The Martin Baker ejection seat – what a ride – it saved my life. Oskar, Amira and the people of Beric – if you are still around – I owe you one. The ultimate professionalism and flexibility of A21 SAS: you guys don't get paid enough. Misha for the cigarette-holder and Mary for the stitch-up job. The French special force Puma crew: you are the best. Captain Terry Loughran (Big Tel) and all of the members of 801 NAS (1994) for their support and understanding. Mark Lucas and Nick Cook, without whom this book would never have been possible. Yvonne and the kids, for giving me the will and determination to make it out. And last, but not least, June, for her love and support through the good times and the bad.

# PROLOGUE

The yellowcoat's hand changed from a balled fist into the signal that gave me my instruction to roll: fingers and thumb of the right hand splayed wide, the gesture held there in freeze-frame for a good long moment.

I felt *Ark Royal* heave as another big wave started to ride the length of her. The swell merged uncomfortably with the steel claw that was already raking its way through my guts. No matter how many times I launched off the deck of a ship, each time seemed like the first. Controlled bloody mayhem, rendered more interesting by a two-minute infusion of high-octane adrenalin.

The Sea Harrier's Pegasus engine was already belting out tons of thrust, but still I toggled the throttle for more. The aircraft bucked against the brakes and held there, its entire rear half hanging over the fan tail, with nothing but the height equivalent of a six-storey block of flats between me and the surface of the Adriatic. A little extra power never hurts at this stage if you want to keep from deep-sixing over the side.

Out of the corner of my eye I caught a glimpse of angry grey eddies and white foam whipped up by *Ark Royal*'s powerful screws, then the rear of the ship started to haul back up again. Never mind the yellowcoat. This was the real signal to move.

I released the brake and eased the Sea Harrier forward.

The yellowcoat gave me a thumbs-up and pointed to the flight deck officer, the FDO, distinguishable by his white vest; my next point of contact.

I manoeuvred the aircraft down the tramlines, reached the 500ft marker and stopped. My wingman was visible in my mirror a respectable distance behind me.

Five hundred feet between you and the ramp exit feels like nothing when you're sitting in a fully loaded aircraft – a thin skin of aluminium wrapped around several tons of fuel, a quaking power-plant and several million quid's worth of electronics. On this occasion, because of the high threat level, I had the additional weight of a 1,000lb bomb to contend with. Why we bothered, I couldn't really fathom. No one had dropped a bomb on the Serbs yet. And if the UN carried on the way it was going – moving the goalposts every time Karadzic and his cronies pretended to step into line with UN resolutions – no one ever would.

The FDO was standing 30 feet to my right. He was holding his red flag in the air and the green one down low, his eyes fixed intently on the lights by the bridge that would tell him when he was clear to launch. Seconds from the signal, there was still one last big check I had to do. If the Pegasus was going to fail on me, I needed to know now.

I rotated the engine nozzles all the way down and spun up the power. The Pegasus's fan is as wide as a big family saloon car and the noise that it throws out is deafening. Even with his ear-defenders on, the FDO winced visibly.

He was so close I could see the tautness of his expression and rivulets of spray on his face. The poor sod had been out here long enough for a thin crust of salt to form like fine powder on his cheeks and in little drifts in the corners of his mouth. Even though I was only seconds away from being launched across the tops of the waves, I knew where I'd rather be.

The rule book said you needed to be registering 100 per cent or more as you thundered down the deck. After one second of roll, though, I was committed to launching whether I got full power or not. A carrier deck is a place of simple truths.

The light on my instrument panel told me I was riding a good engine. I brought the throttle back to idle, rotated the nozzles aft, and then, almost immediately, shoved the power back up to 55 per cent. Ahead of me, I could see the bow starting to fall and the first licks of ocean swelling beyond the grey metal of the ship. Come on, I found myself willing the FDO as I risked a last glance at my flickering engine instruments. Let's light the bloody candle.

I got my wish.

I had a momentary impression of the lights changing below the bridge, then the FDO brought up his green flag. I slammed the throttle forward. There was a seemingly interminable pause as the Pegasus fought to reach full power. The sound of its screaming machinery filled the cockpit. I stood on the brakes and felt the vibration transmit through my feet into my body. The aircraft wanted to go, but not yet, I told it, not yet.

I shoved the throttle to the stops and the power hit 100 per cent. The aircraft started to skid across the deck. I released the brakes and felt a giant boot in the back as 21,000lb of thrust shot out of the nozzles and propelled the Sea Harrier forward.

The FDO and the bridge disappeared in a sickening streak of colour on the periphery of my vision.

A quick glance at the rpms, a minute adjustment on the rudder bars to keep the aircraft straight and I was heading for *Ark Royal's* ski-jump at the speed of heat. For a brief moment it filled my vision: a grey mountain, almost indistinguishable from the sea beyond. Then I shot over the ramp, gasping as the aircraft, no longer supported by the deck, lurched towards the waves.

Before it lost all its ballistic energy, I rotated the nozzles 35 degrees and felt the cushioning downward thrust of the Pegasus as I clawed for airspeed.

Only when I heard the ker-klunk of the undercarriage as it folded into the belly of the plane did I relax my grip on the stick and tilt the Sea Harrier towards the Dalmatian coastline.

Twenty minutes later, a crackle in my headset signalled I had a message inbound. The voice of the AWACS controller steadied on the ether.

'Vixen Two-Three, this is Magic from Chariot. Proceed to Italy and contact Fortune Zero-Five on TAD Three.'

I acknowledged before I had absorbed all the information. My sixth sense must have already got the gist of it, though, because the hairs on the back of my neck were standing up. Something big was going down and we'd just flown into the thick of it. The exercise had switched to something infinitely more deadly.

I checked my map. 'Italy' – codename for the besieged town of Gorazde – was 20 miles to the south-east of my present position, 10,000ft over the battered ruins of Sarajevo.

I banked the Sea Harrier and reached for the bundle of OS maps tucked under my left leg.

Keeping one eye on my instruments, I picked out the main map from the fan of charts, shoved those I didn't need back under my thigh, then did a swift bit of one-handed origami to ensure that the folds of the main map took me away from the Sarajevo area and out over Gorazde.

My last move in this cockpit version of Twister was to open up my notebook – an aircrew companion known as the 'green brain' – at the page containing the authentication codes the forward air controller, the FAC, had to provide to demonstrate that he was genuine.

I looked up and saw the weather closing in. The cloud cover over Sarajevo had been intermittent, but the base of the dotted cumulus stacks had steadied at around 12,000ft. As I rocketed towards Gorazde, I found myself reluctantly forcing the nose of the aircraft down towards the 10,000ft mark. To see the target, I needed to stay below the angry wisps of grey steam vapour that seemed to be bunching over the target area.

I cursed under my breath. I was heading for SAM City and there was not a damned thing I could do about it.

Before I had taken off, I had refamiliarised myself with the locations of Serbian SA-2 and SA-6 missile batteries. These were ancient but formidable Soviet-supplied surface-to-air missile systems – SAMs – with operating altitudes of 90,000ft and 50,000ft respectively. Because our intelligence was up to speed on the positions of these weapons it was easy enough to steer clear of them, but what the intel guys couldn't plot, because there were just too many of them, were the Serbs' man-portable air defence systems, or

MANPADS, shoulder-launched missiles. On top of that, there was the Triple-A, anti-aircraft artillery. That was bloody everywhere, too.

Normally, neither the MANPADS nor the Triple-A bothered us that much, because we spent most of our time above their effective height range of 10,000ft. But as I watched my altimeter dip below the magic safe base height mark, I kissed all that goodbye. I'd just crossed into a very dangerous patch of sky.

The green brain contained the codes that hooked me into the new frequency. Trying to read this shit as I'm thudding through the choppy air spinning up from the mountains below is like trying to read a telephone directory while driving round a pot-holed version of the M25 at 120mph. At last the numbers swam into view. I reached up and twisted five dials low down on my left-hand side.

'Vixen Two-Three. TAD Three. Go.' I checked with my wingman that he was tuned in as we readied ourselves at the top of the switchback ride.

I'm a family man with three kids. I pictured them back home, savouring the sunshine of a warm, mid-April afternoon, or dodging the showers on a shopping run in the local town. This isn't really happening, the voice in my head attempted. It's just another alert. It'll all be over by the time you get there, mate. You wait. You'll see.

Sixty seconds to target.

'Vixen Two-Three,' I checked with the wingman.

'Two-Four,' his reply crackled back.

As a pair, a fighting unit, we're locked and loaded. Now to make contact with the FAC.

'Fortune Zero-Five, this is Vixen Two-Three.'

There was a brief pause, then a voice burst in my ears: 'Vixen Two-Three, this is Fortune Zero-Five. You're loud and clear.'

At the first attempt, I failed to get the necessary authentication off the guy. As I was wondering what the problem was, I heard what at first I took to be an irregular jamming signal, like a series of thumps. Then it started to dawn on me what was happening.

'We haven't got time for this shite, mate!' the voice on the ground yelled in between more artillery bursts. 'We're getting bloody shelled here!'

Through the head-up display, the HUD, I could now see a pall of smoke between the ground and the cloud base ahead of me.

'Authenticate, X-ray Yankee,' I insisted.

Three or four seconds ground by. The airspeed indicator was clipping 440 knots. The tension was killing me.

Suddenly, there was a crackle in my headset. 'Bravo. It's Bravo.'

I heard several more bursts of shellfire. Then the FAC said: 'We know there's a tank or two above the ridgeline to the north of Gorazde. That's what you're gonna take out, mate. All right?'

I grabbed the map and scoured the topography. A moment later I found it, a sharp divide between two alpine faces running north–south about 10 miles north of the besieged Muslim enclave. I was now down to only 8,000ft, right in the heart of the MAN-PADS and Triple-A envelope.

I shot over Gorazde, banking the Sea Harrier to the left. Columns of smoke were rising from the houses below, but in the still air it could have been wood smoke. It was not what I imagined at all. From my vantage-point, there was little discernible damage.

The ridgeline suddenly veered towards me. For a brief couple of seconds, it undulated and coiled below the aircraft. And then it was gone. I was out over the mountains again and pulling into a 'dumb-bell' manoeuvre that would bring me back again, this time from another direction.

As I hauled back on the stick, feeling the gs wrenching at my oxygen mask and sucking my guts into my boots, my brain tried to review every nook and cranny of the densely wooded topography I'd just seen.

'Vixen Two-Four, spot anything?' I asked.

He was positioned 500 yards behind me and a little to the right, in strike formation. I was about 500 feet below the base of the clouds. He was a little higher. As wingman, his job was to watch out for me. Over this place, that meant keeping his eyes peeled for SAMs.

'Negative.'

I heard the disappointment in his voice. The FAC must have caught it, too. 'We're pretty bloody sure there are two tanks down there, mate,' he yelled, hope in his voice. 'Do you see 'em?'

The ridgeline loomed large in the HUD again. I banked the

aircraft and peered hard past the canopy glare. My eyes watered with the effort.

'Come on!' the FAC yelled, incredulous when I told him I'd found nothing, 'you must have seen 'em.'

I elected to give it one last try. This time I pressed even lower, scanning the terrain feverishly as I tore towards the ridgeline. For a moment I could see nothing but trees. Then, quite unexpectedly, a plume of smoke broke through the branches.

Instinctively, I made a minute course correction towards it and shot overhead. As I did so, I caught the unmistakable outline of an olive-green main battle tank. And then I spotted another. The second vehicle was on the move, sending a stream of thick, clogging exhaust into the air.

'Tally!' I yelled. 'Two T-55s.'

'Tally!' the wingman responded. He'd seen them, too.

'That's your target,' the FAC announced drily.

As we started pulling round, I asked to be 'cleared live' by Vicenza. This was the authorisation I had to have to drop the bomb. In the meantime I armed the fuse. I was in the middle of this instinctive routine when I heard Vixen Two-Four shout a warning.

'Flares!'

As I hit the countermeasures button to release the flares, I threw my head around, wondering if I'd catch a glimpse of the sliver-thin frame of the projectile as it slammed into the aircraft. Instead, I saw a trail of smoke rising vertically from the ground and disappearing into the cloudbase to my right. My relief was tempered by the realisation that the missile had passed between our two aircraft before I'd had a chance to react.

The voice of the FAC was back in my headset. 'Come on, man. We're getting shelled to shit down here. Do something, for Christ's sake!'

I switched the HUD to ground-attack mode, lined up on the ridgeline and rolled the Sea Harrier into a dive. The tanks slid neatly into the middle of the sight. I pressed the accept button, waiting for the radar to range the distance between me and the tanks, but nothing happened. The diamond symbol that had flashed up with unfailing regularity every time I'd done it on exercise failed on the one occasion I really needed it to materialise.

I hauled back on the stick and pulled into a 5g, 30-degree climb. I went into another dive, but the same thing happened again. Then Vixen Two-Four had a go. The same thing happened to him.

I looked at my gauges. My fuel state was pretty iffy, but I was determined to have one last go. I approached from the north and went into the dive. Once again, the tanks were lined up perfectly in my sights. And once again I failed to get a radar lock.

I was pulling out of the dive, 30 degrees nose-up and feeling sick about the whole thing, when there was a massive bang beneath the aircraft and a violent jolt upwards. For a moment, the force that propelled me against my straps threatened to rip my shoulders off. Then, as a black curtain snapped around my head, there was a fearsome ripping noise, as if my brain and body had just parted company. I found myself falling into a cold place with a beguiling absence of sound. I was still falling when a flash of searingly bright light cut through the darkness, accompanied by an angry, grating noise that seemed to emanate from somewhere behind my eyes.

And then, suddenly, I was staring at a wall of flashing cockpit lights with the master warning horn going off in my ears. I'd been out for less than a second, but it felt as if I'd been to the end of the universe and back.

The Sea Harrier was upside down and hurtling towards the ground.

# CHAPTER 1

When I reported for the shareholders' meeting – a session colloquially known as 'hairy shoulders' – shortly before eight o'clock on the morning of 5 January, it was situation normal: no one had told us anything about anything, even though we already knew something was up. Over the Christmas and New Year break, the TV news bulletins had been full of stark images of the conflict in Bosnia following the collapse of the latest round of EU-sponsored peace talks two days before Christmas. The Serbs had been shelling Sarajevo repeatedly, in blatant contravention of the seasonal ceasefire, and fighting between Muslim and Croat forces in central Bosnia had also escalated sharply. As a result, the rumour-mill at Royal Naval Air Station Yeovilton had gone into overdrive. We were, it was said, poised to sail at any time.

Like so many other people, I didn't begin to understand the centuries-old tensions that had led to the war in the former Yugoslavia, even though I had already been closer to it than most. In the first six months of the previous year I had been deployed with 801 Naval Air Squadron aboard HMS *Ark Royal*, one of three Invincible-class aircraft carriers operated by the Royal Navy, in the Bosnian theatre of operations.

In strictly operational terms, it had been a pretty good waste of our time. Even though the pilots and Sea Harriers of Naval Air Command were the only force in the UK trained for the entire spectrum of air-combat operations – for air-to-air, air-to-ground and reconnaissance missions – for six months we had been relegated to combing the waters of the Adriatic for the low-key threat posed by the former Yugoslav Navy.

The deployment from January to June 1993 had been about showing our face alongside those of the French and the Americans. And now it looked like we were about to go through the motions all over again.

While I was all for doing my duty, I looked forward to the prospect of another stint in the Adriatic, scanning the waves for ancient Croat and Serb torpedo boats and the odd armed trawler, with less than my customary relish. My wife, Yvonne, was due to give birth to our fourth child within the month, and the law of probability said it would not be an easy birth. Alexander, our second child, had come into the world still-born and James, our first, had been delivered in a difficult Caesarian section. Little Hannah had arrived without complication, but the trauma and loss associated with the births of her two brothers were still with us.

As I sipped my coffee outside the shareholders' meeting room, listening to the banter among the other pilots, I confess that it was these family matters that preoccupied my thoughts. It was hard to concentrate on flying, let alone on events taking place in Bosnia.

Every day began with a 'hairy shoulders' meeting. It was the moment when we discussed the upcoming business of the day and received vital meteorological and air-traffic data. On this particular morning, there were some grumbles of dissent about the fact that our new boss, Mel Robinson, had moved the meeting from 0830 hours to 0801 hours in corny if well-meaning homage to the title of the squadron that had just fallen under his command. Rob Brunswick, known as Beasty, was stumbling around lamenting the extra half-hour he could have spent in bed and muttering darkly about what he would do to Mel if he ever caught him in his gun-sight.

A minute or so before eight o'clock, Smitty, the senior pilot – always known as the Splot – ushered us into the shareholders' meeting room, where chairs were laid out for the nine pilots and assorted squadron regulars who are integral to the day-to-day business of keeping eight Sea Harrier FRS1 combat aircraft in the air.

Ranged along the front row, just in front of the overhead projector and the briefer's lectern, were the five people crucial to this operation. They were the CO, Mel; the Splot, Smitty; the air warfare instructor or AWI, a guy called Henry Mitchell; the operations officer or 'Opso', me; and the air engineering officer, or AEO. The AEO, who is responsible for the airworthiness of the Sea Harriers and is known as Big Engines, rarely goes anywhere without his sidekick, the deputy AEO, or Little Engines. Little Engines sat just behind him in the second row.

As I settled into my seat, I was nudged by Dave Ritchie, a pilot who had come up through the system with me, from the helicopters we'd started out on all the way to the élite fixed-wing seat we now occupied. Dave was known as Deke, a gentle corruption of the initials DQ. Deke doesn't like this to get around, but DQ stands for dancing queen, on account of his extraordinary gyrations on the dancefloor.

'Christ, would you take a look at him,' he whispered as Smitty walked past. I hadn't noticed it before, but our senior pilot was hobbling. 'I don't suppose that would have anything to do with the fact that we're about to be informed we're heading for a bloody war zone.' I turned to see a wicked smile on Deke's face. Smitty, it had to be said, was not in the running for the most popular guy on the squadron.

The Splot is central to the smooth running of the unit. It is he, through his close collaboration with Big Engines, who ensures the safe running of the squadron in the air. The Splot is responsible to the CO for all the flying we do and devises our week-in, week-out flying schedule. Having been fortunate enough to have been picked for the Navy's top flying job, we are accorded a fair amount of freedom. But if we start to go off the rails, it is the Splot who whips us back into shape – and, with luck, before the CO ever gets to hear there's been a problem.

But in Smitty's case, for some time it had been apparent that he'd been bending the rails to suit him, not us. With flying hours ever scarcer due to the post-Cold War budget cuts handed down from Whitehall, we needed all the time in a Sea Harrier we could get. Yet somehow, Smitty, the guy in whose hands this allocation rested, always seemed to get twice as many hours in the air as the rest of us, and it did not endear him to us. In the nine months I'd been working for Smitty I'd also learned the hard way not to confide my innermost thoughts to him, as they often had a nasty habit of bouncing back at me from some quite unexpected quarter.

So, all in all, if Smitty had a back problem, I'd be sorry for the guy, but I wasn't going to lose any sleep over it. I didn't have time to ponder the mystery of Smitty's limp any further, however, because on the dot of one minute past eight he called us all to rise for the CO. A second or two later, Mel Robinson breezed in.

Everybody liked Mel and few doubted that one day he'd go all the way to the top. He'd certainly amassed ticks in all the right boxes to make rear-admiral. Mel had started out as a Sea Harrier pilot, but had transferred as a lieutenant at the apogee of his flying career from the 'supplementary list', the personnel pool to which pilots and other non-seafaring oddities get attached, to the 'general list', that part of the Royal Navy reserved for pukka seafarers. Supplementary list careers are capped at lieutenant commander, but general list types can go all the way.

As his penance for deserting the aviation community, however, fate had handed Mel some pretty rough commands, forcing him to earn his bridge watchkeeper's ticket on vessels that routinely slogged along at 15 knots – a far cry from the 450-knot cruising speed of a Sea Harrier. After a few years Mel's need for speed must have been too great, because following a short refresher course on the Sea Harrier, he was back with us at Yeovilton. Mel was a straight, cool bloke who commanded great loyalty from all of us. If the shit was going to go down, I was glad he was in charge.

For the first ten minutes it was business as usual. There were met briefs and air-traffic control briefs and then Big Engines and Little Engines ran through the availability of the aircraft, giving details of the technical problems that would keep some of them on the ground that day.

While all this was going on, I glanced occasionally at Mel, two seats to my left. I tried to read his expression, but the CO wasn't giving anything away. I should have known better from a man who was the self-styled squadron supremo at spoof balls, an absurd game, usually played for drinks in the mess after dinner, in which you have to guess the total number of marbles that are being held in the hands of the participants. Each pilot has three spoof balls in his possession, allowing for a total of twenty-seven if all nine of us are taking part. The game, like its better-known counterpart using coins, is simple enough, except you're not allowed to pitch in a number that's already been offered from the floor and if you do, you're automatically back in the pool. It's largely a game of luck, of course, with some memory skill thrown in, but for Mel it's a deeply personal thing and he throws his all into winning. At his turn, he'll cock his head, stare intently at each clenched hand, suck his teeth a little, and then, following a moment in which you think he's just carried out some highly complex calculation, call out his guess in an intense and sombre tone, like a judge informing a petty criminal how many days he's about to receive in jug.

I could sense the eagerness of every man in the room to know, one way or another, what the hell was going down, but the military is ninety-nine parts bureaucracy to one part action and occasional sheer bloody terror, and 'hairy shoulders' operates at its own set pace irrespective of anything that may be happening in the outside world. So before we found out whether we were sailing for war, we needed to clarify whether there were any divisional issues that needed attending to.

Each officer had divisions of ten men and women from the ranks in his charge and to these people, many of whom were straight out of school and away from home for the first time, he was expected to act as surrogate father, confidant and guide. On this occasion, so soon after our return to the air station, none of us was yet apprised of the inevitable problems that had arisen over the Christmas break. But I braced myself for the usual diet of family and financial difficulties, exacerbated, as they are for us all, by the pressures of Christmas and the New Year.

At long last, the CO got to his feet. After all the preamble, his words might have come as an anti-climax, but the sense of anticipation had not dissipated and Mel, the spoof ball king, milked it to dramatic effect. He stood ramrod straight, looked at each of us in turn and tapped the side of his nose with his forefinger, as if he were trying to probe exactly what we knew.

'I've heard all the banter, so you obviously know that something is going down,' he said, adopting a magisterial tone. 'You've seen the same images I have on the news and so what I'm about to tell you won't come as any major surprise. For your information, however, I've had a signal that *Ark Royal* will be sailing for the Adriatic and that we'll be going with her. I've had no specific date yet, and no specific instructions, but you should count on the fact that we'll be heading for the Med soon – probably in about a week's time.'

He paused for a moment before continuing. 'I've got ultimate faith in you and in your professionalism. I know you'll do a great job in the Adriatic. I know you all pretty damned well and I consider it a great honour to be going into war with you. But this situation has cropped up at short notice and we've all got a lot of work to do before we can declare ourselves ready in all respects to go to theatre.'

His last remark was directed primarily at Smitty, Henry Mitchell and me. As Splot, air warfare instructor and Opso respectively, we were the individuals on whose shoulders most of the preparations fell. My mind worked quickly to try to compute where we'd need to direct our training in the little time we had left before we were declared to the coalition force assembled off the Yugoslav coast.

Aside from our one week on land, we'd also have some preparatory time on board *Ark Royal* before we arrived in the Adriatic. We were fairly up to speed on the air-to-air portion of the Sea Harrier's three-pronged role as we'd practised the air defence mission pretty much exclusively since our return from theatre six months earlier. But without the 'spins', those 'specific instructions' telling us what would be required of us when we got to the Adriatic, it was impossible to know on what to concentrate our precious training time. Nonetheless we couldn't afford to sit twiddling our thumbs and waiting for news.

I was still pondering this conundrum when the meeting broke up and the three of us assembled in Henry's office for further discussion. As AWI, it was Henry's responsibility to formulate all our air-combat tactics and to determine what munitions we'd need to take with us on board *Ark Royal*. The nature of their jobs – plotting moves and manoeuvres designed specifically to kill the enemy in the air and on the ground – means that AWIs need to be fairly aggressive individuals and Henry was no exception. His favourite expression was 'fucking one-eye', directed with feeling towards anyone who prevented him from fulfilling his duties. More often than not, it was some unfortunate 'fish-head' – a naval aviation term for RN personnel who serve on board ships – who bore the brunt of his venom.

Henry was also a man of prodigious musical talent, especially on the piano, and this would be utilised in the mess after dinner for colourful renditions from the squadron songbook. His speciality – one that required infinitely more skill than at first seemed obvi-ous – was off-key dirges punctuated with bum notes and facial contortions in the manner of the late Les Dawson.

'Bloody typical,' Henry bristled, his face reddening under his fair hair. 'No spins yet. So what the hell do we do? You know what it's like once we get on board ship: the moment the bloody fish-heads get their hands on our jets, they don't want to let us off again.' Henry continued to rant, pacing up and down and paying little attention to either Smitty or me. 'It's always the way, but it drives me nuts. As Mel so rightly observed, we've got a lot of work to do before we're ready.'

He paced on, chin in hand, for a moment or two, then he looked at me. 'Nick, when was the last time you did any steep-dive work?'

I told him it was about a year ago. I could see which way his thoughts were heading. We would be in the Adriatic in three weeks' time, four at the most. If things stuck to their traditional pattern, we could be arriving on station still with no real direction from the top brass on the specific nature of our mission. That gave us less than a month to prepare for all eventualities. We were fairly proficient in the air-to-air role, but in air-to-ground the squadron was most definitely lacking.

Steep diving was about the most demanding aspect of our air-to-ground work. It was a bombing method we relied on for delivering our trusty old 'iron' bombs – bombs that did not rely on any form of 'smart' guidance – on to the target. The steeper the dive, the higher you could release your weapons. If we were ever called to account in the former Yugoslavia, our bombing height would be critical, since the place was supposedly awash with man-portable air defence systems and Triple-A, venerable anti-aircraft artillery. Triple-A was a throwback to the Second World War, but it had cost the Royal Air Force dearly during the campaign against Saddam Hussein in Iraq in 1991. As a general rule, if you stayed above 10,000ft, you kept yourself outside the MANPADS and Triple-A engagement envelope. Knowing exactly when to pull out of the steep dive over a place like Bosnia could well prove the difference between life and death.

The trouble was, steep diving required a lot of practice – and over land, not sea. And between Portsmouth and the Adriatic, with one notable exception, land was going to be in pretty short supply. The exception was Decimomannu in Sardinia, an air-to-air and air-to-ground weapons range which was the closest thing to the US Navy's famous 'Top Gun' school NATO had this side of the United States.

'Do you think you could work out the logistics of booking us into Deci en route to the Adriatic?' Henry asked me between pacings. 'If we fly off the carrier somewhere close to Gib, we could get maybe a week's worth of practice on the ranges there and still arrive on station just about on schedule. *Ark Royal*'s captain isn't going to like it, but we'll have to persuade him that the risks of not doing it are too great. I'm thinking particularly of the newer squadron members, people like Mowgli and Beasty. Without some serious steep-dive practice at Deci, they'll get creamed. Shit, maybe we all will. So, see what you can do, eh?'

I told him I'd get on to it straight away. In my mind's eye, I could already see the magnitude of the task ahead. Basically, it entailed flying the Sea Harriers off *Ark Royal* as the carrier neared the Straits of Gibraltar. A quick refuelling stop in Gib and then we'd be off again, destination Sardinia. The distance involved would necessitate a top-up en route and that meant air-to-air refuelling courtesy of the Royal Air Force. As Opso, organising all of this was my responsibility. The interesting bit would be at Deci itself. Deci was one big war-gaming operation, with whole areas set aside for air-to-air and air-to-ground work. From what we had just agreed, it looked as if we'd want to spend most of our time over the bombing range at Capo Frasca. I made a mental note to inquire about availability on the air-to-air range – the dogfighting facility – while I was about it. Something at the back of my mind told me we might need it.

Henry turned to Smitty, who had just lowered himself awkwardly on to a chair next to me and was now performing a one-handed massage on the lower part of his back.

'Splot, is there any chance we could work up a decent idea of the threat? Chances are nothing's changed since the '93 deployment, but the picture is confusing out there and, well, you never know.'

Smitty grunted. It was interesting to watch the shifting relationship between these two key players on the squadron. With Smitty's back playing up the way it appeared to be, I could see the way things were drifting. Smitty was still the boss when it came to all matters aerial on the unit, but to look at him now, all quiet and subdued, it was almost as if he had wiped himself out of the picture already.

'From memory, the Serbs are using MiG-21s in the air intercept role and Galebs, Oraos and a mixed bag of helicopters for strike and close air support,' he said. 'But for the details, I'll get Beasty on to it.'

We found Beasty outside the briefing room engaged in some banter with three other pilots, Oz, Shaggy and Deke, about how many kills you required to become an ace. The mood among the pilots – young, predominantly single guys with little in the way of family ties – was bright and breezy. It was twelve years since the Falklands, British naval aviation's finest hour since the Second World War, and the guys were eager for action. I confessed to feeling a ripple of excitement myself, but from a markedly different perspective. I was thinking about what I was going to tell Yvonne, eight months' pregnant and with our two small children in tow. Word of the deployment would already be travelling like wildfire and I wanted to be sure she heard it from me and not from anybody else.

I picked my moment during a lull in the preparations, jumped in the car and drove home. I was due in the cockpit for an air combat manoeuvring sortie against Deke at three, but if I put my foot down, I reckoned I could be back on the base soon after lunch, before anyone had really missed me.

There is no good way to break the news to people you love that you're heading for a place from which you might never come back, but during the drive home this did not stop me from trying to find a form of words that would soften the blow. I was still wrestling with this impossible task when I pulled up outside the house we had bought in a village close to the base.

I got out of the car and crossed the road. Sunlight glinted off a fine layer of dew lining the roofs above the main street. From somewhere, I could smell wood smoke. As I placed the key in the lock of our front door, the silence of the Somerset countryside was broken only by muffled sounds inside: the dull clank of activity as Yvonne moved around the kitchen, a low burble from the TV.

Then my ears pricked to a new sound: a Sea Harrier climbing away from Yeovilton on a training sortie. I could still hear it as I stepped into the house and shut the door behind me.

Yvonne was standing in the kitchen, her back to the window. With the light behind her, I could not see her face, but she could clearly see mine. She took a step towards me, then stopped. 'You don't have to say a thing, Nick. All I really need to know is how long we have before you leave.'

It took me a moment to gather myself. 'Who told you?'

'The TV's been full of it all morning. Bosnia this, Bosnia that. No one told me. I just knew.' She half turned and I saw that she'd been crying. 'The look on your face when you walked in didn't help.' She managed a half-smile. 'Never get captured, Nick. You'd be lousy under interrogation.'

'*Ark Royal*'s got to be in the Adriatic by the end of the month,' I told her. 'We sail in a week's time.'

Yvonne passed her hands briefly over her stomach, feeling for the baby. She told me she'd seen pictures on the lunchtime news of a young Muslim woman, heavily pregnant, dodging a sniper's bullets in Sarajevo. At that moment something had told her that I wouldn't be spending much of 1994 at Yeovilton.

'Why you again?' she asked, after a long silence. 'Last year, they hardly used you at all. You were bored. And pissed off, I seem to remember.'

I struggled to decide what to tell her. It was obvious to me that FONA – Flag Officer Naval Aviation – would not have pushed for this deployment if we were simply going to be used for another round of hunt-the-fishing-boat; that the only reason we would be going to the Adriatic so soon after our last excursion was because someone high up the UK chain of command had hinted that, if it came to a fight, we would be among those seeing action.

But this wasn't the moment to talk about such details. 'I should think it'll be much of the same this time,' I tried.

She touched my cheek. 'Thanks, Nick, but you're also a terrible liar. The kids and me will be fine. Just look after yourself, OK?'

The conversation had been punchy and terse, but I knew she meant what she said. It didn't make it any easier, but at least it had broken the ice.

Over lunch, we discussed anything but the deployment. Naval wives are part of a close-knit community and I knew that our friends would rally round to ensure that Yvonne was well looked after while the squadron was away. I'd been at sea for so much of our married life that Yvonne and I slipped into a well-rehearsed routine. For the sake of the children as much as for ourselves, we decided to make the best of the little time we had left together.

An hour and a half later, I was cruising at 24,000ft in the cold blue somewhere above the Bristol Channel. Ground Control had just vectored me on to Deke's Sea Harrier and I was head down over the scope waiting for the moment when I picked him up on radar. An air-combat manoeuvring sortie was normally something I relished, but today I couldn't shake from my mind the image of Yvonne in the kitchen, staring at me, cradling her stomach.

Maybe it would have been better if we'd said all the things that we'd held back from saying over lunch. I'd been around for less than six months of the previous year while our two kids had been growing up, and now it looked as if I wouldn't see our third until he or she was crawling across the living-room floor.

High on the centre of the scope, I caught the first faint image of a radar return.

'Judy, Judy,' I called over the radio – the signal to Ground Control that I had acquired Deke on my radar.

I checked along the wings for the snub nose of the dummy AIM-9 Sidewinder missile that we carry on ACM sorties like this. The 'pod' is an AIM-9 tube with a fully representative seeker in the nose, but, lacking the rocket motor of a real missile, it never leaves the wing. When its infra-red sensor picked up the heat source of Deke's jet, it would give me all the cues I would get from a real AIM-9, culminating, I hoped, in the growl in my headset signalling that I had him 'locked up'.

For the purposes of the exercise, the first pilot to lock on to his opponent and call 'Fox Two' – Sidewinder missile kill – was the winner. Depending on how things went, we normally expected to carry out five or six individual dogfights in an hour. The limiting factors are exhaustion brought on by lengthy exposure to high-g manoeuvres – manoeuvres in which, if the turn is tight enough, your body can end up weighing almost seven times its normal weight – and, of course, fuel state.

Within seconds, I had acquired Deke visually, a tiny glint in the pale band of sky between the curvature of the earth and the black expanse of space beyond. In another second, we were on each other and I was hauling back on the stick, grunting against the onset of g, as we went into the fight.

The inflatable bladder in the upper part of my g-trousers kicked me in the stomach as the turn tightened. It might have stopped all the blood in my upper body from draining into my boots, but I still felt myself mushing towards g-induced loss of consciousness, which we call g-loc, as I fought to keep Deke off my six o'clock position. After the excesses of Christmas, everything bloody hurt.

Seconds later, we were in a spiralling right-hand turn and still pulling a hideous amount of g. I knew that Deke was right on my tail and getting closer, narrowing the angle on me, eating into my six.

I cursed into my oxygen mask. All my co-ordination was out. The hairs on the back of my neck prickled as I sensed the tail of my aircraft pulling into the viewframe of Deke's heat-seeking AIM-9. To stand any chance of getting away from him, I had to tighten the turn. But try as I might, it wasn't happening.

I had pinpricks of pain all over my upper body as blood vessels popped under the pressure of the turn. Ahead, I could see only a narrow stretch of horizon as the edges of my vision began to grey out.

And that was when I lost it. In a moment of apparent clarity, I felt I knew how to outwit Deke, but it turned out to be the worst thing I could have done. When someone is chewing into your six o'clock position in a hard and sustained turn, you never, ever reverse the turn by rolling out of it. Yet that's precisely what I did; and the moment it happened, sense got the better of me, because I realised I was dead.

'Fox Two,' I heard Deke call, a mixture of surprise and relief in his voice.

I felt sick with disgust at my performance. 'Roger. Terminate, terminate,' I announced, almost spitting out the words. I knew there was no point in continuing. Any attempts on my part to get back at Deke would simply be a waste of fuel. We might as well head home.

As soon as we landed, taxied and switched off, I jumped down from the aircraft and headed for a place where I could have a quiet smoke prior to the debriefing. I was in the shadows of the squadron office, pulling on my second cigarette and wincing at the memory of the fight, when I heard footsteps behind me. I braced myself for a string of insults as Deke followed up the success of his engagement with a homily to his own flying skills and a poke at mine.

But Deke and I went back a long way and I guess he knew when it was OK to lay on that particular piece of Top Gun panto and when it was time to ease back.

'Did you go and see Yvonne this afternoon?' he asked me.

I nodded.

'How did she take the news?'

I looked up at him. 'Surprisingly well.'

'Then what's the problem, Nicko? I've never known you to make a fundamental error like that.'

I threw the cigarette on to the ground and stubbed it out. 'I'm just not sure I should be going to theatre right now. The baby's due in a month and I'm trying to put it all in focus. You know, kids, career, wife, flying – the whole shebang.'

'In six months' time, you're going to look back on this moment and wonder what the hell you were worrying about.'

'Right. But the Yugoslavs aren't the Iraqis, Deke. They're good. Read the threat reports.'

'Nicko, this is what we've trained for all our professional lives. This is the whole damned reason you and I joined the Fleet Air Arm, isn't it?'

'Yes,' I said. 'It is.'

Deke paused, then said: 'If anyone had asked me yesterday, I'd have said you'd be the one making this speech and I'd be the guy in your shoes. Yvonne and the kids will be fine, Nick. Stick to worrying about yourself – and us – and you'll be fine, too. We're the best damned pilots this country has, and we're good at looking out for each other. The Serbs aren't going to know what's hit them. Trust me.'

At midnight, an hour after I had lapsed into a fitful sleep, Yvonne nudged me in the ribs. At first, I was not wholly inclined to believe what she was telling me. There was another month to go before anything should be happening, I stammered blearily. But Yvonne, who'd had three more kids than me, and was more than fed up with carrying our fourth, told me that the contractions were real and gathering in intensity. If I didn't want to be delivering the baby myself, she suggested with a forced grin, I'd better start getting the car warmed up.

We left the kids with neighbours and drove hard for the hospital in Taunton. Within an hour, despite initial fears that she'd have to undergo an emergency Caesarian, Yvonne gave birth naturally and we had a new baby boy: Kristian Alexander. But he was dangerously premature, weighing in at a mere 4.5lbs, and almost as soon as we had had our first look at him he was rushed off and placed in an incubator. For the next few days it would be touch and go, the doctors told me. After the trauma of Alexander's birth three years earlier, Yvonne and I felt shattered.

I stayed with her as long as I could, but by daybreak, all she really needed was rest. And as Kristian was in the full-time care of the hospital staff, there wasn't anything I could usefully contribute by hanging around. Yvonne's mother was already on her way down from her home in the Midlands to look after James and Hannah. For one unnerving moment I felt like a lone navigator adrift in the eye of a surreal storm. As I walked out of the hospital and into the bright sunlight of a crisp, blue January morning, I looked desperately for something to cling on to.

With the sailing so soon and plenty to do to prepare for it, I found myself driving on automatic pilot back to the base. The plan was for the Sea Harriers to join the aircraft carrier a few hours out of Portsmouth, somewhere in the English Channel, as she steamed for Gibraltar. It wasn't just a matter of deploying the eight jets. Everything the squadron needed would have to be in place by the time *Ark Royal* slipped her moorings in Portsmouth in six days' time. That meant not only bombs and fuel, but also spare parts for the Sea Harrier's airframe and Pegasus engine, as well as all the admin that was required to keep the planes in the air. This spanned everything from the flying and technical manuals that detailed every nut and bolt of the airframe right down to marker pens for the overhead projectors for our briefings on board ship.

On top of all this, we had just learned that the squadron would be moving to a new location at Yeovilton while we were in the Adriatic and, in the worst traditions of British bureaucracy, the move had to be completed on time, whatever else was happening in the big, wide world. I knew the Navy would be sympathetic over Kristian's traumatic arrival, but at the same time, life on the squadron and my central role in its operations went on. I was still expected to pull my weight, but more importantly – and this was what continued to drive me on at a time when my emotions were all over the place – I did not want to let my colleagues down.

Over the next five days, life slipped into a curious kind of routine. After our regular shareholders' meeting I would get down to the business of the day. Much of this entailed detailed preparations for our stopover at the Decimomannu training range in Sardinia. Permissions had to be sought for our brief touchdown in Gibraltar and for a tanker aircraft to bridge the gap between Gib and Sardinia – and the paperwork, inevitably, was a nightmare. A big part of the overall problem was that we still didn't know what missions we would be called upon to perform over the Balkans. This would only be rectified when the Royal Navy arranged for a carrier liaison officer (LO) to join the Combined Air Operations Centre (CAOC) at Vicenza in northern Italy. The CAOC was a sophisticated ops room from which all NATO air movements over the former Yugoslavia were controlled.

Every NATO air force taking part in the Bosnian operation had an LO attached to the CAOC, and part of the brief of these people was to secure the best possible missions they could for the air forces they represented. The US Air Force, US Navy, Britain's Royal Air Force plus the French Air Force and Navy all had good representation in the CAOC. If we weren't going to be chasing trawlers round the Adriatic again, we needed a Fleet Air Arm officer in Vicenza who could pull his weight in the company of the big boys. This wouldn't be easy, as we were a tiny percentage of the overall NATO force. But we did have one key advantage, one that an adept LO could work in our favour: the Sea Harrier, being a multi-role platform, was capable of fulfilling just about any mission asked of it. The RAF, by contrast, had Tornado F3 air defence aircraft capable of taking on the Serbs' MiG-21s, and Harrier GR7 and Jaguar GR1 strike aircraft for bombing ground targets, but no aircraft that was capable of performing both roles simultaneously.

Henry Mitchell, our AWI, was right. Our bombing skills were more deficient than our air-to-air skills, and this was where we would concentrate our training when we arrived at Deci. But until we had LO representation at the CAOC, we had to proceed as if we'd be called upon to do everything.

As a result, even while we were preparing things on the ground, our air-to-air training continued. And while I wasn't in the air, working off the Christmas fat, or on the ground, berating hapless individuals over the phone for dragging their feet over arrangements for our transit between Gib and Deci, I had one eye on the clock, waiting for the moment when I could jump in the car to be with Yvonne and Kristian, having first touched base with Yvonne's mum and spent a bit of time with Hannah and James at home. A couple of times I took them to the hospital with me, but mostly I went on my own. Kristian was improving, but he was still on the critical list and I didn't have the wherewithal to explain, nor the kids the capacity really to understand, the reasons for this sudden emotional upheaval in all our lives.

One consequence of these solitary excursions was that I often did not get home until the small hours. A few hours' kip and I was up again and heading off to work. How I was any use to anyone over this period still remains a mystery to me.

The day before the unit made the drive to Portsmouth, ready to embark on *Ark Royal*, I had to give a pep talk to my division on the dos and don'ts of sailing into a combat zone. My division was composed of eight men and two women, all of them either air engineering mechanics (AEMs) or leading aircraft engineering mechanics (LAEMs), the two most junior ranks in the Navy. Part of my job as guide and mentor to these, on the whole, startlingly young individuals – a role I embraced reluctantly – was to ensure that they had everything squared in their personal lives before we left port.

All of them had read the papers and knew of the risks involved. The Yugoslav Navy might not have been equipped with battleships or cruisers, but it possessed enough firepower to do some serious damage to *Ark Royal* while she was steaming off the rugged Dalmatian coastline. The last thing I wanted to do was to put the fear of God into them, but as I stressed the importance of preparing wills and checking that life-insurance premiums were topped up and in order, I could see the penny dropping.

Worried that I may have over-egged the cake, I pulled one of the division members aside as soon as the meeting was adjourned. AEM Billy Borland was a character, but he was also someone I relied upon to present a true picture of a situation when I needed one. If there were any rumblings of dissent within the division, I knew I could trust Bill, whose identical twin brother was on one of the other squadrons at Yeovilton, to give me some warning before things turned nasty. When we were alone, I made a couple of coffees, sat him down and asked him if there were any members of the team I should keep a special eye on while we were at sea.

Billy thought for a moment before answering. I knew that he understood the value of these sessions. If there were problems, they could reverberate not just within the division, but around the squadron itself – and perhaps spread to other portions of the ship. Through our informal get-togethers, Billy and I endeavoured to make sure that nothing reached that stage.

'Leading Arnold's not at all happy about this,' Billy said at length, staring into the depths of his mug as if the dregs of the coffee somehow contained the answers I was looking for. 'You know he's trying to get drafted to Hong Kong, don't you, sir?'

I shook my head and pulled a face. 'No, I did not. Why Hong Kong, for Christ's sake?'

'It's that new Singaporean wife of his. For some reason, the authorities here are holding out on her immigration papers. Arnold's going nuts about it, sir. He's requested the draft to Hong Kong so he can be closer to her.'

I nodded, recalling now snippets of Arnold's case. If I remembered rightly, he had married the girl during a port visit by *Ark Royal* to Singapore Harbour. They had known each other less than a week at the time of the nuptials. Given the circumstances in which they had met and tied the knot, I admired Billy's diplomatic glossing over of the possible reasons why the UK immigration authorities were being a tad tardy in giving the green light for her relocation to these shores. Leading Arnold's wife was an 'exotic dancer'.

'Well,' I answered truthfully, 'we really can't afford to lose him. Arnold's a good man. Let me know how things develop, will you, Bill? Any other problems I should know about?'

Again, Billy stared into his cup. 'Well, Wren Alexander seems to be having boyfriend problems again.'

I rolled my eyes. Wren Alexander was 5ft 3 and stocky, but she was pretty, too, and this, it seemed, had often conspired with her somewhat accident-prone nature to get her into trouble where matters of the heart were concerned. 'What on earth is it this time?'

'He doesn't want her to go, apparently, sir.'

'Does Wren Alexander's boyfriend realise that he doesn't have a whole lot of choice in the matter?' I replied testily. 'I seem to recall that somewhere along the line she volunteered for service at sea.'

I was beginning to wish I'd never asked, but Billy drained his coffee and offered some reassuring remarks about how, on the day, the division, like the squadron itself, would be fine. He, at least, gave me the impression that he was excited and raring to go. I said goodbye, knowing that the next time I saw him would be on *Ark Royal*, somewhere in the English Channel.

There were two other significant developments that day. The first involved Smitty, the 801 Splot whose limp had indeed been brought on by a back injury sustained over the holiday period. It was announced that he would not be flying with us on account of his condition, but he was deemed fit enough, someone senior had decided, to act as our LO at the CAOC in Vicenza. He promised to make up for his absence from the skies over Bosnia by making sure that we were allocated a decent spread of missions – a generous sentiment, of course, but not so reassuring if you're the one in the firing line. The best bit of this development, however, was that Henry Mitchell was to fill the vacant Splot position with immediate effect.

The second development concerned Yvonne and Kristian. Late that afternoon, I got a call from the hospital. While there were still concerns for Kristian, the doctor told me, our baby boy was improving all the time and was at last deemed to be off the danger list. Yvonne, he added, had made such good progress that they were letting her out a day early. I could collect her any time I liked.

As I put the phone down, an enormous feeling of relief washed over me. There was something neatly symmetrical about the way things had panned out. At the eleventh hour, I could fly to the carrier with most of those little loose ends in my personal life tied up. After the lecture I'd given the division, anything less would have been wholly inappropriate.

# CHAPTER 2

On the morning of the squadron's departure for *Ark Royal*, Yvonne drove me into the base and we said our goodbyes. It was a routine that had become all too familiar during our eight years of marriage, and we had learned not to draw it out. One significant difference from earlier deployments, I told her, would be our ability to phone home regularly, and this made my departure a little easier. Someone on the squadron had persuaded Motorola to lend us a mobile satellite phone – a huge, ungainly thing that was sort of a prototype of today's infinitely more portable devices – and this would enable me to keep in touch with Kristian's progress. None of us knew how long the squadron would be away, but the general feeling was that some time over the next month or so NATO jets would deliver the warring parties in Bosnia a lesson they wouldn't forget, the bad guys would fall in line, and before we knew it, we'd be home again.

I told Yvonne that I hoped to see her in six to eight weeks' time.

With most of the squadron's aircraft maintainers already on board ship and steaming full tilt for the Mediterranean, our particular corner of RNAS Yeovilton felt eerily quiet when I arrived.

A light mist still clung to the airfield and was only just beginning to burn off as I headed into shareholders for the briefing that would give us our instructions for joining the ship. Lined up on the apron were our eight Sea Harrier FRS1s. The few remaining groundcrew scuttled around them, hazy silhouettes that appeared, disappeared into and reappeared out of the mist.

In a couple of hours, I thought, the only link between me and Yeovilton will be that aircraft. I'd learned to love the Sea Harrier, but as planes went, she could be a temperamental beast, too. She was no longer in the first flush of her youth. Derived from the original Harrier GR1 that had entered service with the Royal Air Force in the strike role in 1967, the Sea Harrier had adapted well to the maritime environment, but it still retained one or two vices inherited from the original aircraft. The most critical of these was its poor payload-range performance compared with an aircraft that took off and landed conventionally.

The Harrier's inability to carry as much or fly as far as a regular jet fighter was a trade-off born of its most outstanding characteristic: its unique ability to take off and land vertically. In the 1970s, the Russians had made a stab at designing their own vertical/short take-off and landing (V/STOL) naval fighter, but the Yak-38, also known by its NATO name, Forger, was always a pale imitation of its Western counterpart, and by the early 1990s it had been phased out altogether, leaving the Harrier and its derivatives to soldier on as the only operational V/STOL combat aircraft in worldwide service. The derivatives were the AV-8B and GR7 variants, developed by British Aerospace and its partner McDonnell Douglas during the 1980s, and lumped together under the banner programme name Harrier 2. The US Marine Corps and the RAF had several hundred Harrier 2s on order between them, but fine aircraft that it is, the Harrier 2 is primarily a ground-attack plane, a function that has always set it apart from the multi-role Sea Harrier.

In 1982, less than three years after the first examples were handed over to the Royal Navy, the Sea Harrier underwent its most fundamental test when it was dispatched on the carriers HMS *Hermes* and *Invincible* as part of the UK expeditionary force sent to the South Atlantic to oust the Argentinians from the Falkland Islands. During the six weeks that the twenty-eight aircraft flew against the Mirage, Skyhawk and Super Etendard fighter-attack aircraft of the Argentinian Air Force and Navy, the Sea Harriers destroyed twenty-two enemy aircraft in air combat for no losses on their own side (although four were lost in accidents and two to groundfire). In what some have likened to the exploits of 'the few' who defended Britain from the onslaught by the Luftwaffe in the summer of 1940 – though on a much smaller scale – the Sea Harrier FRS1 and its small cadre of pilots kept the Argentinians beyond the range where they could launch Exocet missiles at the two carriers, their primary naval targets. If either of these ships had been disabled, let alone sunk, it is arguable that the British task force would have had the capacity, or the will, to retake the islands. It was truly the aircraft's finest moment.

But twelve years on a whole lot had changed in the big, bad world of combat aviation and the dear old Sea Harrier had failed to keep up with the times. As I headed into 801 Squadron's all but deserted offices that morning, I knew that we were just a small step away in capability terms from being outflanked by the fighter aircraft deployed with the air arms of the former Yugoslavia.

The Bosnian Serbs, the aggressors in Bosnia and the faction viewed as our most likely opponent in the event of a fight, had access to the MiG-21 multi-role fighter and several squadrons' worth of Orao, Jastreb and Super Galeb attack jets. None of these represented a particular threat to us, although the MiG-21, despite its age, came closest. The real question – one with which I hoped Beasty had got to grips following Henry's instruction to get us the gen on the threat – concerned the Bosnian Serbs' access to the Mikoyan MiG-29, NATO codename 'Fulcrum'.

In theory, the MiG-29 was the most potent fighter we would face over the Balkans, although the received wisdom was that almost all of the aircraft in the Yugoslavs' possession – a single squadron's worth, or around a dozen aircraft – had been badly hit by the arms embargo imposed on Belgrade and the other capitals in the region. No MiG-29s had been detected in the air for the best part of a year, leading to the inevitable conclusion that the aircraft were grounded for lack of spares. This was just as well, as the Fulcrum's performance far outstripped the Sea Harrier's.

While the Sea Harrier could barely muster Mach 1 in a dive, the MiG-29 was capable of more than twice the speed of sound in level flight at altitude. And while the Sea Harrier's Blue Fox ranging radar enabled us to sweep the skies up to 30 miles ahead of us, the MiG-29's multi-mode pulse-Doppler model allowed its pilot to see three times as far, and to fire radar-guided air-to-air missiles with a range of 40km or more.

The Sea Harrier's only air-to-air weapon, apart from its optional 30mm gun pods, was the heat-seeking AIM-9M Sidewinder, which was highly effective in a close-quarter dogfight but useless beyond a range of around 8km. We had developed tactics against the MiG-29, because not to have done so would have been suicide. But there was no doubt in any of our minds that our best form of defence against the Fulcrum was to avoid all contact with it – at least until our replacement aircraft arrived.

During the next twelve months, we were due to receive a completely revamped version of the Sea Harrier known as the FA (for Fighter Attack) 2. The FA2 embodied a pulse-Doppler radar of superior performance to the MiG-29's, a vital ingredient that would allow the Fleet Air Arm to wage aerial warfare at beyond visual range (BVR) for the first time in its existence. This was by virtue of the American-designed AMRAAM (advanced medium-range air-to-air missile), which would supersede the Sidewinder as the FA2's primary air-to-air armament. The FA2 would be able to ripple fire up to four AMRAAMs in 'fire-and-forget' mode at four separate targets. But that capability, as wondrous as it was, was still tantalisingly beyond our reach. And for a moment, as I cast my eyes over the rest of the guys as they lolled casually in their flights suits, waiting for Mel to show up at 0801 precisely, I wondered whether someone, somewhere in the upper echelons of the Navy, hadn't been just a little hasty in rushing us to the Balkans.

But if there were any pre-match nerves among my fellow pilots in the moments prior to Mel's arrival, they weren't visible. Henry, who'd eased neatly into his new role as Splot, was pacing up and down, telling anyone who'd listen how little he was looking forward to spending the next few months in the company of so many fish-heads. Deke, who'd made mincemeat of me during our ACM exercise, caught my attention and gave me a hesitant thumbs-up when I joined the throng. I gave him a reassuring nod, a sign that everything was OK at home, and he returned contentedly to reading Shaggy's newspaper over his shoulder.

For Shaggy – Kev Seymour – the Bosnian deployment would be his first flying tour. Shaggy was the only GL – general-lister – other than Mel and, like the boss, he had done plenty of seatime. Because of Shaggy's GL credentials, people who didn't know him thought he was simply biding his time with us supplementary-list types till he could get back on the bridge of a ship. Nothing, however, could have been further from the truth. Shaggy had embraced his stint at the Fleet Air Arm like a zealot and was fiercely proud of his aviator's wings. I had little doubt that Shaggy, like Mel, would end up going a long way.

All the pilots were present except for Gary Langrish, or Gazza, who'd gone on ahead with the rest of the squadron since there were nine pilots and only eight jets. Gazza was a quiet, unassuming sort of bloke – except when he'd had a few drinks, whereupon he became a social hand grenade. After he'd downed his second rum and Coke, you never quite knew what he was going to do or say. There was a time on our previous deployment to the Adriatic when Gazza had administered such a slap-down to the XO of the ship, its second most senior officer, over some clash of culture between us and the fish-heads that he ended up getting ROBed. To be 'required on board' is a bit like being gated at school: tedious and a little shaming. We, of course, were very amused by this, but Mel's predecessor as CO found it a lot less funny. He had to go out and bat for Gazza on several occasions, but always ended up doing so enthusiastically because Gazza was such a fine pilot. I only hoped Gazza would have managed to keep his mouth shut these past twelve hours without our guiding influence or Mel's authority to see him through.

On the other side of the room I spotted Beasty. Anxious to know if he had any fresh gen on the MiG-29 business, I started to make my way towards him, but was beaten to it by Oz Phillips, our resident Australian. In the couple of seconds it took me to cross the floor, they had started to argue. This, in some ways, was inevitable, as Oz is a livewire, known to us as the squadron tannoy system, and Beasty quite the opposite: the quiet, brooding sort. Such a mix, of course, is extremely volatile and when Oz and Beasty were in close proximity the sparks often flew. It was usually good-natured stuff, but with Beasty you could never be sure where or how it was going to end.

Beasty was a fitness freak and the only one among us who had done the All-Arms Commando course at Lympstone in Devon, the headquarters of the Royal Marines. If you're not seeking to become a marine commando or to join the SBS, the marines' equivalent of the SAS, going on this six-week endurance trial is entirely voluntary. Reports from Lympstone had it that Beasty had been in his element, making some of the instructors look like sissies. This must have been particularly galling for them, since Beasty looked like an accountant. But for most of us, it was that dark side of the man that kept us guessing – a subtlety that was lost on Oz, for whom observational niceties were anathema.

The argument was standard fare. Beasty had told Oz to turn down the tannoy and Oz had responded by calling him a poof. This was brave stuff, as there was more than enough time between now and when we flew for Beasty to wedge a horse's head into the footwell of the Australian's cockpit.

I was about to call time when Henry announced Mel's arrival and the CO swept into the briefing room, pulling the rest of us in his wake. There was a palpable sense of expectation as we settled into the session. Take-off, Mel told us, would be at 1100 hours and in two lots of four ships. It would also be a 'simsto' affair – a simultaneous short take-off – which meant four aircraft all rolling on the runway at the same time, then punching into the sky with a puff of downward thrust from the nozzles, followed immediately by the second four-ship formation. This spectacular departure has a dual purpose: it gets our blood pumping a little faster and gives those on the ground something to remember us by while we're gone.

We were given the rendezvous position with *Ark Royal* in the South-Western Approaches, but warned about the weather: it was piss-poor, with rain and mist reducing visibility to a minimum, so everything would be down to our ability to find the carrier on final approach with our Blue Fox radars in sea-search mode. The radar was a big help, but it wasn't infallible. On a radar screen, a large bright blip can be a carrier, but it can just as easily be a supertanker.

Before we left, Mel spent a couple of minutes reminding us what we might expect when we arrived in the Adriatic. A summit meeting of NATO leaders in Brussels had just reaffirmed the alliance's decision of the previous year to use force against the Bosnian Serbs if their attacks on Sarajevo and UN convoys continued. While we'd heard this kind of language before, the big difference this time was that the UN secretary-general, Boutros Boutros Ghali, had expressed his organisation's readiness to accept NATO air strikes, as long as they came from UN Protection Force (UNPRO-FOR) commanders on the ground. The big question was whether the French UN commander in Bosnia, General Jean Cot, had the balls to see the attacks through. In the meantime, Operation Deny Flight, the enforcement by NATO air forces of a no-fly zone over Bosnia-Herzegovina, continued. It looked like we were going to be working our socks off.

'In view of the likelihood that we will be called upon to fly into the threat zone the moment we arrive in theatre, I'm sure I don't have to remind you how much pressure there is on us to deliver,' Mel said. 'As soon as we touch down on deck, we're going to be working up our training routine for the voyage. Sorry, guys, but this ain't going to be no pleasure cruise.'

And that's before anyone starts shooting at us, I thought. I turned to give Deke a theatrical wince, but caught Beasty's eye instead. Beasty wore an expression not unlike one Hannibal Lecter might adopt upon glimpsing his next meal.

The meeting was adjourned and we drifted outside. Just beyond the door, I was stopped by Phil Mould, our newest recruit. None of us knew Phil particularly well, but that hadn't prevented us from giving him his new moniker. Mowgli had hair that stuck straight up in the air, a look that made him seem a bit demented much of the time, although now he looked plain worried.

'What's up?' I asked.

Mowgli coughed nervously. 'What's it like, Nick?'

'What's what like?'

'Being on ship for all that time.'

I thought for a moment. 'It's like doing time, mate,' I replied with a sigh. 'It's like doing fucking time.'

If that didn't help Mowgli's karma, worse was to come. Deke, who'd overheard the exchange, gave the new guy a dig in the ribs. 'Don't let him fool you,' he said with a grin. 'He's not telling it like it is.'

'Oh?' Mowgli said, his face brightening.

'Yeah,' Deke said, in his best Geordie. 'It's like doing fucking time with a better than even chance of drowning.'

I was the third man in the lead four section, sitting on the tarmac, gazing out across the Somerset hills, wondering when I would see them again. It was a moment of mixed feelings; excitement about going to sea, but dread at the same time, the thought of being locked below deck, possibly for months, far from a life that most of the time you take for granted.

At this precise moment, though, as I looked fore and aft and saw three other Sea Harriers lined up for the simsto, and with the thrum of the Pegasus at idle behind me, it was difficult to feel anything other than a great sense of pride and exhilaration. This was it. Into the unknown. No more talk. Just action.

'Vixen Three, ready,' I said, responding to Mel's instruction. His aircraft was 500 yards ahead of mine, its skin reflecting the glare of the high, bright overcast sky.

I counted off the responses from the other pilots behind me, waiting for the order to roll. The remaining four aircraft were in line off the runway, waiting for us to take off.

Then Mel's voice in my headset again: 'Vixen, rolling, rolling, go.'

I caught a puff of black smoke from the nozzles of the two Sea Harriers in front of me as I released the brakes and slammed the Pegasus to full power.

There was a moment's delay before the revs bit. The aircraft kicked me in the back and the hills jarred momentarily across my vision. Then the Sea Harrier leaped forward.

Mel and Henry disappeared in a cloud of spray and steam as the hot exhaust gases from their engines blasted the rainwater off the runway. I glanced constantly between them and the airspeed indicator.

Four seconds later, at 150 knots, there was a clipped instruction from Mel and I pushed the nozzles to 50 degrees. The Sea Harrier jumped into the sky. Mel, Henry, Mowgli and I were airborne in the same instant. I raised the gear and watched my speed climb.

In a few more seconds we were into the clag and setting course for the coast. Five minutes later, when we were cruising happily above the clouds, the back four aircraft formated on us and we banked as one in the direction of 'Mother', a hundred or so miles to the south.

The cloud base was thickening by the minute. There seemed to be an incontrovertible law, drawn up, I suppose, the moment some bright spark decided to land an aircraft on a ship, that a carrier will always sail into a fog bank the first time you fly out to her. According to transmissions from 'Homer', our very own air-traffic control centre on the ship, we could expect some nice, thick stuff when we rendezvoused with her in twenty minutes' time.

Although Homer would talk us down using the ship's radar, before departure we'd entered Mother's co-ordinates into our onboard nav-kits. This was a belt-and-braces procedure. The moment you got within 20 miles of the carrier's position, you fired up your own radar and – if you'd done everything right – there she was, a nice, strong blip on the edge of the screen.

Ahead, I watched as the lead pair, Mel and Henry, dropped into the clouds. Moments later, Mowgli and I followed them down in radar-trail formation: me in front and to the left, Mowgli tucked just behind, within 30 feet of my starboard wingtip. Flying in cloud is like flying into a big, grey fishbowl. Unless you trust your instruments, you can get disorientated in an instant, confusing down with up and vice versa. As I monitored Mother's position on my screen, I followed Homer's instructions and throttled back as he talked me down to the sea.

The idea is to bring the approaching aircraft on to a heading that is the same as the ship's, only slightly off to the right-hand side, dropping all the while to 600ft, by which point the pilot should have his eyes on the carrier. At 800ft I was down to 350 knots and still in the fishbowl. I looked down, hoping to see the first white flecks of the wavetops against the black of the ocean. But left, right, up and down everything looked exactly the same: a wraparound blanket of white steam vapour broken only by the silhouette of Mowgli's jet as he decelerated and we descended towards the sea.

And then, without warning, the cloud evaporated and we were over the water, the wave trails of a large ship's wake fanning out in a perfect chevron in front of me. At the head of it was a faint dot below a low cloud base, tendrils of angry grey vapour reaching towards the sea. The carrier was exactly where she should have been, several miles ahead and slightly to the left of my nose. Between them, Homer and Ferranti, manufacturer of my slightly rusty Blue Fox radar set, had done it again.

But the best bit was yet to come. It had been a few months since my last carrier landing and no two were ever alike.

Mowgli and I tracked the dot until it grew into the familiar outline of an Invincible-class carrier. At 20,000 tons, she is not a big ship – tiny, in fact, compared with the floating cities that the Americans use. As she began to fill the frame of the forward canopy, her details moved into focus. A line of helicopters was snugged up against the superstructure, their blades folded aft for stowage. Sea spray from the bow wave spewed over the ski-jump, sending rivulets of water across the deck as the ship bucked in the choppy swell. Henry's jet was touching down in a cloud of steam on the landing zone amidships as Mowgli and I swept alongside, 600ft above the water. Mel's aircraft was already down and manoeuvring towards the graveyard – the stowage area for the Sea Harriers when they are on deck – just in front of the bridge.

I waited until I was exactly level with the bridge, then hit the airbrake and pulled the throttle back to idle. I hauled the Sea Harrier into a hard turn to the left, dumping 4g on the airframe to bleed my speed down to 300 knots. At the moment I hit idle, the Pegasus growled, a noise that is so disconcerting to those who haven't heard it before that we brief students not to eject the first time they attempt this manoeuvre.

As I hauled on the stick and executed the turn that would bring me on to the port side of the ship in preparation for landing, I started lowering the nozzles and powering up to fly the approach. The Rolls-Royce Pegasus is the enabling technology at the heart of the Sea Harrier's unique V/STOL capability. In forward flight, the four nozzles that eject its 21,500lbs of thrust are tilted all the way aft, giving the aircraft the performance characteristics of any conventional jet. But in transition to V/STOL mode, the four nozzles are moved progressively downward as the aircraft decelerates, until, in the end, they're pointing vertically and the aircraft is held aloft by nothing other than the brute force of its exhaust thrust.

Once you've mastered the technique, landing on a pitching, heaving deck in a V/STOL aircraft is infinitely preferable to slamming down in a conventional jet at close on 200mph and praying you'll catch an arrestor wire to stop you shooting off the other end of the ship.

Yet as I pulled back on the silver nozzle lever with my left hand and juggled the throttle, I was far from being home and dry. On the final approach to the ship, there's a critical speed band – approximately 120 down to 40 knots – coupled with the aircraft's angle of attack and yaw angle (its nose-up attitude and nose position relative to wind direction) that can still conspire to kill you.

I was always mindful at this moment of a film we showed student Sea Harrier pilots after they graduated. It depicts the final moments of a US Marine Corps pilot who has timed his turn on to the ship all wrong and is fighting desperately to try to pull back the nose on to the carrier's centre line. In hauling heavy-handedly on the controls he unwittingly enters the aircraft's zone of unforgiveness: the nose comes up past the 12 alpha mark ('alpha' describes the relationship between angle of attack and airspeed), his speed drops and the aircraft begins to sideslip. Without warning, the AV-8B flips on to its back and rolls, inverted, into the sea. Its pilot, of course, never stood a chance.

As I increased power, progressively handing over the full weight of the aircraft from wingborne flight to the Pegasus and decelerating past 150 knots, I made sure I maintained the aircraft at a steady 8 degrees of alpha and kept the nose into the wind. With the aircraft's weight now all but transferred to the four belching columns of thrust from the Pegasus, I lined up exactly where I wanted to be, around 150ft off the water, just behind and slightly to the left of the ship, and put the aircraft into the braking stop – angling the nozzles as far forward as they will go – the airborne equivalent of slamming on the brakes in mid-air.

For a moment, as I fell forward against my straps, my view was filled with the carrier's stern and her sprawling superstructure. As the Sea Harrier wobbled on its thrust axis, I could sense the power of *Ark Royal's* engines from the eddies that boiled up as grey-white froth immediately behind the ship.

I began toggling the speed trim on top of the throttle, still trading forward momentum against the downward thrust of the Pegasus. The speed trim allows you to control the nozzles 10 degrees either side of the vertical and is so precise that you can almost think your way towards the part of the deck you're aiming for.

At 100 knots, I checked engine temperature to ensure that I had a sufficient thrust margin to go into a full hover as I drew alongside the ship. By now, I was 'wet committed', which meant that a powerful pump was belching water into the engine to prevent it from overheating while it supported the full weight of the aircraft. As soon as the water starts pumping, there's no stopping it. You have ninety seconds before it runs out and you spike the engine. If for any reason you're not lined up to land when you're wet committed, you face a choice: land anyhow, anywhere you can, ready or not, or drop like a stone into the oggin.

With the water flowing, I eased the stick across and felt the jet slide over the deck. There was an unnerving moment when it seemed that the aircraft would keep going and slam into the sheer wall of the superstructure, but deft movements of the control column brought me back over the tramlines that indicated where I was meant to set down.

The aircraft was buffeting now from the dense, spray-laden air moving constantly across the bow of the ship from the starboard side – what we call a 'green' wind. I was scanning the markers below and around me to ensure that I maintained the hover over the right spot. The pummelling effect of the wind forced me to toggle like fury on the stick just to hold position. I was sweating profusely and straining to keep my eyes on the markers. It was an effort to focus on anything because of the salt spray streaming in rivulets down the side of the canopy.

I had forty seconds of water left when I began to lower the Sea Harrier towards the deck with a half-inch reduction on the throttle. As soon as the jet began to set down, I forced myself into a routine which, no matter how many times I'd done it, still felt strange: reapplying thrust to the engine. This is to compensate for the hot gases from the exhaust nozzles that were now being reingested into the Sea Harrier's engine air intakes. The reingestion of these gases causes thrust levels to drop off significantly, compelling you to power up, not down, as you descend.

You always strive for a solid landing, setting her down hard and square on all four wheels. Attempting to kiss the deck is not a good idea, as too gentle a descent leaves you in the air longer than you'd want to be while those hot gases are swirling all around you. Too much hot gas reingestion and the Pegasus pop-surges and you fall the last 20 feet like a brick.

With my eyes all the while on the lieutenant commander flying in Flyco – a place on the ship with a window overlooking the deck, much akin to an air-traffic control tower – who was watching me intently from his position just aft of the bridge, I slammed the aircraft on to the deck and reduced the power. The aircraft rocked from side to side as three wheels hit the steel plate, followed a split second later by the fourth.

I glanced up and saw lieutenant commander flying shaking his head in mock reproach. Behind my oxygen mask, I smiled sweetly, raised the middle finger of my right hand and gave him the bird. Any landing you walk away from is a good one.

Ahead of me, a yellowcoat appeared, his head ducked down against the spray blowing across the deck in sheets. He quickly marshalled me forwards, pulling me off the spot on which I'd just set down. Hang around too long on a surface which has just been toasted by the hot exhaust gases of a turbo-fan engine and you risk having your tyres explode beneath you. I angled the nozzles aft again, gave the Pegasus another dose of the throttle and taxied into the graveyard. As soon as I was in position, the yellowcoat gave me the balled fist signal that denotes 'brakes on'. Four more deckcrew appeared from nowhere and started strapping me to the deck. Only when they had finished and I'd closed down all the electrical systems did I shut down the engine and open the canopy.

An icy blast hit me in the face. It felt as if it was freezing on my skin. I turned in time to see the first aircraft in the next four-ship sliding over the deck, its pilot, Oz Phillips, struggling to hold steady as the wind eddied around the underside of his jet.

To my right, Mowgli was being marshalled into position on the graveyard, his aircraft bunched hard up against the other two to make room for the four jets still to come. I hung around until Mowgli was finished, then slid down the ladder that had been placed alongside the cockpit. I beckoned Mowgli to follow me and scuttled towards the watertight doorway halfway down the superstructure which led to the aircraft control room (ACR), where I needed to sign in the jet: the final stage in its journey from land- to sea-based fighter.

Mowgli and I stepped into the airtight 'citadel' and shut the door behind us. Both of us had learned about watertight procedure during mandatory courses at Whale Island, Portsmouth, where they teach you the dos and don'ts of life on ship. Maintaining safety discipline is one of the lessons that you pick up quickly. During 'action stations' the doors are always sealed tight, primarily to keep the water out, but increasingly also because the threat of nuclear, biological or chemical (NBC) warfare is deemed to be omnipresent.

As the door boomed shut behind us, Mowgli's eyes widened slightly. The sights and sounds of a ship were less familiar to him than they were to me. I didn't tell him this, but the truth is, you never, ever quite get used to it.

I opened the door on the other side of the citadel and stepped into the ship proper. The first thing that grabs you is the smell. It's indefinable, but there are elements to the bouquet – the tang of steel, the heavy aroma of polish and the ambiguous scent of a thousand people locked in each other's company below decks – that are just about recognisable. That smell is enough to induce a flood of memories, each of them suffused with a mixture of excitement, trepidation, longing and loathing, and it momentarily stopped me in my tracks. *Ark Royal*, *Invincible* and *Illustrious*, it didn't matter which one of them you found yourself in, they all smelled alike. It was the ship's way of saying she had got you back again. It felt like I'd never been away.

'What is it?' Mowgli inquired.

I shook off my reverie. 'Nothing, mate. Come on, I'll show you where we go to check the jets in.'

The ACR is half the length of a tennis court and divided into sections. It is here that all the admin relating to the ship's complement of Sea Harriers and Sea King helicopters is kept up to date. I made my way to the Sea Harrier section in the far corner, where I found Little Engines and the watch chief, Chief Petty Officer Squashy Morton.

On board ship, the squadron's engineering personnel are split into two watches, port and starboard, giving us thirty-five aircraft maintainers per eight-hour watch. Squashy, a big fellow with a huge, red face like a tomato, was the port watch chief. I had known Squashy since the dim and distant days of my time in 899 Squadron, the Sea Harrier training unit at Yeovilton. He was a jovial sort and I liked him immensely, but he was a tough son of a bitch when he needed to be: a vital attribute for a watch chief, whose role and status are not dissimilar to those of a sergeant-major in the army. The other watch chief, Bob 'Vic' Vickery, had also come to the ACR to make sure that none of the aircraft had suffered any problems in transit. Vic had a habit of looking you straight in the eye and saying, 'Splendid, sir, splendid,' whenever you gave him the good news that an aircraft was problem-free. Between them, Squashy and Vic were the chief roadies who kept the whole show going backstage. In the room with them were five maintainers whose responsibilities spanned most of the engineering disciplines – radios, engines, electrics, etc. – required to keep the aircraft in the air.

'Morning, Squashy, how have you been?' I asked, placing my helmet on the table beside him.

Squashy beamed and his big, pudgy face almost creased in two.

'Great, sir. Good to be back on board, isn't it, sir?' He pulled a face, a look just short of a gurn, that was hard to read. Squashy had been on board two days longer than me, but I was never quite sure whether he loved the sea or loathed it.

I signed the aircraft into a large ledger known as The 700 and gestured to Mowgli to do the same. Mowgli's hair, which gets particularly spiky when it emerges from the sauna-like microclimate of his bone-dome, was treated to some facetious glances from the ACR troglodytes. Neither Mowgli nor I had anything wrong with our aircraft, so we headed down to Two Deck, Vic's cries of 'Splendid, sir, splendid' still ringing in my ears.

In a system that's slightly arse-about-face, the landing deck is referred to as One Deck, with decks numbered upwards all the way down to the bilges. Everything above One Deck is given a zero prefix – the next level up, for example, being O Two Deck. The ship is also divided lengthwise into sections, the letter A denoting the area closest to the bows. To signal where you are in the ship, you compose a set of co-ordinates comprised of a letter, a deck number and the side of the ship you happen to be on.

Mowgli and I were headed for the SE (survival equipment) Section to hand in our helmets and life preservers. SE Section is down and about 150 feet forward of the ACR. I reminded Mowgli to watch his head as we progressed along the corridor, moving through watertight doors and dodging people coming the other way. As soon as we'd handed in our survival equipment, we popped into the nearby squadron briefing room. A computer printout on the door said: 'No hawkers, gypsies or tramps.' Below this, someone had written: 'And definitely no pingers' in an effort to keep out anyone involved in anti-submarine warfare (ASW) duties.

Inside the briefing room, we found Mel and Henry. Henry was rummaging through a pile of boxes and bags brought on board by the maintainers. They were supposed to contain all the kit we'd need for our voyage, including our day-to-day clothing, but it was not unknown for things to get mislaid. As he delved into boxes stuffed full of computers, books and other paraphernalia, searching desperately for his kit, Henry's face got redder and redder.

'Some fucking one-eye has forgotten to load my stuff.'

I laughed. 'What, all your kit?'

My mirth only made Henry's face go a deeper shade of red. 'Too bloody right.'

'Sounds like a trip to stores for you, then,' I said.

'But what about my cummerbund?'

He had a point. You could buy just about anything you wanted on the ship from clothes to CD-players, but you couldn't buy an 801 Squadron cummerbund, a natty little black-and-white check number hand-tooled in the squadron colours.

'Then it's a trip to the Choghi tailor for you instead,' I suggested.

It may be hard for those who have never been on board an Invincible-class carrier to believe, but the ship has its own tailor, and very good he is, too. In three days, for the right price, he'll knock you up a very creditable three-piece suit. In fact the skill of the Navy's tailors rivals that of the best in Hong Kong and Singapore. The only snag is that the *Ark*'s Choghi tailor, Mr Wong, is located in a secret corner of the ship and getting to him is like embarking on Dante's journey to the underworld. Henry pulled a face, but accepted that a trip into the bowels of the vessel was the price he had to pay for maintaining squadron propriety in the wardroom.

I sat down and logged the statistics of my flight, then picked out my own bag from the detritus left in Henry's wake and went in search of my cabin, again with Mowgli in tow.

The atmosphere when you get back on ship is not dissimilar to the first day of school after the long summer break.

Looking for my cabin, I ran into a number of pingers and bagmen known to me from earlier voyages and my previous incarnation. The Sea Harrier community liaised closely with bagmen, the crew members of the Airborne Early Warning (AEW) Sea King helicopters that act as the eyes and ears of the fleet. They get their name from the inflatable radome housing the AEW radar that hangs off the side of the helicopter.

I know exactly how it feels to be a bagman, because I used to be one.

'Hey, Richardson!'

The shout came from an open doorway as I manoeuvred down

the corridor looking for my room. I stepped back a few paces and saw an old friend from my AEW days, Mark Fulford, call sign Fluff.

'Have you seen the latest OAL?' he asked breezily.

The officers' appointment list is a regular bulletin in which new appointments and promotions are announced. This was an unusually serious opening for Fulford.

'Er, no,' I replied cautiously.

'You've been appointed senior pilot of 849 A Flight,' he said, a big grin spreading across his face. 'Congratulations!' He held his hand out in an exaggerated display of bonhomie. 'You're going to be a bagman again.'

Eight Four Nine Squadron was a Sea King AEW unit. Although most naval helicopter pilots will tell you that they are doing the job they always dreamed of, this is almost always untrue. Deep down, every Navy pilot wants to end up on the Sea Harrier, because the aircraft is fast and sexy and there's only a handful of them, around twenty-four all told, of which eight are allocated to training.

Of course, any military flying job is a good one, especially if it's your first, but looking back on my time as a Sea King AEW pilot, much of it was the flight-duty equivalent of watching paint dry. For two years, my job had been to fly three-and-a-half hour sorties at a flight level of between 2,000 and 10,000ft. It's the guys at the back of the helicopter who are actually having all the fun, determining what's a threat and what isn't, and then directing the action accordingly. As the pilot, you're little more than a taxi driver, stooging around the sky at 90 knots under the direction of the bagmen in the back. During air defence exercises, these guys would vector the Sea Harriers on to whatever simulated threats happened to be attacking the fleet. It was in listening to the interaction between them that I caught the bug and resolved to end up on the Sea Harrier myself. Making the move isn't easy, however, since, if you fail to make the grade, your helicopter crewmates will never let you forget it.

'Yeah, right. Piss off, Fulford. It's good to see you again, too.' I kept going.

'Was he serious?' Mowgli asked, a small voice behind me.

'Nah,' I said. 'He always tries that one on me.' But just to be on the safe side, I thought I'd better check the OAL as soon as I got the chance.

There are two ways you can become a Sea Harrier pilot. One is to direct-entry: straight through the system from *ab initio* all the way on to fast jets. The other is to come up through the rotary community, as I had. Mowgli was one of the direct entries and had not been exposed to some of the subtleties of bagman humour. One of these days, I reflected ruefully, Fluff might actually get it right. But what he didn't know was that, having tasted life in the fast lane, I wasn't going back.

After showing Mowgli to his cabin, I found my own and surveyed my home for what was likely to be the next couple of months. An officer's cabin is around 8ft long by 7ft wide. It comprises a fold-down bed on the wall opposite the door, a desk and cupboard on the left-hand side and a sink on the right. Whatever anyone may tell you, there are only two kinds of people in the Navy: those who piss in the sink and those who tell lies. I had never sunk so low, of course, but I did note that the heads were a couple of hundred feet away from my cabin.

The folding bed is an ergonomic marvel, although it does have a tendency to snap shut in the event of a particularly violent swell. If a pilot has gone missing during the night, there's a better than even chance the search party will find him swallowed by his own bed.

The only other feature of note in the cabin is a wall safe for securing confidential and secret material, which more often than not ends up as a repository for gin, smokes and porn mags. It really is just like being back at fucking school.

I was officially woken by a steward at 0630 the following morning, but I had actually been awake some time before the knock came, listening to the faraway pulse of *Ark Royal*'s engines and feeling about as sorry for myself as Martin Sheen pondering life and death on his Saigon hotel bed at the start of *Apocalypse Now*.

The cabins for the Sea Harrier pilots are split between Two and Five Deck. I was glad now that I had chosen a berth on Two, because it had given me almost a whole night's sleep. Sea Harrier pilots are divided over which is the better level to be on, but for my money, there's no contest. True, on Two Deck you do get Sea Harriers taking off and landing a few feet above your head, something that is particularly irksome during night ops. But while the whoosh and thump of aircraft coming and going is disturbing, it is at least infrequent. There is no escape, on the other hand, from the constant rumble of a carrier's engines or the continuous whine of her propeller shafts. To be next to these perpetual-motion machines all night is my idea of hell, but some of the other guys don't mind it. Their *bête noire* on Two Deck isn't so much the roar of the Sea Harriers as the scraping sound made by the chains as the maintainers move around the deck securing aircraft that have just touched down or releasing those ready for launch. It really is each to his own taste.

I headed towards the showers, fighting the nauseous, light-headed feeling that accompanies you everywhere you go during your first few days at sea. I could tell the weather had worsened in the night because of the increased levels of g I was experiencing as the ship ploughed through the crests and troughs of the waves. In heavy sea states, the gs can really pile on: plus and minus 1.5 to 2g, depending on whether the ship is rising or falling. The answer to the nausea problem in the short term, I'd found, was to down a hearty breakfast. Eating somehow always seemed to settle my stomach. It helped that the food on board Navy ships – in my experience, at least – was usually pretty good.

I jumped into the nearest available shower, remembering to shout 'switching on' moments before I opened the taps. If you forget to issue this simple warning, there is a chorus of protest from the other cubicles as the temperature yo-yos, scalding or freezing other bathers.

A low-pressure stream of cold water hit me in the chest, accompanied by an oily waft that's known as eau de diesel, because it clings to you like a delicate perfume throughout the voyage. It is explained, apparently, by the close proximity of the water tanks to the ship's fuel supply, which is something else to curse the fish-heads for.

I changed into my Number 12s – white shirt and black trousers –

and headed down to Five Deck to get some breakfast. The dress code for anyone not used to life on the ocean in the service of Her Majesty must seem arcane, but if you're not flying in the first wave, you don't get to wear your flying gear at breakfast, which is a pisser, because given half a chance, it's what we'd all pad around in most of the time.

When I reached the wardroom, it was about three-quarters full. There were approximately seventy officers spread around the twenty tables, most of whom had congregated in their respective professional groups. I cast my eye over tables of fish-heads, pingers and bagmen, looking for our tiny Sea Harrier group. Eventually I spotted them in the far corner, plonked myself down, grabbed a steward and ordered coffee, cereal and toast. Only then did I turn to my fellow pilots to bid them good morning and observe that there was none of the usual banter.

'What's up?' I inquired casually.

'Do you want the bad news or the really bad news?' Beasty replied.

I looked at each face in turn. It was like we'd hit an iceberg during the night and someone had forgotten to tell me.

'Well, tell you what,' I said, 'why not hit me with the bad news first?'

'The UN has requested the removal of General Cot,' Shaggy said, his face a picture of deep concern.

'Why?' I asked, as I struggled to remember who General Cot was. I seemed to recall from Mel's pep talk at Yeovilton that he was the head of the UN military force in Bosnia.

'Because of some disagreement with the secretary-general over air strikes, apparently,' Gazza said.

'But I thought Boutros Ghali had just agreed to air strikes,' I said, keeping one eye on the steward who was teetering towards our table with my food.

'Cot was insisting on authority to call in the strikes without prior approval from the UN Security Council,' Shaggy said. 'Boutros Ghali refused. He wants sole authority to direct NATO air strikes from the Security Council in New York. The general wouldn't give way, so he walks. It was on the news this morning.'

'This is all very interesting, but what does it mean?' I asked of no one in particular. To tell the truth, I was a whole lot more interested in the arrival of my breakfast, which had just been set down on the table in front of me.

'It means that the UN military force is leaderless,' Mel said. 'And the warring parties are taking full advantage of the power vacuum. There are reports of an escalation in the fighting just about everywhere.'

'What I meant was how does it affect us?'

No one said anything.

I put down my coffee and looked at Mel. 'Boss,' I said. 'From the little i know and read about the place, Bosnia's been in a fucking mess for years and probably will be for decades to come, with or without our intervention. I don't see why we're getting strung out by some French general's recall because of a tiff with the UN. Or am I missing a trick here?'

There was an unnaturally long pause. Then Oz said: 'That wasn't the really bad news, Nicko. That was just polite conversation, mate. The signal came through during the night from NATO headquarters. There were several no-fly violations during the past twenty-four hours. It seems the Serbs are testing our reaction times and building for something.'

'And guess what made an appearance in among the ragbag selection of planes they managed to get in the air?' Beasty said.

It was only then that the reasons for the long faces dawned on me. 'Our old friend, the MiG-29?' I ventured.

'Bang on,' Beasty said, giving me, I could have sworn, a momentary flash of that Lecter smile.

I sat there absorbing this news for a moment. My appetite disappeared. It wasn't the prospect of meeting a MiG-29 over the Balkans that had put me off my food – though God knows that was worrying enough – but something else; the germ of a thought at the back of my mind that something I had seen over the past twenty-four hours, some knowledge I had acquired, could make a difference here.

And then it came to me. In among the signals that had come back from Decimommanu, I recalled a list of the other NATO units that would be at the training base during our stint there. There are dozens of fighter aircraft from as many as three or four different NATO nations at the Deci 'Top Gun' range at any one time. But on this occasion, during the very period we were due to stop by for our week of intense air-to-ground weapons training, so were the Germans.

I looked at Mel. 'What would it be worth to you, boss, if I could fix us some training time against a real MiG-29 – or better still, several of them?'

Mel gave me a withering look. 'What are you suggesting, Nick? We stop off and ask the Russians if they'll lend us a Fulcrum or two?'

'The Luftwaffe is going to be at Deci while we're there.'

Mel stopped chewing on his toast. 'You're kidding me.'

I shook my head. 'Scout's honour, mate. They're going to be there. And so are their MiG-29s.'

In 1989, when the Berlin Wall fell, the Luftwaffe inherited the MiG-29s of the East German Air Force. This gave NATO its first opportunity to get inside the aircraft and see how it ticked. Ever since, the sole Luftwaffe unit that still operated the MiG had obligingly volunteered its services to NATO as an 'aggressor' unit, simulating the tactics of the bad guys who flew the revered Russian-made fighter for the benefit of people who needed to hone their flying skills against it. The unit in question, JG73, based at Laage, was currently at Deci and would be there for the next fortnight.

Mel asked me to give them a call to see if we could book in a couple of sorties against the MiGs in among our practice sessions over Deci's bombing ranges. In the meantime, he told us, we'd better work on the tactics we'd need against the Germans so that we didn't suffer any undue humiliation when we came up against them in the clear skies over Sardinia.

After breakfast, I sprinted back up to the briefing room, where I was booked in to make a quick call to Yvonne on the Motorola prior to the mass flying brief, which is the equivalent of school morning assembly for all aircrew. We were due to be addressed by

Commander Air, for whom it definitely pays not to be late. I sat down at the clunky-looking phone and tapped in our home number, praying that the line wouldn't be busy. The Commander Air, who's also known as Wings, is in charge of all flying on the ship and renowned for his quick temper. I couldn't afford to hang around.

The seconds ticked by as the signal hit the satellite uplink, crunched through the satellite itself and shot on towards Somerset. Finally, I heard the phone ring. When it answered, it wasn't Yvonne but her mother. Yvonne was at the hospital seeing Kristian. Nothing to be alarmed about, her mum told me, but could I call back later? There was a constant queue for the Motorola and to be sure of getting a slot, you had to make arrangements well in advance. I said I'd do my best, asked her to kiss the kids for me, and hung up. Then I dashed for the Number One Briefing Room, just down the corridor. The Number One Briefing Room belongs to the pingers and, being quite a bit bigger than ours, is ideal for mass briefs.

As we waited for Wings, I surveyed the scene. There were approximately fifty people in the room, a mixed selection of squadron COs, pilots, fighter controllers and AEOs representing the three flying communities: bagmen, pingers and 'stovies'. 'Stovy' is bagman and pinger slang for us, derived from stove-pipe, a nickname from way back for jets.

At 7.29 and 45 seconds, the briefing officer walked in and announced Wings' arrival. As he strode into the room, I found myself checking my watch. I counted him down as he approached the front row. Bang on 0730 he sat down and we followed suit. Whenever I saw Wings, I was reminded of a song that we sang on the squadron when we were several sheets to the wind:

> There's a chap up in Flyco that everyone knows
> Where he gets his three gold rings from nobody knows
> But he sits up in Flyco where he rants and he shouts
> And he shouts about things he knows fuck-all about.

This particular Wings, Ian Stanley, was an ex-helicopter pilot. He'd earned himself a medal during the Falklands for picking up a load of soldiers off a fog-bound hillside, the enemy all around them. I liked Wings and I respected him greatly, but the words of the song still stood.

There was a short preamble from the briefing officer concerning general housekeeping – a reminder about call signs, codes and frequencies, plus the weather and sea conditions for the day – and then he got to his feet. He took us through a number of aspects of carrier lore, reminding us of procedures that were integral to the running of a tight ship.

One of the fundamentals concerned the need to meet our 'Charlie times' when we landed back on the carrier. This is important, because whenever we launch and land, the ship has to be facing into wind. If the wind is coming from an inconvenient direction relative to the ship's final destination, this is too bad. To conserve the ship's fuel and the time spent heading in the wrong direction, therefore, we need to keep our Charlie times tight.

Another fundamental is the need to maintain radio and radar silence anywhere in the vicinity of the carrier. Wings rammed home the point. 'Even though we're still days from the war zone, I want us to remain as stealthy as possible throughout the voyage, because you never know who's bloody listening in.'

He didn't say it, but there were plenty of other ships in the busy sea lanes of the Atlantic and the Mediterranean, and you couldn't be altogether sure who they were or where their sympathies lay. If the Russians picked up our signals on the way to the Adriatic, it was a safe bet that they'd pass on the details to their brother Serbs in Belgrade or Pale. Wings told us that this strict EMCON silence policy – EMCON standing for emissions (in the form of radar and radio signals) control – would apply to us as much as the carrier herself.

We were left in no doubt as to what he would do to us if we broke this sacrosanct policy, except in an absolute emergency. 'I want no radars shone within a 10-mile radius of the ship,' he barked, sweeping us with a menacing glare. 'But the flipside of this, of course, is I don't want to see anyone doing a Suds Watson, either.'

Poor Suds. He had been my instructor at 899 training squadron.

He was quite an aggressive pilot and if you didn't meet his tough expectations, he'd let you know it. Trainee pilots who badly transgressed under his tutelage were put through what came to be known as the Walk of Shame, in which Suds stormed away from his parked aircraft leaving the hapless student pilot trailing in his wake all the way to the briefing room.

The ultimate Walk of Shame – a mercifully rare event, and one that I somehow managed to escape – entailed Suds shutting down the engine wherever he happened to land the aircraft, ejecting the miscreant from the cockpit, and then starting the engine up again for a solo taxi run back to the apron. The student, meanwhile, would have to make his own way back, usually from a far-flung corner of the airfield, irrespective of the weather.

Suds' students nursed one vital piece of information, however, that always sustained them in such moments. Soon after the Falklands campaign, he himself had managed to land his Sea Harrier on the wrong ship. This was all the more embarrassing as the ship in question wasn't the Royal Navy's, or even a warship, for that matter, but a Spanish freighter.

During a voyage, we're handed what are called ramrod and covec codes that enable us to communicate with and then locate the ship in secure conditions whenever we're returning after a sortie. A covec code gives us the range and bearing of the ship, but to confuse the enemy – and, more often than not, us – these details are always so many degrees and so many miles out of true. The precise number of degrees and miles varies daily and is signified within the code, which we're given before we take off.

The problem is, with the best will in the world, the carrier is rarely in the position that has been transmitted to us. Due to all kinds of drifting errors in the navigational maths, she's quite likely to be as many as 10 miles away from the position given, even after the covec code computation. Hence the need to do a quick sweep with the radar, pick out the carrier on the screen and then fly the correct bearing.

When we're working the aircraft to its limits, we're very restricted on landing weights. The Pegasus engine is hugely affected by ambient temperature conditions. On a particularly hot day, it's quite impossible to land on deck with more than a few hundred pounds of fuel remaining, because the engine simply runs out of puff. If you haven't already dropped your bombs on something, it's mandatory to dump them in the sea.

In Suds' case, he picked out what he thought was the carrier on radar, but only acquired it visually when he was a couple of miles away, by which time he was desperately low on fuel. When he realised that it wasn't the carrier at all, but a freighter, he was already committed to land.

A few minutes later, one very surprised Spanish sea captain looked up from his bridge to see a Sea Harrier touching down on the forward part of the ship. Suds stayed with it till the ship berthed in its home port on the Spanish mainland several days later.

The incident made all the papers, of course.

The last part of Wings' brief concerned us. 'Spider launch time is at 0930 and Charlie time is at 1045,' he announced drily, just before the wrap-up.

This would give us an hour and a quarter to practise the tactic that we fervently hoped would give our Sea Harriers parity with, and maybe even the edge over, the MiG-29s.

# CHAPTER 3

It takes three or four minutes to reach Flyco from Two Deck. Henry's brief to Shaggy and Beasty, the two other pilots flying the ACM sortie, had run way over time – as it usually does with Henry. By the time he eventually concluded, there were less than twenty minutes to go before launch time.

I'd wanted to spend a few moments in Flyco composing myself for the exercise to come – an engagement sequence known as One Versus Two AI (for airborne interception) – but no such luck. I had a headache before I'd even started, not good prior to a session in which you're going to spend the best part of an hour and a half bent over a radar screen.

You get a spectacular view over the flight deck from Flyco, which is why you often find the place packed with people who technically have no right to be there. As I opened up the door, there was an unusually heavy presence of these hangers-on. Today, I recognised the ship's chaplain, the education officer and the weapons engineering officer for starters. Because they're all commander rank, you can't exactly tell them to hop it, although the look I gave them when I walked in probably said it anyway. Some people, I guess, are just born very thick-skinned.

Matt Cuthbertson, the lieutenant commander flying, one of the two people apart from me who was meant to be in Flyco, a room that's little bigger than a privy, greeted me warmly. 'Morning, Nick. Not flying this wave?'

'Full marks for observation, Matt,' I said, pulling a face and nodding in the general direction of the goofers.

Matt shrugged. 'The Lord moves in mysterious ways, Nicko. And we certainly have Him to thank for the weather today.'

The vicar, who hadn't quite got the point of Matt's remark, looked down at him and beamed beatifically.

It was indeed a beautiful day. I looked left along the length of the ship and saw the three aircraft ranged around the fan tail, deckhands crawling all around them, doing the pre-launch checks. Above them, the sky was a bright blue, its colour sharpened by a stiff wind. Free of haze, the horizon was clearly delineated.

I checked my watch. Another twelve minutes to the time when the ship turned into wind.

The door between Flyco and the bridge opened and the captain walked in. Terry Loughran was a truly great guy, although as unlikely-looking a figure to command a carrier as you'd ever meet. He reminded me of the *Carry On* actor Sid James, with a smile and laugh to match. He was so short that they had to bring a soapbox on to the bridge so he could see out. It was a great testimony to his abilities, however, that the men would have followed him anywhere.

I'd sailed with him the previous year. Terry used to rev up the ship's complement by playing 'Simply the Best' over the tannoy system. It sounds cheesy, but it worked and the men loved him for it. He was also crazy about bikes and was the proud owner of a Harley Davidson, on which he'd lavish much of his time when he was back on dry land. He even had a leather jacket with 'Big Tel' marked out in studs on the back. This, of course, was what he came to be known as behind his back. 'Ah,' Big Tel said, his gaze latching on to me after he'd gone through the motions with Matt and Wings, 'not flying this morning, Nick?'

I was busy running over the launch calculations in my head and momentarily forgot myself as I drew breath to deliver another 'full marks' riposte. I just stopped myself before the words popped out.

'No, sir, the B team's on this morning. The A team flies this afternoon.'

Loughran chuckled, then turned to the CAG. 'Are we launching on time, Wings?'

'Yes, sir. In ten minutes' time.'

Loughran nodded, apparently satisfied. He looked on the Sea
Harriers as his pride and joy. He was an aviator himself, but had
spent his flying career on helicopters, not fixed-wing aircraft.
Rumour had it they had to attach blocks of wood to the Wessex's
yaw pedals so that he could reach them.

'So, what's on today's programme?' he asked me. 'I gather we're
going to be on the look-out for MiGs when we get to the Adriatic.'

I told him that the tactics Henry, Shaggy and Beasty were practising this morning were designed specifically with the MiG-29 in
mind. It was the superior performance of the MiG-29's radar, coupled with its excellent weapons capability and supersonic speed,
that combined to make it such a formidable opponent. I mentioned to Captain Loughran, however, that we had a couple of
moves that we wanted to try out under representative combat conditions. For the purposes of the exercise, Beasty was to act out the
part of the MiG-29 and Henry and Shaggy would be playing themselves. If either of the moves worked, we knew we'd at least stand
a chance of survival if we ever came up against the MiG for real.

The two sets of opponents had shipborne team-mates to back
them up. Fighter controllers, known as freddies, control the fight
from the ground by using radar to vector the pilots on to the
enemy. The relationship between pilot and freddy is a close one
and the team has to work well if it is to come out on top.

Today, Al Good, the 801 Squadron freddy, was to act as fighter
controller to Henry and Shaggy, using his God's eye view of the
fight to try to outwit Beasty and his controller.

Both controllers were perched over their respective radar screens
in the ops room on Five Deck, their two consoles separated from
each other by about 6 feet. In previous AI engagements, I'd caught
Al Good and his oppo giving each other mutually suspicious
glances, much as a couple of chess grand masters might in the seconds before a high-stakes game. I told Big Tel that as soon as I'd
finished here, I'd be heading down to the ops room to watch the
fight develop. To my dismay, the vicar popped up his hand and

asked if he and his cronies could come too. I smiled back as warmly as I could. It is, of course, impossible to refuse such requests, especially with the captain looking on. To shield my true feelings, I returned to my vigil over the flight deck.

As LSO, it was my responsibility to see that the aircraft got off the deck all right. With only five minutes to go before launch time, I was relieved to see hot exhaust gases streaming from the nozzles of the Sea Harriers, and their pilots with their heads down in the aircraft doing their pre-launch checks.

It's in this moment that the LSO is vested with about as much authority as a lieutenant ever has on a carrier, since it is down to him to ensure that the ship does exactly what is required of it to launch the aircraft. On some voyages I'd had to step over rank to achieve this, ordering a reluctant captain to flash up another two engines – the ship normally cruises on two out of the four – to get enough wind over the deck. It's also down to the LSO to compute the take-off run the aircraft need before they hit the ski-jump. This is a calculation based on the weight of the aircraft, the ambient temperature and windspeed. On this voyage, thank God, I didn't need to get shirty. When it came to the Sea Harriers, Big Tel had an intuitive feel for what was required.

There was a lurch and a rumble as the ship turned into wind. I could hear Loughran through the open doorway to the bridge calling for more power and then a deeper vibration as the other two engines opened up many deck levels below. I needed 30 knots windspeed over the deck to get the aircraft into the sky and the gauge was still reading 25. As the power of the two new engines was transmitted to the ship's screws I watched the needle creep up to and then inch past the 30-knot mark. We were in business.

Three minutes to launch.

I glanced back towards the fan tail and saw Spider One, Henry's aircraft, taxiing up to the bracket.

Matt turned to Wings and asked him if he was happy. Although, practically speaking, Matt – call sign Little F – ran Flyco, Wings was technically in charge. Wings looked at me and I nodded back: we still had 30 knots over the deck.

'Clear to launch, Little F,' Wings told Matt.

Matt moved his hand up to the button that controls the traffic-light system situated just below Flyco. He waited while the flight deck officer (FDO) had a final look underneath the aircraft, checking for any obstructions. Then the FDO stood up, raised his green flag and promptly crouched back down again so that the jet efflux of Henry's aircraft didn't blow him into the sea as it shot off the deck.

Matt hit the green light. There was a momentary delay as the engine reached max revolutions, then Henry released the brakes and it pelted towards the ski-jump. I watched it hit the ramp and lurch into the air, then turned back to see the next aircraft move up to the bracket.

It might have been only day one, but the FDO was already firing on all cylinders. Spiders Two and Three were both airborne within the next minute.

I heard a grunt of satisfaction from Wings and felt a roar and rumble from the bowels of the ship as she was brought back on course for Gib. Then I made my way to the ops room.

As I watched the three aircraft fly out in escort formation on the scope, I reflected on how little had changed since the summer of 1940, when WAAFs used to shuffle model aircraft around a big table. The only real difference was that we were watching things develop on a radar screen 2ft in diameter – and, of course, that this was just an exercise.

Even so, given the background presence of the MiG-29, today's test had a palpable sense of urgency about it. The feeling that there was more to this than business as usual had been picked up by the goofers, who had begun to gather round the scopes. Despite the gloom, I could make out their faces and expressions in the reflected light of the radar scope and associated electronics which gave the assembled entourage an almost theatrical appearance as they gazed down on the proceedings.

Among the crowd that had encircled our screen, I spotted Chris, a twenty-one-year-old kid from my village whom I'd helped months earlier to join up. Chris was heavily into computers and aircraft. Even though he'd had a good job working in a local software company, all he'd ever really wanted to do was to fly. Seeing this passion, I'd asked him if he wanted me to endorse him for a career in the Navy, something that can sometimes help you get past first base. He leaped at the chance, was accepted, and was now waiting for a place at RAF Topcliffe, where they teach student pilots the basics. In the meantime, he'd volunteered to 'hold with' our squadron, which is a bit like doing unpaid work experience. It looks good on the CV, especially if it gets you to a war.

In Chris's hands I noticed a couple of cups of coffee. He passed one of them to me.

'Have you ever seen one of these things before?' I asked him.

He shook his head. 'No, sir, I haven't.'

'Well, watch the screen. Things are about to get interesting.'

Behind us, over the loudspeakers, I heard Henry and Shaggy checking in with Al Good. Seconds later, there was a slight echo as Beasty, the surrogate MiG-29 pilot, did the same and his freddy acknowledged.

Al adjusted his head-mike and gave Henry and Shaggy the bearing information they needed to commence the fight.

'Spiders One and Two, you're loud and clear. Vector one-four-zero for CAP.'

I leaned forward. The three tiny arrows that signified the aircraft began to split up. After each 360-degree sweep of the radar beam, the arrows would move forward with a little jump. Behind them, the direction they'd come from was clearly visible thanks to their ghostly fluorescent trails.

'The controllers are vectoring them to their respective combat air patrol (CAP) positions,' I told Chris. 'The freddies need a 35-mile split between the CAPs before they can turn them in to fight.'

At 420 knots, or around 7 miles per minute, it would take the two teams four minutes to reach their CAP positions.

The vicar, who'd been listening in on me and Chris, began to rub his hands excitedly. 'I say, it's a bit like watching a jousting tournament, isn't it?' He nudged me and gestured with his head to the other freddy. 'How does each side know who's addressing whom?'

'They each have discrete frequencies,' I replied, pointing to the paired set of arrows moving now almost at right angles away from the third. 'Henry and Shaggy can hear each other – and Al, their freddy, here – but they are not privy to conversations between Beasty and his freddy. It's what you'd get in a real combat situation: each set of fighters being directed by their own controllers on the ground.'

There was a crackle on the speaker, then Henry's voice came through: 'Spiders fence out.'

'Fence out?' Chris queried.

'It means they're preparing the jets for action.'

I didn't bother to elaborate, but in my mind's eye I saw the combatants making their final preparations for the fight. The dummy Sidewinder missiles strapped to the underside of each aircraft needed coolant to flow through the seekers before they could pick up the heat signature of another jet; radar warning receivers (RWR) – the electronic gizmo known by us as the 'raw' that told you if the enemy had you 'locked up' on his radar – had to be switched on and set to the right mode; the head-up display (HUD) had to be preset with the right symbology, which meant feeding the wingspan dimensions of the Sea Harrier into the sighting system so that when it filled the aiming circle, you knew it was at the correct 350-yard range for a good gunshot with the Aden cannon. Then there was the engine to attend to. During rapid manoeuvring, such as you get in a dogfight, the flow of air into the engine intakes gets severely disrupted and, without special precautions, can cause a 'surge' or compressor stall. To overcome this, there is a 'combat switch' in the cockpit which for short durations can put the Pegasus into a higher power setting, thereby preventing it from dying on you in mid-air. Finally, you do a quick check of your g-suit to ensure that it's working properly. If it's not, you'll black out quicker than the other guy in the turn and he's got you.

'Spiders One and Two, first merge,' Henry's voice crackled, 'Tactic Alpha.'

Beside me, Al responded instantly. 'Spiders One and Two, bogey bears two-seven-zero. Thirty. High.'

Short, sharp and sweet. Beasty's surrogate MiG was at a bearing of 270 degrees, 30 miles from their position and at a higher altitude than them.

'Bogey bears two-seven-one. Twenty-nine miles. High,' Al continued, his voice beginning to find its rhythm.

I watched as the two arrows swung in Beasty's direction, still in battle formation, 2 miles apart and maintaining parallel tracks.

Then Al again: 'Bogey two-seven-two, 28, high.'

I turned to Chris, dropping my voice to a whisper. 'Al's guiding them to a point where their own radars will be able to pick up the MiG. Once that happens, they'll commit and go into Tactic Alpha. Henry and Shaggy will split up, forcing Beasty to go after one of them. If it works, the aircraft he's forced to ignore will snap on to an intercept course and hit Beasty in his blind spot. That, at any rate, is the theory.'

The vicar chortled amid a rustle of appreciation from the other goofers.

Henry and Shaggy maintained radio silence until they were 23 miles from Beasty, at which point Henry called 'Judy, Judy,' over the ether, signalling that he had spotted Beasty on his own radar. Fifteen seconds later, at 20 miles separation, he called 'Spiders, commit,' and he and Shaggy went into Tactic Alpha.

I watched on the screen as the two aircraft split up, Shaggy peeling 45 degrees to his right and Henry 45 degrees to his left. There was a tense moment as Beasty's arrow continued on its same, steady, dead-straight course, then it, too, changed direction.

'Good,' I said, 'Beasty's fallen for it. He's going after Henry.'

The two tracks began to converge head-on. Now for the moment when Al would snap Shaggy on to a course that would bring him into Beasty's blind spot amidships.

But instead of a barked command from beside me, all I heard was a muffled oath. 'Shit. I've lost Shaggy!'

I looked at the screen to see what Al had seen – or not seen, as it turned out. Shaggy's aircraft had disappeared from the scope.

'He must have flown into some atmospheric distortion,' Al said. His voice rose only fractionally above its normal calm intonation, but I knew he was panicking. 'I can't see him anywhere.'

Nor could I. It happened sometimes. Temperature inversions,

unusual cloud activity – sometimes aircraft flew into these met phenomena and disappeared from the view of the ground controller. For it to happen now, however, was not good news. It could not have come at a worse moment.

On the right of the screen, Beasty's arrow scudded inexorably towards Henry.

Shaggy – desperate, I knew, for information from Al – burst through on the speaker. 'Freddy, bogey dope for Spider Two!'

Precious seconds ticked by. Then the speaker crackled again: 'Freddy, for Christ's sake, I need bogey dope!'

As Al took a deep breath to give him the bad news, suddenly Shaggy's aircraft reappeared as a bright blip on the left of the screen. In the seconds that had been lost, Beasty's aircraft was now too close in his head-on merge with Henry for Shaggy to do much about it. But Al gave it his best shot anyway.

'Snap south!' he yelled at Shaggy. 'Bogey two-one-zero, 15 miles.'

Shaggy grunted as he whipped the Sea Harrier into an impossible turn in a bid to get Beasty inside the 5-mile kill envelope of his Sidewinder. But Beasty was way out of range and it was already too late.

Behind me, I could hear Beasty and his freddy engaged in an increasingly animated dialogue as Beasty closed in for the kill.

The other freddy leaned back and gave Al a sickening smile. 'Fox Two kill, Spider One, Al,' he announced smugly, then went back to his set again.

'What does that mean?' the vicar asked.

'It means,' Chris told him, 'that the MiG-29 just killed our senior pilot.'

'Who is not going to be at all happy,' I added, my gaze still glued to the radar set.

Sure enough, the speaker almost fell off its mount when the news was passed on to Henry. Out of the game, he exited stage right as the fight moved on to the endgame: a one-on-one merge between Shaggy and Beasty.

I looked down at the screen as Beasty's MiG-29, vectored by his freddy, snapped over to engage Shaggy.

'Spider Two, bogey committing to you,' Al told him, the urgency audible in his voice. 'Bogey two-one-zero, 12 miles.'

They were pretty much head-on to each other. Had Beasty been flying a real MiG-29, Shaggy would have been in the heart of its missile envelope. The MiG-29 carried a longer-range missile than the Sea Harrier – the R-27, known to NATO as the AA-10 Alamo – but the weapon needed to be guided all the way to its target by the MiG's radar. I knew that Shaggy's only hope now was that by some miracle Beasty hadn't seen him. At a 1,000-knot closure speed, all would become clear within the next minute.

'My raw's clean,' Shaggy announced, more in hope than anticipation, 'I'm committing.'

I turned to offer some explanation to Chris and the vicar. 'Shaggy's radar warning receiver isn't registering Beasty's radar. He thinks he's in the clear, but—'

I was interrupted by a muffled 'tally' from Beasty over the neighbouring speaker. My worst suspicions were confirmed.

'Beasty's seen him,' I said.

'Oh dear,' said the vicar.

Seconds later, the other fighter controller tapped Al on the shoulder. 'Fox Two kill. Grand Slam Spiders.'

'Does that mean what I think it means?' the vicar said.

Chris nodded. 'Shaggy's dead. Game over.'

Al pushed his chair back from the scope and kneaded his eyeballs. 'I don't suppose Henry'll be buying me any beers tonight,' he said sheepishly.

'Nor Shaggy, either,' I told him cheerfully. 'Never mind, Al, there's always Tactic Bravo.'

'What's Tactic Bravo?' the vicar asked.

'Ah, well,' I said, not sure who I was really trying to convince here. 'Tactic Bravo is our secret weapon against the MiG-29, isn't it, Al?'

After his trouncing by the opposition, Al didn't look too hopeful, either. He spoke into his head-mike again. 'Spiders One and Two resume CAP,' he told Henry and Shaggy. 'Get ready to play again.'

'Bloody one-eye!' Henry said.

Al shrugged off the insult. The vicar, mercifully, was pondering the wonders of the radar scope and missed it.

'There's something that's troubling me here,' the man of the cloth said at length, straightening up to look at me.

'What's that, sir?' I asked.

'If a lone Sea Harrier, acting as a MiG-29, can beat two Sea Harriers acting as themselves, what hope does a Sea Harrier have against a real MiG-29?'

I was about to go into the rudiments of Tactic Bravo, but the finality of the vicar's sentiment stopped me short. I glanced at him and then at Chris. They were both giving me the same, quizzical look.

'Well, I hate to have to say it,' I replied, concentrating my gaze on the vicar, 'but that's where, as a pilot, I'd be looking to you, sir, for that winning piece of inspiration.'

It was then that Henry announced over the air that Spiders One and Two were ready to play again.

The Mikoyan MiG-29 is in most respects an awesome fighter, comparable to the mighty American F-16. But it does have one fatal, if little-known, flaw. To be fair to its designers, it is not the only aircraft to suffer from this affliction. Most modern fighter aircraft, Western and Eastern, share the same fundamental deficiency. But for once, we in the Sea Harrier community were perfectly placed to exploit it. The flaw in question pertains to the pulse-Doppler radar that is fitted to most modern fighter aircraft.

PD radars are excellent in almost all respects. They are highly discriminatory, particularly good at picking out fast-moving, low-flying aircraft against background 'clutter', the unwanted ground reflections that fill the return signal of a non-PD radar when it is angled earthwards. PD radars filter out clutter because they 'cue' on to things that move. The signal-processing computer at the heart of the system filters out all stationary objects, giving aircraft fitted with PD radars their much-coveted 'look-down/shoot-down' capability – in other words, if you can look down with the radar, you can shoot down with a missile. I say coveted because the good old Blue Fox radar of the Sea Harrier has no such capability. The Blue

Fox is steam-age technology compared with the Phazotron radar in the MiG-29.

Herein lay the guts of Tactic Bravo.

We drew around Al's position again. On the screen, I could see that the warring parties had just turned in on each other from their respective CAPs.

'A pulse-Doppler radar, such as the one fitted to the MiG-29, is a wonderful thing,' I explained to Chris, 'because it gives me speed, range and bearing – precisely the kind of information that I want as a fighter pilot. But if I can stop moving relative to the sweep of the beam, guess what? I disappear from the MIG's scope.'

Chris looked at me, startled. 'That's Tactic Bravo?'

I nodded.

Now the vicar was intrigued. 'You mean, the Harrier stops in mid-air? It just hangs there and vanishes from the MiG's radar screen?'

'No, sir, that's not what I mean. Technically, it could do that, since the Sea Harrier is a V/STOL fighter. But it would be risking everything. One of the golden rules of air combat is that he who has the most energy wins the fight. Broadly speaking, that means you want to keep your speed up prior to the engagement to give yourself enough stored energy to outmanoeuvre your opponent.'

'But I don't understand,' Chris said. 'How can you keep moving and stop at the same time?'

'Ah, well, that's the trick. I never said we stopped moving. I said we stopped moving relative to the beam.'

Chris's eyes widened slightly. With his keen interest in aircraft and aerospace technology, I could see that he had got it. The vicar urged me to continue.

'The beam works on the Doppler-shift principle. The speed of anything moving forward or backwards can be measured with infinite precision.'

'But if you move at 90 degrees relative to the beam – bingo! – you vanish from the scope,' Chris said, picking up the baton.

I smiled. 'Right.'

'Bloody hell,' the vicar said, dropping his guard. 'That's a bit sneaky, isn't it?'

'We're talking about a MiG-29, sir,' I said. 'But in any case, there's no guarantee any of this will work. It takes a very skilful pilot to pull it off.'

I turned to the screen just as Henry told Al that he and Shaggy were committing to the fight. They were head-on with Beasty again, separated by around 25 miles.

We called it the spike-and-drag manoeuvre for reasons, I hoped, that would quickly become clear. It opened with Shaggy and Henry dropping chaff, tiny bundles of iron filings, designed to spoof enemy radar.

Billowing in the slipstream, the chaff bloomed into a pair of 'splashes' on Al's radar screen. The arrows that had hitherto depicted Shaggy's and Henry's aircraft with clarity disappeared within the splashes.

Four seconds later, Henry's aircraft appeared from out of his chaff cloud, dragging away 80 degrees to his left. This bearing made him highly visible on Beasty's radar, but he maintained a minimum rate of closure with the MiG to keep out of its missile envelope.

A second later, Shaggy appeared out his chaff cloud. He was spiking – dropping vertically like a stone – perpendicular to the radar beam of the MiG. We could see him, because the ship's radar was a non-PD system. The question was, could Beasty?

Beasty's aircraft held its course for a second or two longer than I'd have liked, but then began to crank round towards Henry.

'It's working,' I whispered. Shaggy's plummet from 30,000ft ended at around 5,000ft, where the Sea Harrier pulled out of the dive and began climbing again. Beasty was still at 30,000 and closing on Henry in the right of the picture. His course had not deviated. It was clear now he had no idea where Shaggy was.

Shaggy's nose was 20 degrees up, his radar probing the clear sky ahead for a signal from Beasty's aircraft. Having practised this manoeuvre myself, I knew that this was the critical moment when it either all came together or fell apart.

The sound of Shaggy's breathing, hard in his oxygen mask, filled the speaker. 'You know the enemy is there, but you can't see him. Why not? Where the hell has the fucker gone?'

'Spider Two, tally!'

Shaggy. He'd found Beasty.

Al's response was instantaneous. 'Clear, engage.'

Shaggy pulled up even harder until Beasty was within the 5-mile kill radius of his Sidewinders.

The missile's seeker head is 'slaved' to the radar antenna: where the radar looks, so does the missile. Shaggy needed the growl in his headset that would tell him his Sidewinder had picked up the heat of an aircraft against the cold blue of the sky. As the lock-on improves, the pitch of the growl note increases. You check a volt-meter on the HUD display – to make sure you haven't locked on to the heat of the sun instead of the hot exhaust trail of a jet – wait for the diamond symbol to come up on the HUD screen, check you're within the maximum and minimum launch zone of the missile, and wait, wait, your thumb poised on the button, until it seems as if the high-pitched note from the missile's seeker is going to burst your head open . . .

. . . *deeeeeeeeeeeeeet!*

'Fox Two!' Shaggy yelled. Sidewinder away.

And from that bloody range, he couldn't miss.

Al Good gave an uncharacteristic chuckle of satisfaction before pushing his chair back from the screen and tapping his oppo on the shoulder.

'Missile kill,' he said, giving him a big smile.

I resisted the temptation to deliver a congratulatory slap between Al's shoulder blades. Instead, I turned and said calmly to Chris and the vicar: 'That, gentlemen, is how we will deal with the MiG-29.'

On my way back up to Flyco, I popped into the squadron briefing room on Two Deck and got the news I'd been looking for. The Germans were happy to play. The wording of the signal went fur-ther: they were relishing the chance of going up against the Sea Harrier.

I was still running over all the things I needed to do to make the Sardinian detachment proceed as smoothly as possible when Henry, Shaggy and Beasty shot over the carrier and entered the circuit for touchdown. Half an hour later, I was back in the briefing room listening to Henry's debrief. His conclusions on the sortie came as no great surprise.

The pincer manoeuvre – Tactic A – was clearly too dangerous to attempt against the MiG. With its high speed, manoeuvrability and excellent radar and missile performance, the MiG-29 would make mincemeat of us if we stuck to such conventional tactics. Tactic B, on the other hand, worked well. Given the weak link inherent in the performance of the Russian-made fighter's PD radar and our ability successfully to execute the spike-and-drag manoeuvre, we were confident we had a strategy up our sleeve that could get us out of an otherwise suicidal encounter. The fact that the Serb pilots were probably getting only around fifty or sixty flying hours every year also played in our favour.

The real test would come against the German MiG-29s of JG73. To be honest, I think we were more keyed up about our perform-ance against our old adversary than we were about the Yugoslav Air Force.

That afternoon I found myself with plenty still to do. Top of the agenda was sorting out final items of paperwork for our trip over to Deci. I sat down in my cabin and drafted a couple of signals, one to thank the Germans for their co-operation; the other to let Deci's UK liaison officer know what time we'd be arriving – 1600 hours on Thursday, a little under seventy-two hours away.

The plan was to get six jets off the deck while we were still about ten miles from Gibraltar. There we'd have a quick refuelling stop and a confab with the RAF tanker crew that would top us up on the leg to Deci, and then we'd be airborne again and on our way to Sardinia.

The 100 or so maintainers, fighter controllers and other support staff who would be coming with us would be ferried by helicopter flights from *Ark Royal* to the compact RAF airbase nestling under Gibraltar's famous rock. They would then board an RAF C-130 and proceed to Deci by air. This way, we'd be able to do our thing while at the same time allowing *Ark Royal* to take up station in the Adriatic for the shortest possible time.

In the meantime, there was more training to carry out on the flying side. All of us had to practise our one-versus-two AI techniques, particularly the now approved spike-and-drag tactic, and there were mock anti-ship missile strikes to carry out against *Ark Royal*. The last exercise was less to give us practice than to hone *Ark Royal's* air defence capabilities in the face of the anti-ship missile threat. Memories of the Falklands and the damage inflicted by Argentinian air-launched Exocets were still uppermost in the minds of anyone who'd served on board a ship in the past dozen or so years.

But my main priority was to talk to Yvonne. After my last, unsuccessful, attempt to call her, I had looked at my watch, calculated that she'd almost certainly be at home an hour later and booked my turn on the Motorola. Oz, who was using it before me, promised to deliver the monstrous machine to my cabin. I'd have to make it quick, he told me, because the boss was next in the queue, fifteen minutes after me.

I picked up the two signals I'd composed and headed towards Five Deck, looking for Steve Mather or Stumpy Wylde, the ship's two ops officers, who were responsible for vetting all signals before they were transmitted off the ship. This was standard procedure. Everything had to be checked – some would say censored – before it hit the airwaves.

I hoped Steve would be on his own in the lower ops office, as Stumpy could be a bit fierce, dealing with the signal you brought to him as if he were a short-fused schoolmaster reviewing a piece of sub-standard Latin prep. A word out of place with Stumpy and you felt you were a hair's breadth from a whack over the head with a blackboard rubber.

In idle moments, I have often found myself wondering how it is that I have remained trim during long deployments, despite all the good food. The answer, of course, is to be found in the many miles you tramp every day between decks on just this sort of duty. It's tedious, but there are compensations, and the positive effect on my waistline is one them. It took me around five minutes to get down to the relevant part of Five Deck. You can't rush it: those who do almost always end up braining themselves on the kidney hatches that divide the ship into supposedly watertight compartments. To get into the lower air ops office, you have to cut through the ops room, the nerve centre of the ship. It's from here, during battle stations, that all aspects of the carrier's activities are controlled.

I'd once been in the ops room during a mock anti-ship missile attack by Sea Harriers. It was like a manic version of the Stock Exchange with added pitch-and-roll as the officers manning the various consoles yelled warnings and instructions to the captain, as well as to each other, while the 'bruisers' – anti-ship missiles – came inbound in rapid succession and the ship's defences were mobilised to engage them. Now, however, everything was quiet. Out of the gloom, figures took shape, hunched over electronic display tables, monitoring radio traffic, drinking coffee, their faces reflecting the blue, green and red lighting of their equipment. The air was filled with the background static hiss of radios on standby.

The two centres of gravity in the ops room are the surface warfare plot table and the air warfare plot table. The former displays the status of every ship picked up by the ship's sensors; the latter every aircraft. During a battle, mock or real, the guys in charge of these two tables – the principal warfare officer (PWO) and the air warfare officer (AWO) – call the shots to the captain. Of the two, it is the PWO who shouts loudest.

The captain will make almost all his life-or-death decisions on the basis of what the PWO is seeing. The romantic image of the captain on the bridge in the teeth of a sea battle went out with Jack Hawkins and *The Cruel Sea*. The quickfire nature of the modern sea battle, with its threats on, below and above the waves, requires the most powerful man on the ship to be here, close to the equipment that gives him as much information as he can absorb in real time. The Russians are currently marketing anti-ship missiles to anyone who has the money to buy them and some of these weapons travel at speeds in excess of Mach 4. This is more than four times faster than the speed of the subsonic Exocet that wrought so much havoc on the Royal Navy in the South Atlantic in 1982.

As I manoeuvred my way across the floor, trying to avoid various bits of kit that loomed murkily at me at or around groin height, my eyes adjusted to the sight of the PWO lolling at his station with a cup of coffee in hand. Though we weren't close friends, we'd been on nodding terms for some time after several voyages together.

'Quiet day at the office?' I inquired as I made my way forward.

'While I'm in charge, it's always like this,' he quipped.

I stopped myself, just, from saying, 'Yeah, yeah,' as I recalled the Bad Day at the Stock Exchange atmosphere of my visit during the anti-ship missile exercise.

'How are you fly boys managing so far?' he probed, in a typically sceptical, fish-head kind of way.

'Oh, you know, pretty good,' I replied, anxious not to get caught up in a conversation I really didn't have time for. My mind was already on that telephone call to Yvonne.

'Must have a drink some time,' said the PWO as I reached for the door handle.

I mumbled a reciprocal sentiment and stumbled into the light of the narrow corridor that separates the ops room from lower air ops. I paused briefly outside the door, muttered a prayer to the gods who determined the movements and whereabouts of Stumpy Wylde, and crossed the threshold. To my relief, I found myself confronted with Steve.

'Hi, where's Stumpy?' I asked.

'He's off watch,' Ops One said. 'Why? Worried he might be keel-hauling someone or something?'

'As long as it's not me,' I replied, slapping the two signals down on Steve's desk, 'I really don't mind.'

Steve laughed. 'Up a little late last night, were we, Nick? Celebrating our return to the ocean with the odd rum and Coke, perhaps?'

I apologised for sounding tetchy and mentioned the phone call I had booked. Steve took the hint and began to read the signals. Behind him I could hear the tick of his wall clock as he checked and double-checked each sentence. After he had finished and given the signals the all-clear, I still had twenty minutes in hand, to my relief.

From lower ops I went on to Comcen, the ship's communications centre, just down the corridor and asked the Wren on duty to send the signals. Then I made my way back along the length of Five Deck, heading for the stairs that would return me to parts of the ship where I knew the air hadn't been recycled a dozen times before it reached my lungs.

Just before the stairs I ran into Paul Snow, the ship's marine engineering officer. When it came to the delicate handling of the ship's engines, Snowy was the number two guy. Snowy was different from most hands-on engineers, in that he was much more interested in the human condition than in sprockets and widgets. I liked him enormously, but inwardly my heart sank, because Snowy talks for England. As he so rarely emerges from the bowels of the vessel and the constant company of pounding pieces of machinery, when he does, it's as if he's face to face with another human being after a long stretch in solitary. Sometimes it's impossible to get away.

We shook hands after Snowy had wiped a dubious-looking residue off his hands and on to his trousers. 'Guess what?' he said enthusiastically. 'That little personality trick I tried on you the other day worked perfectly the other night. Spot-on, it was. Remarkable.'

Snowy had worked up a little party piece that, he claimed, allowed him to calculate anyone's likes and dislikes from the answers they gave to four innocuous-sounding questions. As I recalled, these were: 1) What's your favourite colour? 2) What's your favourite animal? 3) You're in a completely white room: how does it make you feel/respond? 4) You're overlooking a stretch of water: where are you and what's the water like? The animal, apparently, denotes how you like other people to see you and the colour what your character is really like. How you respond to the white room is how you view death, while the water question – the one that induces sniggers from those already in the know – the state of your sex drive.

I looked at my watch. There was now less than fifteen minutes left before my phone call booking and God only knew who else I might run into on the way.

'Look, Snowy, I'd love to stop, mate, but—'

'You don't understand, Nick. It was that Wren I was telling you about. Blimey, you should have heard how she reacted to the water question, mate. Storm-tossed waves, the lot. Incredible. I think I'm in with a chance there, you know.'

I held my hands up in protest. 'Don't want to know, Snowy.

Sorry, mate. Got to go. I'm booked on the phone in ten minutes. Got to call home.'

I left him standing there scratching his head and pounded up the stairs, happy I'd got off so lightly.

As I embarked on the last leg of my return journey, satisfied now that I'd make it to the Motorola in time, I thought back to Snowy's questions and how I'd answered them. For a party trick, they did seem to shed an alarmingly accurate light on my own personality – or at least on how I perceived myself.

My favourite colour was blue, denoting a strong conservative bent. My favourite animal was a dog, for loyalty and honesty – two qualities I try to maintain in myself, with intermittent success, and admire greatly in others. It was my answer to the water question that caused Snowy's eyebrows to lift momentarily into his hairline. I'd seen myself on a beach, watching storm-tossed seas crashing down on to rocks. I'm still trying to figure that one out myself.

The white room response, however, was probably the most revealing, because I felt distinctly uncomfortable about it, so much so that I wanted to repaint it in something bright and garish.

When Snowy told me what that meant, I was taken aback. When you volunteer as a fighter pilot, even in peacetime, the realities of the job mean that death is never that far away. The interpretation of my vehement response to the white room question was that I did not want to confront it in any shape, way or form. It left me wondering what on earth I was doing as a Navy fighter pilot. It was true, though. Death was something that never, ever crossed my mind; and this was as true today, as we steamed full-tilt towards a war zone, as it had ever been.

I sat down at my desk and stared at the Motorola for a second or two, catching my breath and doing my best to picture things at home. Part of me, too, was bracing myself for any left-of-field information that could hit me about Kristian. All the indicators were that he was improving with every passing hour, but there's always that little bit of you that prepares for the worst on a long-distance call, and this one was no exception.

When I felt suitably composed, I lifted the receiver. My finger was heading for the first digit of my number when there was a knock at the door. I clucked, cut the line and somewhat imperiously shouted: 'Come!'

The diminutive figure of Wren Alexander appeared in the doorway.

'Wren Alexander,' I said, trying not to display any irritation, but conscious that the sigh I emitted probably said it all. 'What is it?'

'I was after a word, sir.'

'Well, can't it wait?' I pointed towards the phone. 'I'm about to call England.'

She faltered momentarily and then burst into tears. For a second or two I just sat there, phone in hand, staring at her. Then I was on my feet, out from behind my desk and offering her the seat I had just vacated. I shut the door and produced a handkerchief from one of my pockets. When her tears had subsided a little, I inquired a little nervously what the matter was, though I thought I already knew. Details of the short conversation I'd had with Billy Borland back in Yeovilton about looming problems within the division burbled into my conscious thought. Wren Alexander's domestic difficulties had been right at the top of the list.

'I want to go home,' she said. 'Right now. Not another moment on this ship, sir. I want to go back to Yeovilton.'

I sat on the edge of my bed and considered this for a moment or two. 'Is this anything to do with your boyfriend?' I asked.

She gave an almost imperceptible nod. She was staring at the hanky crumpled between her hands.

'Wren Alexander,' I said softly, 'you did volunteer for sea service.'

'I know, but—'

'Listen,' I interrupted gently. 'We're all in this together. I know it's hard, but we are kind of at war here . . .'

I winced at the way the words came out, aware that they sounded as if they'd been borrowed from a second-rate war movie. I took a deep breath and tried again, casting my mind back, all those years ago, to my first time at sea.

'It seems worse than it really is, especially in these first few days,' I told her. 'It does get better, honest. Believe me, lots of people feel the way you do. It's just that not everyone shows it. You know what the remedy is?'

She looked up and shook her head.

'Work. Throw yourself into the work. That helps – a lot. Also, write to your boyfriend. Try to make him understand what we're doing here.'

She held my gaze. 'What are we doing, sir? What is Bosnia to us? I don't understand. Do you?'

I paused. 'You must have seen the pictures on the news. We're part of a force that is trying to prevent a humanitarian tragedy from taking place. Bosnia has become a bloodbath, a massacre on our own doorstep. The last time anything like this happened in Europe was during the Second World War. It's important that we stop it happening.'

She stopped crying and looked at me. 'Do you believe that, sir?'

The intensity of her gaze unsettled me. I hesitated, but only for a beat, and answered that I did.

Wren Alexander took a deep breath and got to her feet. She thanked me and took a step towards the door. 'My boyfriend and I spent two weeks last summer in Corfu,' she said, turning back to me. 'It's close, isn't it? To where we're going, I mean.'

'Yes,' I replied. 'Pretty close.'

'It shouldn't be possible in this day and age for there to be a war next to a place you go on holiday, should it?' she said.

I didn't answer, because she'd put it in context a lot better than I had. I was about to tell her that that particular sentiment was probably as good a place as any to start in her letter, but she was already out of the room, the door closing behind her.

As I reached for the phone again there was another knock at the door. I muttered something threatening under my breath and reached for a box of Kleenex to hand to Wren Alexander as she re-entered the room.

Instead, however, I was greeted by the sight of Leading Rob Arnold, the man who had married the Singaporean lap-dancer and was now making noises about a posting to Hong Kong to be closer to her.

'What is this,' I said, 'a doctor's surgery or something?' I briefly

wondered if this was someone's idea of a wind-up. Beasty's perhaps. Or Oz's.

Leading Arnold stared at me blankly.

'Sit down, Rob,' I said, as kindly as I could. 'What is it?'

'It's about my wife, sir.'

'Ah, of course,' I said, casting a rapid glance at my watch. I still
had some time left on the clock. 'You're looking for a transfer to
Hong Kong, aren't you?'

'Yes, sir.' He paused. 'Actually, sir, I'm thinking of putting in for
an emergency draft. Right now.'

I raised my eyes to the ceiling, not quite believing what I was hearing. I wanted to shake the man by his shirt and point to the odds of
this marriage panning out. He'd married a prostitute, for Christ's sake.

'You want to get off the ship as quickly as you can – is that what
you're saying?'

'Yes, sir. I love her, sir.'

'I see.' I was disturbed by the look in his eyes. There was no mis-
taking the man's depth of feeling and, to be honest, it knocked the
wind out of my sails.

'Look,' I said, too tired to argue, 'I'll see what I can do. I'll have
a word with the AEO, but I'm not sure it'll do any good, Rob. The
truth is, we need men like you – and especially now.'

The air engineering officer, Big Engines – the guy with whom I
shared responsibility for the division – was a tough old Scot and I
pretty much knew what he'd tell Arnold. But I found myself penning
the aide memoire anyway: 'Speak Engines – Arnold and HK.'

'Thank you, sir,' Arnold said, craning over the paper as I
scrawled out the words.

'Pleasure,' I replied, looking up at him and smiling reassuringly.
'Now do me a favour.'

'Yes, sir.'

'Piss off. I'm trying to call home.' I shot a glance at the Motorola.

Leading Arnold beamed as he backed towards the door. ''Course,
sir. Thank you, sir.'

I picked up the handset and started to dial. Then, unbelievably,
there was another knock at the door.

'For fuck's sake!'

The door began to open before I could request either Wren Alexander or Leading Arnold to go straight to hell. I crashed the handset back on to its cradle and prepared to deliver the mother of all bollockings to the sorry-arsed individual who'd had the temerity to interrupt me again.

As the door swung open, I saw the boss, standing in the corridor, his hand outstretched.

'Time's up, Wings,' he said, wearing that spoof-balls grin of his.

'What do you mean?'

He tapped his watch, stepped into the cabin and picked up the sat phone. 'You've been hogging this thing far too bloody long. Time to give someone else a turn.'

Three days later I climbed into the cockpit of my Sea Harrier and prepared for take-off. It was a little after eight-thirty in the morning, twenty minutes from launch time, and the sun was already high in the sky. We were now just a dozen miles off the coast of Gibraltar and I liked to think I could smell the dust of North Africa on the warm breeze that blew across the deck. In the space of a few days we'd sailed from winter into spring.

The six jets that were bound for Deci via Gib were ranged around the fan tail. Three of the eleven Sea King helicopters tucked up against the ship's superstructure were being readied for the hop to Gib. These were Sea King Mk 4s, transport variants known as Commandos, and they would be shuttling squadron maintainers for much of the day between the carrier and Gib.

For their passengers, the leg would be nigh-on two hours of bone-rattling fun in the back of an RAF C-130 transport. One of the advantages of being a fighter pilot is that you rarely, if ever, have to strap into one of these hellish contraptions.

As I watched the buzz of activity around me, I uttered a quiet prayer for everything to proceed to plan. If there was a fuck-up between here and Deci, the buck stopped with me, because I was the guy who'd organised it all. But as we started the engines and the ship swung into wind, my mind settled into the job. Everything else was suddenly behind me. I'd even managed to speak to Yvonne and get the good news that Kristian was continuing to improve.

We took off and joined up in 'radar trail' at 2,000ft, using the ranging capability of our Blue Fox radars to maintain a precise distance of a half-mile between each of our aircraft. The carrier was so close to Gibraltar that I was able to see the rock the moment we reached our cruise altitude. Minutes later, we were 'dirtying-up' for the approach, dropping the landing gear and lowering the nozzles as we decelerated towards the airfield.

On paper, the landing looked pretty. We were all competent pilots and it's always nice to put on a bit of a show for the locals. But I remembered from previous landings that the unusual topography at Gib did funny things to the air currents, and as we came in to land, the turbulence seemed especially bad. As Mel touched down, with the wind blowing all over the place, he power-nozzle-braked a little too smartish. PNBing – putting the nozzles as far forward as they'll go and applying huge amounts of thrust – is the aerospace equivalent of hitting a brick wall.

What started as a picture-perfect approach ended with us all bunching up with nowhere to go. Because the runway at Gib is so short, we were fortunate we didn't shunt into each other like a load of dozy commuters on the M5. Fortunately we always brief an overtake lane, but if I'd had a horn on the joystick that day I'd have used it.

The culmination of this embarrassing sideshow was Shaggy whistling past us, his left-hand outrigger almost in the grass. For a moment, I thought he'd resorted to this drastic tactic because his brakes had failed, but it later transpired he hadn't noticed the traffic jam on the centre line until it was too late. Our only warning of near-disaster was the jolly shout, 'Coming through!' followed by the sight of his Sea Harrier shooting past our wingtips. Henry, needless to say, took a dim view of this.

As soon as we'd straightened ourselves out, we taxied over to the visiting aircraft facility. Gib is normally a busy staging post for all kinds of aircraft, but today it seemed quite quiet. Among the ragtag bunch of aircraft nestling under the rock, I was relieved to spot the C-130 tanker and the transport aircraft that would get us and the maintainers to Deci.

A couple of hours later, having co-ordinated with the tanker crew on the ground, we were off again. At 20,000ft I settled into the cruise and prepared myself for the ordeal of tanking.

It sounds straightforward enough, but air-to-air refuelling is a very precise art and if you get it wrong you can dump yourself and your team-mates in the shit. On the long leg to Deci, it would take around half the total journey time for all six of us to get the fuel we needed to make the distance. Deci was simply too far to do it all in one hop. The tanking window would commence a quarter of the way into the sortie and end when it was three-quarters through – as long as everything went to plan. A number of factors conspire with Messrs Murphy and Sod to put a stick through the spokes of such well-laid plans, however. The unusual refuelling probe of the Sea Harrier sticks a long way out on the left-hand side, making for a challenging hook-up with the refuelling 'basket' that trails in the slipstream of the tanker.

The basket is pretty much as it sounds: a thing that looks like a shuttlecock attached to the end of the fuel hose, into which you must rudely but accurately insert the tip of your refuelling probe if the hook-up is to work. You are best advised not to watch the basket, but to line up with the aircraft, which gives you a much better measure of distance. If you're not on form, if your mind's not on it, it can end up being a bit of a joust.

A Sea Harrier can carry a full fuel load of 8,000lbs. On an oper-ation like this, the first guy in line is down to about 5,000lbs when he mates with the tanker, while the last has only around 3,000lbs sloshing in his tanks by the time he hits the basket. As we cruised towards our rendezvous with the tanker, which had taken off forty-five minutes before us, I was third in line. By my turn, I'd be down to about 4,000lbs.

It's the last guy you have to bear in mind as you go into the joust, because if any of us takes too long to hook up with the basket, it's the tail-end Charlie who hits what's known as 'tanker bingo', the moment when he has insufficient fuel to make his destination, and has to divert to the nearest available airfield. On this mission, that would mean somewhere in France.

A glint of sunlight on metal up ahead and the tanker suddenly sprang into focus against the deep blue of the stratosphere. Like migrating birds, we formated on our new leader and began to take on fuel. Everything went smoothly until it was the turn of number five, poor old Mowgli, who'd only ever tanked once before.

It's obvious when a guy's tensing up during a mid-air tank, because the back of his aircraft starts flapping around like the tail of a fish. It means he's watching the basket, not the Hercules. This is only natural as it is what your instincts tell you to do, but you have to fight the urge. Trying to follow the end of a piece of hose that's flapping around the sky like the head of a writhing snake makes you bounce around too. Air-to-air refuelling is something that comes with experience. And, I realised now, Mowgli simply hadn't had enough time to practise it.

Oz was the last guy in line and I knew what would be going through his mind. He'd be glancing between his fuel gauge and Mowgli's brushes with the basket, shouting into a dead mike: 'Come on, Mowgli, make the fucking connection!'

On Mowgli's second attempt, he jabbed at the basket and missed. It was obvious to all of us now that Oz only had fuel for just one more attempt.

Talk about off-putting. Tanking at this point is a real spectator sport; five of us watching one guy who's all tensed up and, no doubt, thinking about the ribbing he's going to get from us when he lands. But there is danger in this procedure, too. If it gets so bad that you start to panic and jab with the probe too hard you can get what's called a 'spokes': one of the spokes of the basket breaking loose and shooting into the yawning hole of your jet intake. A spoke in your Pegasus, and it's goodnight nurse.

Mowgli approached the basket for the third and final time. Above him, the four whirling turbo-props of the Hercules chopped and beat the air into myriad small currents and eddies. I could see Mowgli fighting to control his aircraft as he manoeuvred the probe closer to the basket. From my perspective, it looked as if the Sea Harrier was close enough to clip the back end of the Hercules. And then, suddenly, the probe slid into the basket and locked. Mowgli was connected. Seconds later, he started to take on fuel.

You could hear the relief in the banter that erupted across the ether as we flicked on our mikes and made a load of poor-quality jokes about Mowgli and his defective probe. Mowgli was oblivious of it all. I could see him beaming a big smile behind his mask. He looked like the gang member with bum-fluff on his cheeks getting a ribbing from his mates when they find out he's just lost his virginity. The kid is just chuffed that he's a big boy now and that he hasn't altogether disgraced himself.

Twenty minutes later, we were all topped up and ready to go.

'Vixens, you're clear to detach,' the tanker pilot announced.

'Thanks for your help,' Mel told him. 'See you on the ground at Deci.'

'Roger. You're buying the beers.'

He sounded, I thought, like your friendly BA captain on a 747 out of Heathrow.

'Roger that,' Mel said, and peeled away, heading for a flight level 10,000ft higher than the tanker, our optimum cruise altitude for the final leg to Deci.

The rest of us followed, tucking in alongside him and opening up the throttles.

Within a minute, we were visible to the tanker crew simply as six vapour trails, heading east at over eight miles a minute.

# CHAPTER 4

Decimommanu is where the Western world's fighter pilots gather to joust to the death – except that the bullets and missiles aren't real. Like Nellis Air Force Base in Nevada and Miramar in California, home to the US Air Force and Navy's two world-famous fighter weapons schools, it's a place where the talk and the bullshit end and where real reputations are forged. It's a wide, arid expanse of nothing, nestling beneath the mountains that form the backbone of Sardinia.

To tourists, the countryside and coastline around Deci are little pieces of paradise in an out-of-the-way corner of the Med. To pilots, the island is heaven and hell rolled into one.

It's always exciting to touch down at Deci, because it feels like you've arrived at the finals of some great international sporting event. There are different varieties of aircraft all over the place and the markings on their polished metal skins identify the competitors. As I taxied in with the other five jets, I saw Italian F-104 Starfighters, Turkish F-4 Phantoms, some US Air Force F-16s and a couple of Portuguese A-6s.

The problem with Deci is that it's a dump. The earth is brown all year round and there's next to no vegetation to break up the barren view. Such greenery as does exist isn't green at all, but clumpy, parched stuff that looks like grass, only it'll cut the clothes off your skin should you happen to brush up against it.

The heart of Deci's war-gaming system is the ACMI: Air Combat Manoeuvring and Instrumentation system. ACMI is a giant electronic grid covering the airspace off the north-west coast of the island. Every aircraft that takes off to participate in Deci's war-gaming activities is fitted with an ACMI pod under one of its wings. This device relays all the aircraft's pertinent data – its speed, position, height, heading etc. – to a telemetry terminal on the base which, with the help of a powerful processor, computes and displays everything you need to know about every individual aircraft on a set of giant screens in an ops centre in the middle of the base.

The ops centre gives those watching the battle a top-down view over the proceedings. It allows pilots to fly against each other in the most realistic combat conditions and automatically validates the kill criteria so that there's no doubt over who's been shot down and who hasn't. As a prelude to our arrival in a real kill zone, it couldn't have been a better way to get up to speed on our tactics.

The base is Italian-owned, but several countries maintain permanent facilities at Deci, the Brits among them. I eased the Sea Harrier over to the British engineering section and shut down the engine in the shade of its large hangar. It was late afternoon and the sun was already dipping towards the mountains when I slid back the canopy and sniffed appreciatively at the warm Mediterranean air. After spending much of the day in the cramped confines of a cockpit, it was good to stretch my legs on terra firma.

The British accommodation block is around 2 miles from the engineering section, so I was glad to note that there were cars and minivans already there to greet us. As we journeyed over to the other side of the base, I kept my eyes peeled for a sight of the Luftwaffe's MiG-29s. The MiG-29 made its first public appearance in the West in 1988, but six years on, it was still a rare sight and I felt a ripple of anticipation in my veins when it dawned on me how close I was to seeing the aircraft in the flesh again.

We reached the British accommodation block without catching sight of them; probably, our RAF driver told us, because the Germans were still out on the range, sharpening the tactics they were going to use against us. Whether he was kidding or not I didn't know, but already I got the sense that we weren't the only ones at Deci who were keen to find out how we'd fare against the Fulcrums. Word of the impending showdown had obviously got around.

The following morning, after an early night in the comfort of a bed that never once threatened to snap shut on me or hurl me to the floor, I rose at seven and made my way in our minivans with the rest of the crew over to the ops centre.

Although it was still January, the air was warm and muggy, even at this time of the day. From previous experience of Deci, I knew it would be several hours before the light mist that hung over the base would burn off. Fortunately, the prevailing conditions had not stopped Deci's would-be Top Guns from taking to the air. From several miles away, behind the fog curtain, the air reverberated with the sound of aircraft roaring into the sky from the main runway.

It was when we got to the end of the 2-mile straight stretch of road that led from the accommodation block to the ops centre and rounded a couple of buildings that we saw them. In the mist, with the dull light of the washed-out sun behind them, they were visible only in silhouette, but this only made them seem all the more sinister. There's something shark-like about the MiG-29, though I can't quite put my finger on what it is. Perhaps it is the razor-like vertical tails or the slight curvature of the spine aft of the cockpit that give the aircraft its menacing, yet sleek and sensual look and remind you at the same time of its effortless speed and power.

Aerodynamically, the MiG-29 is superb, although it is let down by its Russian-made onboard electronics. As Luftwaffe technicians scurried around the aircraft, it was just possible to make out the dummy AA-11 missiles on their underwing pylons. These were reputed to be the best short-range dogfight weapons in the business, even better than our own AIM-9M Sidewinders.

The important criteria here, what makes one missile better than another, relate primarily to the seeker, the missile's manoeuvrability and its kinetic energy – how much 'oomph' it has left at the extremity of its range. The combination of these factors yields the missile's 'no-escape zone': a volume of sky in which no matter how many evading manoeuvres a fighter pilot attempts, the missile will always kill him.

The no-escape zone of the AIM-9M was good, but on the AA-11 it was awesome. But because the AA-11 and the AIM-9M are the same class of weapon, we reckoned, rightly or wrongly, that we could defeat it through good flying. The MiG-29, though, had one crucial advantage over our Sea Harrier. It also carried a medium-range air-to-air missile, the AA-10, a radar-guided weapon with a 25km range. As we had nothing comparable, it was like going into a boxing ring knowing that your reach is half that of your opponent's. This is what made the spike-and-drag, or 'Doppler notch', tactic so crucial. If we could stay invisible on the MiG-29's radar until we got it within killing distance of our short-range AIM-9Ms, we stood a damned good chance of coming out of the engagement alive.

The silence from the rest of the minivan told me I wasn't the only one who was mulling over the contest to come.

Today, meanwhile, our orders were to concentrate on honing our air-to-ground weapons skills. As soon as we got inside the ops centre, we were greeted by an old and bold squadron leader called Swampy Lake. Our first obligation was to attend a mass flying brief for new arrivals at the base, a thirty-minute session that covered all the dos and don'ts of operational life at Deci. Since most of us had heard this before, Swampy tried to make it as succinct as possible.

The essential point for the initiates was that there were two main training areas: the instrumented ACMI range over the sea to the west of the island for aerial dogfighting, and the Capo Frasca range in the north-west corner of the island for gunnery and bombing work. Each of these had tightly regulated entry and exit points and there were a number of no-go areas, especially when we were armed.

The guys who had never been to Deci before learned that Capo Frasca had five principal targets: a circle of stones to the north of the range, one to the south used for bombing and three 20ft-long strafe-panels, each fitted with acoustic scoring sensors. These deduced whether or not our bullets were on target and automatically relayed the score of each pilot back to the range controller. In addition to these targets, there were several old tanks and trucks scattered around the range. We were pretty much free to have a pop at these whenever we liked.

As soon as the welcome talk was finished, we went into the sortie brief. We didn't have long at Deci – we were due back on the carrier in a week's time – so every sortie over the next few days would count.

Today, our task was to practise our 'steep-bombing' work to the point of perfection. Although we did have access to so-called 'smart weapons', in the form of the Paveway II laser-guided bomb, these were expensive pieces of hardware and were available for use against only the highest-priority targets.

For the rest, we had to rely on our trusty old 'iron' or 'dumb' bombs, weapons that have changed little since the first bombs were dropped in the 1914–18 war. Using the capabilities of our air-craft to the full, we've been able to increase bombing accuracy considerably since those days, but the techniques involved require no less practice. The fact that we'd never dropped 'live' bombs during our steep-dive practice in the UK served only to make our task more difficult.

As a general principle, we target everything through the HUD, which is situated on the coaming in line with the pilot's forward view out of the cockpit. The steeper you dive, the more accurate the drop. If you were ever brave or foolish enough to dive vertically, the laws of physics dictated there would be no errors at all and you'd hit the target bang-on every time.

But here other factors come into play. At all times, you have to be mindful of the threat from surface-to-air missiles. Dip below 10,000ft and these suckers will get you. The steeper the dive, the higher your initial run-in to bomb release needs to be. Based on a 60-degree dive angle, we calculate on starting our bomb run from 20,000ft, releasing at 14,000ft and pulling out at 10,000.

The HUD gives us three different options for bombing. The first and simplest is called ASB1 (Air-to-Surface Bombs One). This is where we use the HUD in its simplest sight mode, bombing through the cross-hairs and praying that the weapon falls some-where near its intended target. In the modern era of warfare, in which collateral damage – that euphemism for the destruction of a church or school building – has become the dirtiest of words, this is a technique we'd only ever consider as a last resort.

ASB2 brings into play the height, speed and wind information that is fed into the weapons-aiming computer, the WAC, significantly boosting accuracy. But we're still talking a miss distance of around 150ft from a bombing height of 8,000ft plus, which isn't great news for any civilians who might happen to be down there at the time.

It's only in the third bombing mode, ASB3, that we start to get really good bombing accuracy, and that's because we're adding the air-to-ground ranging capabilities of the radar to the equation. As soon as the radar has got an accurate reading of the distance between the aircraft and the target, two V-shaped symbols merge into a diamond shape. All you have to do then is wait for a T symbol to pass through the diamond, which signals the moment for weapons release. If everything's working properly, this should give you a bombing accuracy of 100ft CEP (circular error probable, the term that denotes average miss distance from the target).

Getting this right over the next few days would be crucial to the maintenance of our cherished 'swing role' in the Balkans – the ability to perform either our air-to-air, air-to-ground or recce roles at the drop of a hat. There are very few aircraft in NATO with swing-role capability and certainly none, apart from ours, in the UK, which is something that always gets up the nose of the RAF.

The Fleet Air Arm, not surprisingly, prided itself on the swing-role capability of its Sea Harriers. If we could validate our steep-dive work at Deci, we'd be able to declare our swing role to NATO's Combined Air Operations Centre (CAOC) at Vicenza in southern Italy the moment we arrived in theatre. The CAOC was the command and control centre that drew up all the sortie plans for the multitude of aircraft taking part in the Bosnian operation. Our own man, the indomitable but injury-bound Smitty, was on his way to Vicenza to act as our representative there.

With the swing-role cachet under our belts, we'd be assigned all the plum missions, and the honour and tradition of the Navy would be upheld. But this increased the pressure on us to perform now. If we fucked up on Capo Frasca over the next couple of days, we wouldn't get ticks in all the right boxes. And as decent a fellow as Squadron Leader Swampy Lake seemed, I was sure he'd be on to his mates at Vicenza within minutes if we failed to make the grade.

In the rarefied atmosphere of the CAOC, the news would spread in a flash and before we knew it we'd be the talking point of all the other NATO aircrews – but for all the wrong reasons.

That afternoon, we sent up a three-ship to put the theory into practice. I watched Henry, Oz and Shaggy take off, each of them with four 14kg practice bombs strapped under their wings. Then I sprinted the couple of hundred yards from the maintenance area to the ops room to follow the sortie's progress on the radio. The form was for the jets to assume a racetrack pattern, with 2 miles separating them, a few miles from the range perimeter. Each pilot would then await his turn to go in to bomb the target, the northernmost of the range's two stone circles.

After a couple of runs, as I listened to the strikes being called in, I realised that we had a problem. All the bombs were falling about 150ft long and to the right, about two o'clock from the barrel at the centre of the stones. If the strikes had been all over the place, I'd have put it down to plain poor training, but the consistency of the hits suggested that the problem was endemic.

To prove the point, Henry issued instructions to the pilots to introduce an offset aim point – short of and to the left of the barrel – for the last of their bombs. This resulted in some pretty close hits and confirmed that the problem was with the aircraft, not with us.

That night we did some pretty fevered brainstorming. It was obvious that there was a glitch common to all the aircraft. The question was what was it? Someone – Little Engines, I think – suggested that the Doppler aerials under the aircraft might be picking up bad signals off the sea as the jets banked across the water on their final run-in to the target.

In a bomb run, the WAC calculates the aim point for the bombs after number-crunching a range of different inputs from the aircraft's sensors. Height, speed and bearing are easy pieces of data to gather and process, but a fourth, wind, is less so. Its speed and direction are measured by taking data from the inertial navigation system, which works out how fast the aircraft is moving through the sky, and from the Doppler aerials beneath the plane, which calculate how fast it is moving relative to the ground. The difference is the wind drift – and depending on the wind's speed, this can mean the difference between a bomb that is on-target and one that misses by hundreds of feet.

The solution was to fly a longer circuit between bomb drops, thereby extending the inbound leg after the final turn on to the target. This extended period of level flight on the run-in gave the Doppler aerials the thirty seconds of level flight they needed to provide the WAC with good information. If that still didn't work, it was suggested we should take the forecast 5,000ft wind (mid-drop) and type it manually into the system. Because this was something of a lash-up, it was only to be used as a last resort.

We crossed our fingers that this fix would work.

Two hours after daybreak, Gazza, Mel and I took off as Vixens Three, Two and One, respectively, with me leading. We quickly established our racetrack pattern at 20,000ft and received our OK to bomb. As I bled some speed off in the turn, reducing my airspeed to 350 knots, I could see the other two aircraft in the pattern behind me, vapour trails spilling off their wingtips as they followed me round the pattern.

'Vixen One, in hot,' I called, signalling I was ready to bomb. Out of the corner of my eye, even from the height we were at, I could clearly see the circle of stones and the barrel in its midst. To make sure I was adequately lined up from the start, I put the target into the left-hand quarter-light of the canopy, threw a last glance at the altimeter to make sure that I was at the correct height for the commencement of the run, then rolled inverted, pulling the nose down and rolling right-side up in one fluid movement to establish the 60-degree dive angle.

From 20,000ft, 60 degrees looks no bloody different from the perpendicular. I was hanging from my straps with the entire island laid out below me. The speed built up rapidly – 350, 400, 450 knots on the indicator – giving me no time to admire the view. I knew I had only six, maybe eight seconds, to get the two Vs on the HUD lined up either side of the target.

A kick of the rudder and a slight adjustment on the stick and the little white barrel at the centre of the ring of stones slid beautifully into the middle of the sight. Now I pressed the 'accept' button on the top of the stick and imagined the radar doing its thing: squirting radio frequency energy on to the target, receiving the signals as they bounced back to the antenna and calculating the distance between the target and the aircraft in the blink of an eye before feeding the results into the WAC.

Suddenly, bingo, the Vs slid towards each other until they merged as a diamond exactly over the target. The WAC had accepted the data. I maintained the diamond over the target for a few more seconds – it always seems like an eternity – waiting for the moment when the T-bar moved up from the bottom of the HUD through the target bull. And then it started to travel. Wait, wait, wait . . . at last it hit the centre of the diamond, I depressed the pickle switch on top of the stick and the bomb dropped.

Now came the bit I loved: a yank on the stick, wrenching it back into my stomach, to get the nose of the aircraft back up again. The gs hit me with the equivalent of six times my body weight exerted from head to toe, dragging vital body organs – lungs, heart, liver, guts – with them.

Just as it feels you're about to faint from the sudden loss of blood, most of which has by now drained into your boots, training and discipline take over. As the speed started to drop I applied full power. Then, fighting the gs, which were still coursing through the aircraft, I transferred the leaden weight of my left hand from the throttle to the nozzle lever, found the chaff and flare button and punched it with my thumb.

Although there was no danger of any SAMs shooting us down over Deci, it had been drummed into us ever since we'd received news we were heading to Bosnia that we needed to hone our countermeasures discipline in practice sessions such as these so that it would become second nature in the danger zone itself. The most dangerous moment in the bomb run is when we're in exactly this situation – in the pull-out, our minds and bodies depleted by the crippling effects of g, and the jet losing airspeed. If you punch chaff and flares into the airstream now, there's at least a fair chance that the missile that's heading for you at this precise moment will latch on to those little metal filings or those flares and explode among them, not against you.

I was back up to 20,000ft before I knew it. As I looked back over my shoulder towards the target, the controller came on the air.

'Vixen One, score Delta Hotel,' he announced dispassionately. Delta Hotel stood for direct hit.

I whooped into my microphone, then addressed the other two. 'Pressure's off, guys. You can't do any better than that.'

Mel and Gazza gave it their best shot, of course. All the bombs fell within 50ft of the bull: a uniformly good CEP. Gazza excelled himself by achieving another very good score, letting himself down only slightly by targeting the wrong circle of stones – the southernmost set, several hundred feet from the actual target. He was right to brace himself for some heavy piss-taking in the bar that night, but, like the rest of us, he was secure in the knowledge that our remedial action to the Doppler problem had worked. We could declare our swing-role to NATO with confidence. Over Bosnia, there wouldn't be a single mission we couldn't be called on to perform.

That evening we celebrated our victory over the gremlins that had conspired to keep us out of the war. The proceedings took place in the square outside the British accommodation block. It wasn't so much our 'do' as the troops', but everyone was invited, including the other nationalities. The Brits were famous for their parties and at Deci the rule was simple: you worked hard and you played hard.

The festivities began at about six o'clock. The cooking took place on three giant brick barbecues set in the shade of a wood-framed shelter decked out with party lights. In a rare display of interservice harmony, the food was provided by the RAF and the Navy cooked it. The chefs excelled themselves. It was a feast.

As the sun slipped behind the mountains, the air filled with the smoke of roasting meats and grew thick with banter and laughter. After the meal, the beers and wine continued to flow and people from other parts of the base, drawn by the hubbub, music and lights began to show up.

Pretty soon, a bunch of us pilots fell into conversation with a group of blokes from the Special Boat Service, the Royal Marines' equivalent of the SAS, who were in Deci practising for – well, I didn't really like to ask. These guys looked the part. They were all dressed in jeans and T-shirts and built like the brick barbies in the middle of the square. I never found out their ranks or names, and neither were offered, but they all seemed like decent enough blokes and we quickly discovered that we had more in common than our different lifestyles within the service might have suggested.

We were discussing our mutual fondness for *Blackadder* (for some reason best known to the other squadron members, my nickname was Lord Flashheart, after the Rik Mayall character who charms the pants off Queen Elizabeth), when Shaggy reminded me that we oughtn't to get too pissed as the following day we were up against the Germans and we'd need to keep our wits about us. In this rerun of the Battle of Britain, Shaggy and I had drawn the short straws to go up against the MiG-29s.

'Funny lot, the Germans,' Gazza mused drunkenly into his rum and Coke. 'No sense of humour, of course. Did you know, by the by, that there's no word in the German language for "fluffy"? Just goes to show what a sad bunch of bastards they really are.'

'Is that true?' asked Swampy Lake, who'd ambled over a few minutes earlier to join us. 'Or is that something out of *Blackadder*? Don't watch the programme myself.'

Swampy never got his answer, because at that moment there was a huge roar from behind us as Squashy Morton, the tomato-faced watch chief, took on one of the SBS lads at arm-wrestling. The air reverberated with the sound of chanting as sailors and SBS heavies gathered round the table in support of their respective champions.

After just a couple of seconds of battle, Squashy's face looked like a pressure-cooker ready to burst. He held the gaze of his SBS oppo, who'd barely worked up a sweat, his eyes bulging, every sinew and vein standing out on his neck. And then, to another huge roar from the crowd, Squashy's arm was flattened against the table and the champion, looking slightly alarmed now by the sudden turn of events, was picked up by a dozen matelots and hurled into one of the giant wheelie bins containing all the leftovers from the barbie. The SBS boys promptly grabbed Squashy and threw him into the bin as well. Then the lid was slammed shut and the whole ensemble rolled around the square.

I had the grave misfortune to be the person standing closest to this hellish tumble-drier when it ground to a halt, the lid was opened and Squashy and his rival toppled out, covered from head to toe in bits of burger, sausage and bap. They were also liberally smeared with ketchup and mustard.

It was such a sight that I couldn't contain myself and, pointing at both of them, I fell to the ground in fits of laughter. This prompted a howl of anger from both sides of the crowd and the next thing I knew I was being thrown head-first into the bin myself and treated to a ride round the square.

When the bumping and grinding finally stopped and the lid opened, I crawled gratefully out on to the tarmac, pausing only to wipe some mayonnaise from my eyes. Suddenly I became aware of an eerie silence. I made a half-turn and found myself facing Mel, the boss. At his side was a bloke I'd never seen before, immaculately turned out in a pressed flight suit and a very smart black leather flying jacket. He was tall and fair, with piercing blue eyes. They could not conceal a look of mild disgust.

'Ah, Nick, we were looking for you, nice of you to pitch up,' Mel announced without batting an eyelid. 'I'd like to introduce you to Colonel Hartmut Steffens, the boss of the MiG-29 squadron here.'

'Hello, sir,' I managed, dusting myself down. 'Good to meet you.' I was about to proffer my hand but, noticing that it was covered in an unfeasible amount of grease, thought better of it. Instead, for a reason I still don't quite understand, I was moved to fill the vacuum in the conversation with a question. Was it true, I asked in all sincerity, that there was no word in the German language for 'fluffy'? The German stared at me blankly and even Mel looked a little perplexed. Behind me there was some sniggering from the other pilots which I hoped only I could hear.

When my head had stopped spinning and sanity had returned, I

broke the ice by inviting Steffens over to the Pig 'n' Tape, the aircrew bar in one of the buildings on the edge of the square. It was
here, over several beers, that we established that Steffens was a
decent fellow, if a little humourless (which confirmed Gazza's
thesis). By the end of the evening we had the arrangements all
drawn up. In the morning, Deke and Mowgli were due to go up
against a pair of Italian F-104s acting the part of MiG-21s, of which
the Yugoslavs also had a quantity. Then, in the early afternoon, it
would be Shaggy and me upholding the squadron honour against
Colonel Steffens and his wingman in their pristine MiG-29s.

We continued to share pleasantries, each of us rather formal
and reserved, until, on the dot of eleven, there was a squeal of
tyres outside the Pig 'n' Tape and the Italian 'fun police' roared into
the square in their jeeps to break up the party.

Time for bed, said Zebedee.

The F-104 Starfighter is a missile with wings. It was designed by
Lockheed in the 1950s and maintained in the front line by the US
Air Force until the 1970s, when it was phased out of US service
and left to soldier on in other parts of the world.

In 1994, the Italian Air Force was one of a handful of nations
that still operated the Starfighter. This was lucky for us, because its
performance characterstics were broadly analogous to those of the
MiG-21. Both aircraft were almost forty years old, both were single-
engined and both were restricted to carrying short-range missile
systems. If anything, however, the MiG-21 had the edge over its
American-designed counterpart in terms of manoeuvrability.

While we felt we were more than a match for the MiG-21, on its
good days we knew it could still beat us. Sharpening our tactics
against the Italians, therefore, seemed like a good thing to do. Our
real advantage against both aircraft was our missile system, the
latest version of the Sidewinder.

The Sea Harrier had the AIM-9M variant, which allowed us to
take head-on shots against the enemy. The Starfighter and the
MiG-21 had missiles (the AIM-9G in the case of the Starfighter;
the AA-2/AA-8 on the MiG-21) with markedly inferior seeker
performance. These weapons needed to lock on to the heat

signature of an aircraft's jet pipe for their pilots to take the shot, which meant they could only attack from the rear.

Unlike a real battle zone, Deci is bound by safety rules. To stop us flying into the ground, a 'hard deck' is normally established at 5,000ft. The upper level of the fight zone is usually set at 30,000ft. Within these two extremes you can pretty much do what you want. The exceptions are that once you are 'killed' you have to exit the fight quickly, and head-on shots are banned within 1,000ft of two converging aircraft to stop us flying into each other.

The Italians, however, consistently broke fight zone rules and it wasn't uncommon to find yourself canopy-to-canopy at 100ft with an F-104. I reminded Deke and Mowgli of this as they jotted down their briefing notes. Basically, I said, the Eyeties are sneaky bastards, so watch 'em closely.

Because neither the Starfighter nor the MiG-21 was fitted with a modern pulse-Doppler radar, the spike-and-drag tactic we'd practised during the voyage from Portsmouth was inappropriate for this exercise. We decided, therefore, to draw on a couple of other strategies from our tactical box of tricks: trail formation and battle-to-hook.

In 'trail' the lead guy in the pair would fly at around 15,000ft and look up with his radar, while the bloke at the back would fly higher – around 25,000ft – and look down. The trick was for the high-flying pilot to wait for the two enemy aircraft to commit to the leader below, then swoop down and fire on them as they moved to engage him.

In 'battle', the two Sea Harriers would fly into the fight in side-by-side formation, one of the aircraft running straight down the throat of the fight, the other approaching on a parallel heading, but off to the side. With the enemy distracted, we hoped, by the guy running straight for them, the wingman could hook in at the last moment and attack from the beam before they had a chance to appreciate that he was there. So much for the theory. Now it was time to get out there and fight.

An hour later I was sitting on a chair in the ACMI viewing facility watching Deke and Mowgli on the two large screens. A bunch of maintainers had come over from the hangars to add their support in this spectator sport. One of the screens gave you an image of the fight in plan view, the other in cross-section, top to bottom. The aircraft were represented by red and blue aircraft shapes, their progress marked by dotted lines trailing out behind them. At the flick of a button you could switch to a 'virtual' image of the fight from the cockpit of any participating aircraft. It was state-of-the-art stuff, the war-fighting equivalent of watching the big match down at the pub with your mates.

Under the direction of Al Good, the fighter controller – good old Freddy to his friends in the pilot community – Deke and Mowgli were heading for the fight area in trail formation, still 20 miles or more from the Italians, when Deke, the leader, called 'tally,' the call sign for a visual sighting. 'Judy' was a contact on radar.

I turned to Al. 'That's too early. He shouldn't even be able to see them on his radar yet, let alone visually.'

Al nodded to the right-hand screen of the two ACMI screens, the height monitor. 'Check the height the Starfighters are coming in at. Those bastards are up to their old tricks again.'

I saw what he meant. The two F-104s were steaming into the fight at 40,000ft, way above the upper height limit. What the Eyeties hadn't appreciated, though, was that at that altitude their jet exhausts were condensing in the upper atmosphere and they were streaming contrails that must have been visible for miles, which explained how Deke had picked them up so early.

It was all over in a matter of seconds. The Italians committed to Deke out in front and Mowgli, sensing his moment, hooked down and took the shot.

Switching to Mowgli's cockpit view, we saw one of the F-104s slide into the sight on his HUD, heard the growl from the Sidewinder's seeker and then saw the diamond symbol telling us he had lock-on. In my head, I willed him to take the shot and, a split second later, he did. In another instant, Mowgli switched to the second F-104 and repeated the procedure all over again.

Mowgli's voice, distorted by the effects of g, came over the speaker. We all heard his exuberance. 'Fox Two, Grand Slam!'

Both the Starfighters were dead. There were cheers from the maintainers as the screens confirmed the news.

In the second merge, the next fight, both of our jets ran in as planned in battle formation, maintaining 3 miles of separation and ready to carry out the hook manoeuvre.

The Italians, however, clearly having had enough of the proceedings, joined the fight by steaming into the merge at high supersonic speed, signalling that they never had any intention of mixing it with us again. Once had been enough. Typical.

Even though the closing speed was horrendous, Deke was still able to snap into the hook and kill one of the Starfighters with a lucky Sidewinder shot. The second F-104 just kept on going, so fast that it probably made the turn somewhere over France.

Shaggy and I made our way over to the German ops building straight after lunch. I was feeling the tension and I guess it must have been the same for Shaggy, because neither of us ate much.

Inside the enemy's lair, we met Steffens and his wingman, another dead-ringer for every Second World War German fighter ace I'd ever seen pictures of: a tall guy with blond hair and blue eyes, who stood ramrod straight and greeted us with a vice-like handshake. His name was Leutnant Erich Weber.

A couple of minutes later, we were joined by the two freddies. Al Good, our veteran fighter controller, shook hands with his German opposite number. Then we set about establishing the rules of engagement, the RoEs.

For the first merge, we'd use Fox Two shooters only – pure dogfight stuff. For this within visual range (WVR) fight, it would be a straight match between the two short-range weapons, our AIM-9Ms and the AA-11 Archer of the MiG-29s. This was the one I worried about most, since we had no fancy trick up our sleeve to defend ourselves against the AA-11. It was all down to training, individual skill and the missile – and the AA-11 was reputed to be even better than the AIM-9M.

The second and subsequent engagements, we agreed after this, would be no-holds-barred affairs that exploited the full capabilities of the MiG-29. This meant that Steffens and Weber would be free to use their beyond visual range (BVR) R-27 missiles, NATO code-name AA-10 Alamo. Use of the AA-10 required them to operate their pulse-Doppler radars. And that's where we hoped the 'Doppler notch' tactic we'd practised days earlier would come into its own. Using the MiG-29's PD radar to guide the AA-10 was one thing, but first it had to find us.

We quickly agreed the remaining RoEs. The upper and lower limits of the fight were set at 30,000ft and 5,000ft. Each engagement would be preceded by 35-mile 'splits', which meant there needed to be a minimum of 35 miles between our aircraft before the freddies could turn us inbound. And then there were our call signs. The Germans were Gauntlets One and Two. We were Spitfires One and Two. Nice and simple – and not a trace of irony, either.

With everyone clear on what we were supposed to be doing, we said our goodbyes, stiffly and rather formally again, and made our way back to our own ops room for one final tactical briefing session. On the way across, Shaggy clapped Al Good on the shoulder and said: 'Al, lose me on your radar screen this time and I'll fucking kill you, mate. All right?'

Al managed a smile, but it quickly died on his lips. It was one thing for this highly skilled freddy to lose Shaggy against Beasty as had happened during the one-versus-two AI exercise on first day of our voyage, quite another for him to screw up against the Germans. Al looked as nervous as the rest of us. It all added to the overall feeling that we were somehow re-running the finals of the 1966 World Cup.

For the second merge, the BVR contest (we figured, because of its surprise element, that we'd have only one shot with the spike-and-drag trick), we were all agreed. There was nothing more to say or do. We were as ready as we'd ever be. I was glad, too, that we were saving the best for last.

The first merge was pure David and Goliath. The MiG-29 was fast and supremely agile and it had a great dogfight weapon. So where did that leave us in our lumbering old Sea Harriers?

It was Al who made the suggestion, which he borrowed straight from *Blackadder*. The Germans, of course, were highly regimented and always played by the book. So cheat, Al said. Not literally, but do something they are not expecting. Go for massive height splits –

me up at 30,000ft and Shaggy at 5,000ft, with 10 miles lateral separation between us. This, with luck, would force the two MiGs to
split up. If two MiGs targeted one Sea Harrier, we were up the
creek. This should force them to play one-on-one, Al maintained,
allowing each of us to go for a face shot before the whole thing
degenerated into a scrappy dogfight. If that happened, Al noted,
the Germans' speed and manoeuvrability would make the outcome
more or less a dead cert.

At two o'clock I had a last cigarette outside the ACMI building.
Then Shaggy and I strolled out to the aircraft. We broke through a
wooded area and the base was suddenly laid out before us. Out on
the pan were all the aircraft currently at Deci: our Sea Harriers, the
Italians' F-104s, the Turks' F-4s, the Portuguese A-6s and the MiG-
29s. The sun was at its height and Sardinia seemed to be asleep. I
felt like a gunslinger in a spaghetti western.

Shaggy and I stepped into the line hut on the edge of the pan to
do the necessary paperwork. There, behind the desk, was Squashy,
looking slightly the worse for wear. His big face began to crease in
welcome, but today the very act of smiling seemed to cause him
pain and it finished as more of a grimace.

'Feeling all right, Squashy?' I asked as I cast my eyes over the
details in the 700 book. The previous night he had consumed
enough rum to sink a battleship, I remembered.

'Oh, yes, sir. Perfectly, sir,' Squashy assured me, rubbing the back
of his head. 'We gave those SBS poofs a right good trouncing,
didn't we, sir?'

I looked up, not quite sure what planet the veteran watch officer
was on today. Squashy took this as an endorsement of his declara-
tion and added: 'You mark my words, sir, we won't be having any
more trouble from their sort again. Who are you fighting today, sir?'

When I told him it was the MiG-29s, Squashy wished us both
luck and promised he'd go over to the ACMI building with the rest
of the lads to lend a bit of vocal support. If only wars could be settled this way, I thought.

Shaggy and I walked out to the jets, each accompanied by our
own maintainer. We shook hands and headed for our respective
aircraft.

I spent two or three minutes checking the jet over, sticking my head down the intakes, tugging at the ACMI pod and dummy Sidewinders and making sure all the locks were removed from the control surfaces. Then I climbed the red ladder and, with the help of the maintainer, began to strap in. When I was settled, he handed me my helmet and wished me luck. Now I was on my own.

For the next five minutes, my hands flew around the cockpit as I went over all the pre-flight checks. Because it was warm I had the canopy open, but I was not aware of anything outside the aircraft now. Like an athlete who needs pre-race routine to psych up before an important competition, I needed this time to get my head around what I was about to do.

Finally, I closed the canopy and removed the last two pins that primed my ejection seat. There are five pins altogether, and all of them have to be pulled from the seat before it is properly 'live'. Back in the dawn of the jet era, before this routine had been firmly established, maintainers had been known to blow themselves out of cockpits by tripping on the firing handles of live seats.

I stowed the pins and held five fingers up to the marshal to show him that I had done so. When he acknowledged, I gave a winding motion with my finger to tell him I was ready to start the engine. A moment later, I flicked the start switch and hit the button next to it. There was a whistle from the auxiliary power unit, the APU, and then a mechanical whine as it began to turn over the engine. As the engine note built, I found myself humming an old Sea Harrier pilot's song:

> I still can hear the whistle, the thunder and the roar
> Of the mighty Harrier taking off to go to fight the war.

There were now just a few more checks to do. For the last one the marshal shone the beam of his torch into the missile-seeker head. Like an eye surgeon, he directed the beam into the middle of the sensor and then moved it left to right, up and down. From the cockpit, I could see the head of the seeker following the torch. As reassurance, I could also hear a low growl in my headset, the sound the missile gives you when it has picked up a heat source. When this heat source is the jet plume of an engine in afterburner, the noise can be deafening. I gave him the thumbs-up. The weapon seemed to be working fine.

At 1455, I told Shaggy I was ready to go.

'Spitfire check.'

'Spitfire Two,' he confirmed.

'Spitfires loud and clear, channel two, go,' I announced. 'Deci Ground. Request taxi.'

I got the OK, made sure the chocks were clear and powered up. The Sea Harrier rolled forward. I glanced over my shoulder, looking for Shaggy, and saw the two MiG-29s trundling out across the pan behind him. Only then did I feel a pang in my gullet. It felt as if the eyes of the entire Navy were on me. I uttered a quiet prayer for the strength and presence of mind not to fuck up.

Shaggy and I lined up beside each other at the end of the runway. I glanced across at his aircraft, made sure that it looked OK, and gave him the thumbs-up. He did the same for me. When there was nothing else left to do, I made sure I had his attention, looked dead ahead and tapped my bone-dome three times, then nodded – the signal to release the toe brakes and slam to full power.

We reached 100 knots in four seconds. At 150 knots, I nodded again and took the nozzles back to 50 degrees, which punched us airborne.

Colonel Steffens acknowledged his fighter controller, his voice unnaturally calm. 'Gauntlet, ready to play.'

A moment later, he and his freddy changed frequencies and I found myself listening instead to Al Good. 'Spitfire, ready to play,' he said. Behind the professionalism I could hear something else: a note of encouragement. In the loneliness of the high frontier, Al's voice suddenly sounded as warm and welcoming as my own mother's.

'Ready to play,' I told him.

Without warning, Al switched gear. 'Fight's on, fight's on! Spitfires, snap one-eight-zero. Bogeys one-eight-zero, 30 miles, heading north, high and fast.'

I found myself pulling into a heavy right-hand, high-g turn as the cadence of Al's instructions set the pace. 'Bogeys one-seven-nine, 27 miles, battle formation.'

I rolled out of the turn and snapped a glance over my right shoulder. Shaggy, the beauty, was there in perfect battle formation, the sunlight glinting off his canopy, vapour trails barrelling off his wingtips.

Al's voice, still there, solid and dependable; the drumbeat of the slave boat: 'Bogeys one-seven-nine, 21 miles. Bogeys hot. Battle formation.'

The MiGs were pointing right at us. The superior performance of their PD radars meant they were tracking us, too. I looked down at my own radar set and watched the line scan paint its way across the screen: left and right, two sweeps. I willed it to pick something up. But behind the fluorescent back-and-forth motion of the scan, the emptiness of the airspace ahead of me registered as a deep black void on the screen. The Blue Fox was picking up nothing, even though the MiGs should have been inside its range envelope.

Where the hell were they?

A knot of panic formed inside my chest. My breathing quickened against my oxygen mask.

And then, two bright green blips in the centre of the screen.

'Spitfire One, contact!' I yelled, unable to contain my relief. 'Pair. Battle. Twenty miles.'

Al kept his voice steady, maintaining the tempo of the fight. 'They're your bogeys. Engage.'

'Spitfire, execute,' I acknowledged and banged the stick over to my left. I looked over my shoulder again and saw Shaggy peeling away aggressively to the west, each of us building speed steadily for the fight to come.

Speed was energy and energy in abundance was what you needed when you entered the fight. I shot a look at the speedo and saw the needle quivering over the 450-knot mark. Then I looked back at the radar screen.

The two dots were still on the edge of the display. If they were to fight the way we wanted them to, the way we'd rehearsed in the briefing, they should have split by now, rising to meet us one-on-

one. But they were moving forward in 'battle' still, a resolute pair, side by side. I held my breath.

Come on, come on.

Another sweep of the beam. The dots appeared to diverge. I blinked and looked again. The dots *were* moving apart. They'd taken the bait.

'Bogeys splitting,' Al confirmed.

I rolled on to a heading of one-nine-zero, rolling out as soon as I was nose-on to the left-hand MiG. We were now converging at over 1,000 knots. Sixteen miles between him and me. Fifteen miles, fourteen . . .

The back-and-forth movement of his radar beam painting my Sea Harrier with RF energy registered as a steady nick-nick-nick on my RWR. I cast a rapid glance at the threat display beneath the radar screen and saw him in the one o'clock position, the alpha-numerics telling me what I already knew: MiG-29.

He's fast and he's high, somewhere above 30,000ft, and I'm responding at a level beyond conscious thought, pushing the nose of the Sea Harrier down towards the hard deck and increasing my speed. The MiG had the advantage of height. I needed something else.

I let the altimeter unwind as far as I dared and then hauled back hard on the stick. The gs piled on, and for an instant, as I braced against them, the temptation to succumb to the numbing effects of the grey-out – g-induced loss of consciousness – was overwhelming.

Somewhere at the very edge of sensation I felt the clamp of the g-pants stemming the tide of blood rushing to my feet and used it to galvanise my own resolve and kick against the g-loc. I was coming up fast on the other side of the circle now, my nose high, the blue-black vacuum of space pulling me higher.

I was using the g like a sling-shot to propel me into the fight; all the while, the fingers on my right hand feeling their way on the top of the stick for the accept button that would put the Sidewinder into super-scan mode, the setting that primes it to seek out the heat of an aircraft against the cold of the sky.

The radar showed him at 7 miles and still high. I could scarcely believe it: the bastard was still up there. He must have been watching Shaggy all along, not me. Big fucking mistake, guy.

I yanked back on the stick again and commenced the 4g pull-up to the target, waiting for the moment when I'd cross the 5-mile divide that would bring him within lock-on range of my Sidewinder and into its no-escape zone.

Another glance at the radar and I figured I was close enough. I shifted my gaze up and out of the cockpit, but the sun was beating too brightly through the perspex for me to see anything. I pressed the accept button on the control stick anyway. On the pylon, the missile-seeker head snapped towards the target, guided by the radar, transforming the dull growl in my ears into an ear-piercing scream. The signal was so strong I couldn't miss.

I checked the voltmeter on the HUD. It had dinged right off the scale. I was locked on to the sun, not the MiG.

Shit.

I hit the reject button and did a one-fingered dance in a bid to reprime the missile into super-scan mode.

A shadow passed in front of the sun and in the two short seconds in which my view of the outside world returned, I spotted the MiG.

I froze, startled by the size of it. It seemed to fill the entire HUD. In that instant I knew that I was inside my missile's minimum launch zone. No matter that I hadn't managed to reprime the Sidewinder. There wasn't enough distance between me and the target for the weapon to arm itself after it came off the rail.

I kept going anyhow. It was clear that the pilot hadn't seen me. He was cruising straight and level, exposing his soft white under-belly to my gun. I was so close now, I could have a go at him . . .

But before I could switch to the Aden, there were two white puffs from the MiG's wingtips as the pilot flinched, transmitting the jink through the stick to the control surfaces. And then, like a game fish stung by imminent danger, the MiG dropped its left wing and dived. The bastard had clocked me.

For a moment we were canopy-to-canopy, and as we crossed each other I saw him, a mirror image of me, head up, eyes out, craning for a glimpse of my aircraft. I saw his face and I saw his eyes. We were that close.

It was Weber.

He's going down, I'm going up, but I know I have the energy advantage of the sling-shot effect. But he's getting away. I have to get my nose down and fast.

I slammed the nozzles all the way forward to the hover stop. My stomach hit my throat as the Sea Harrier's nose jerked down, the violent lurch expelling the air from my lungs. Then I shot the nozzles aft and, not for the first time, cursed the fact that the Sea Harrier didn't have the luxury of afterburner power for that added punch in the thin air of a dogfight.

The MiG did, and in the time it had taken me to get my nose on his tail, he was already outside the max launch success zone of my Sidewinders. His big wing and powerful twin afterburning engines made his aircraft a natural dogfighter, something the Harrier was not.

Raw panic mixed with sweat and my rapid, short, sharp breaths as I realised I'd had my chance and missed it. The MiG was already down to base height and pulling round to meet me. I was out of places to run to. Now that I no longer had surprise on my side, the natural dogfighting ability of the MiG made the outcome of the contest a foregone conclusion. We were now into a flat fight, our aircraft turning in a circle, his progressively tighter than mine.

Instinctively I transferred my hand on to the flares button on top of the nozzle lever. I couldn't see him, but the short hairs on the back of my neck were a better guide than any RWR: I could *feel* the MiG pilot nibbling into my six, waiting, waiting to fire his missile.

I put myself in his place. When would I fire?

Now. Fucking now.

I punched the flares button and saw the magnesium intensity of the starburst reflected in my mirrors. Al's voice burst into my headset: 'Spitfire One, good flares! Missile defeated!'

I felt weak with relief. My hand shook as I brought it off the lever and back on to the throttle. My whole body was slick with sweat. I was in the turn, pulling with all my might to tighten the circle, my face craned almost vertically, the perspex inches from my nose, eyeballs damned near pushed into my brain trying to get eyes on the MiG. Everything fucking hurt. And it was then, for some reason, that I saw myself a week earlier, in the cockpit up against

Deke over the Somerset countryside. I'd been in exactly this position, an opponent waxing my tail, waiting for that optimum moment to fire.

And I'd rolled out of the turn, a huge tactical error and Deke had killed me for it.

In the days since, I'd rerun the fight the right way over and over again so many times in my head that suddenly I saw in a flash of clarity what I should do now.

With a supreme effort I twisted my head to get a view of the MiG. At the point when my neck felt like it was about to wrench off my shoulders, I saw it. Weber was in the final stages of the endgame, pulling round hard, straightening his nose up for the shot, sucking me into his no-escape zone. He was almost lined up on my tail. If this was going to work, I had to wait two more seconds until he was right on it.

Wait, wait.

Bingo. The second the MiG fell into line behind me, its nose angled in perfect alignment with my direction of flight, I threw the nozzle lever all the way back to the braking-stop position. My body shot forward against the straps. The g-forces almost sucked the skin off my face. With the aircraft rattling like a jalopy, I flung the old girl into a barrel roll, threw the nozzles forward, felt the g fall off, hit the accept button for the missile and opened my eyes.

There, in the middle of the HUD, its outline framed by the diamond at the heart of the sight, was the MiG. The tone in my headset rose like a full-blown orchestra.

*Deeeeeeeeeeeeeeeeeeet . . .*

I punched the launch button. 'Fox Two!'

The wait was agonising, but worth it.

'Spitfire One, good kill!' Al said, and then, much calmer: 'Spitfire Two's bugging out to the north, good run-out range.'

I smiled. Even Shaggy had made it unscathed.

'Suggest terminate,' Al said.

All the players agreed to reconvene for the next fight. This exercise had been no more than a warm-up for the big one: a no-holds-barred engagement in which our opponents would be allowed to use the full resources of their considerable firepower.

Loath as I was to admit to myself, it was the next fight that really counted.

Shaggy and I throttled back to 350 knots to conserve fuel while we confirmed tactics. We were heading south of the fight area at 15,000ft, getting ready to regroup. The Germans were flying north, no doubt going over their tactics – and licking their wounds – in the minutes before the freddies turned us inbound and we started all over again.

Shaggy was 2,000 yards off my right wing and switched to a frequency no one but us could hear.

'Spitfire One and Two, BVR, Tactic Bravo, spike and drag,' I said.

'Roger copied. Tactic Bravo. You spike, me drag.'

I was still battling to reset the missile, waiting for the tone to drop off as the coolant flowed back into the seeker, when Al Good came back on line.

'Spitfires, ready to play?'

'Ready to play.' I was still pumped up. We'd already wupped them on the short-range WVR fight. Now, with Tactic Bravo on our side, I was confident we could teach them a thing or two in the BVR arena as well: the medium-range engagement zone that, by rights, should be the MiG's for the taking.

As we turned in for the fight, Shaggy closed up until he was no more than 30ft from my right wing. This tight, I knew we'd show up as a single blip on the Germans' radar, our point of departure for Tactic Bravo.

There was a crackle and Al started the party. 'Spitfires, snap port, bogeys north, 40 miles.'

I could hear them. The nick-nick-nick of their radars as they combed the airspace in front of them emerged out of the static hiss of the raw gear, my RWR set. If I could hear them, I knew they could see me. The critical moment, though, came at 25 miles, when we hit the outer reaches of the launch success zone for the MiG-29's BVR missiles.

When I rolled out of the turn, Shaggy was still there, hugging my wingtip and looking good. I still had the nick-nick-nick of the

MiG-29s in my headset. I tensed, waiting for the 25-mile mark.

Al counted us down every 2 miles until, at 23, I got a sniff of them on radar, in battle formation dead ahead at 30,000ft. I was just wondering why the hell we'd heard nothing new from the MiGs and pondering the fact that, shit or bust, we were going to have to make our move anyway, when the alarm-bell on my raw gear exploded into life.

It's a sound that puts the fear of God into any fighter pilot, alerting him that an enemy radar had switched to missile-launch mode, but in this particular instance it was exactly what I wanted to hear. It meant they had taken the bait.

'Spitfires execute!' I shouted and rolled immediately left, pulling the nose down with 5gs on the clock. The sea suddenly opened out in front of me as the aircraft plunged into a vertical dive. I had a dim impression of Sardinia stretching away on the periphery of my vision and a momentary glimpse of Shaggy's aircraft pulling hard right into the drag manoeuvre, contrails spilling off his wingtips.

I was two seconds into the dive when the alarm went off. Fucking yes! I'd hit the notch. His PD radar couldn't see me and I'd vanished from his screen. A couple more seconds, then I eased back on the stick, a nice and gentle 5g pull as I levelled off just above the 5,000ft base height.

I toggled the thumbwheel on the radar hand controller, which points the dish fully up, and experienced another rush of adrenalin as I saw the westerly of the two MiGs on my screen at 20,000ft and 15 miles. I felt like singing into my oxygen mask. This was too fucking easy. And that, I suppose, was when I should have got it.

But as you're pressing the accept button for the missile, waiting for the tone to rise in your headset, you don't think about why the enemy's being stupid. Your whole being is waiting for that perfectly pitched note and the moment when (with a real AIM-9M) you can punch the missile off the rail.

So when Al came back to me with the news that the westerly MiG was splitting to Spitfire One and the easterly MiG was committing to Spitfire Two, it took me a nanosecond to absorb it. In fact it was so damned difficult to accept that I almost asked him to repeat it. But then it sank in. Somehow the fucker had seen me.

An nth of a second later, it got much worse: *Brrrrrrrrrrrrrrrrrrrr!*
The alarm on my raw gear went off like a firebell in my ear.

In a desperate bid to break his radar lock, I put the Sea Harrier
into a 180-degree turn, punching chaff and flares as I went. But it
was no use. A couple of seconds later, Al's voice broke in my headset. 'Spitfire One. Time out. Kill.'

As I flew out of the fight, half of me trying to fathom how on
earth the Germans had pulled it off, I followed Al doing his best to
save Shaggy's arse. Both the bogeys were now on his tail and even
though he was running for the sanctuary of the edge of the engagement zone, the end had already been written. Before long, Al,
sensing the inevitable, told Shaggy to knock it off.

The Germans had killed both of us in less time than it takes to
whistle 'Deutschland, Deutschland, Uber Alles'.

But just when I thought it couldn't get any worse, Al came back
on air. 'Spitfires. Gauntlet coming across on your frequency.'

I looked at Shaggy, who'd resumed formation off my right
wingtip, as Colonel Steffens' voice broke on our frequency.

'Spitfire One, radio check,' he said.

'Gauntlet, you're loud and clear,' I replied hesitantly.

'So, who is the fluffy one now?'


There is a curious lore associated with the post-mission debrief at
Deci. Everyone produces some fancy footwork in a bid to emerge
from the fight in the best possible light. It's part *Right Stuff*, part
*Cincinnati Kid*, but the watchword is stay cool. If you can make the
other guy look stupid, good; but no matter how much flak comes
your way, don't get rattled, take it in your stride. I have known
people who've been trounced in the air turn the whole thing
around during the post-mission debrief and make out they were
Tom Cruise and it was the other guys who screwed up big-time.
There's an art to this, of course, and much of it has to do with facial
expression. Wearing a poker face is a good place to start.

So when Shaggy and I walked back from our jets, helmets in
hand, our sweat-soaked flying suits steaming in the cool of the
afternoon, we made sure we plastered broad smiles on our faces,
even though, behind them, our minds were in turmoil. Shaggy

asked me what the fuck had happened and I told him I genuinely hadn't a clue. I'd hit the notch – perfectly, it seemed to me – but somehow the German had picked me up and shot me in the face. I was agog to know how; the trick was not to show I cared.

At the ACMI centre, we trooped into our debrief booth and found all the other participants – Steffens, Weber, the two freddies and some other hangers-on – already there. In the low lighting – the booth is like a small cinema, with a bank of stepped seats and a reasonable-sized screen opposite – curt nods were exchanged, but beyond that, everyone was playing their cards pretty close to their chests.

I clawed for some early points by suggesting that there was really nothing to gain by rerunning the first fight: we were pretty clear on what had happened and I guessed Weber was, too. He'd made the classic mistake of flying through my six o'clock position, allowing me to hit him with the braking-stop manoeuvre, which was unorthodox, but effective. Weber pulled a face, which enabled me to follow through with: 'Unless, of course, you'd like to see the film . . .'

'Nein,' he said quickly, and then laughed lightly as he regained his composure. 'No, thank you. It's OK. Really.'

But I had no more strong cards to play. As we moved on to the second fight, I stood up and told the Germans what we'd attempted to do, keeping it crisp and light, as behind me the fight was replayed on the screen. When I finished and took my seat again, Steffens got to his feet and, with ill-concealed smugness, took us over his game plan, pausing momentarily to allow a red dot from his aircraft to snake across the ACMI screen, close unerringly on my Sea Harrier and then blow me out of the sky. There was nothing I could do but try to absorb the battle damage as best I could. Inside, however, I cringed.

'We had a suspicion you would try zis . . . er, so-called Doppler notch tactic, because of the Sea Harrier's limited capability,' Steffens began. 'We had heard rumours about zis technique for some time, but we didn't know you had taken it quite so far.'

'Meaning what?' I asked.

'Of course, we are only too aware that our aircraft lose targets when they fly perpendicular to the beam of the radar,' Steffens continued. 'But, to be honest viz you, we expected you to fly laterally, not to dive vertically. Zis, I have to tell you, did take me by surprise.'

I appreciated his honesty. Suddenly, I wasn't in the mood for games any more. 'But how did you find me again? You locked me up – I heard the alarm on my RWR – I dropped vertically into the dive and the alarm stopped, which is when I knew for sure that you'd lost me.' I paused and studied him for a beat. 'You *did* lose me, didn't you?'

Steffens smiled. 'No, Lieutenant, I never lost you. I tracked you all the way.'

'But . . .' I floundered, 'that's impossible. The alarm stopped. I broke the lock. End of story.'

'You heard what I wanted you to hear,' Steffens said simply.

'What?'

'I locked you up, sure, and then I saw you go down the dive. I saw you, because I think you didn't hit the notch correctly – how do you say? "Spot-on". Maybe you were at 70 degrees in the dive, or 80, perhaps, but for sure, not 90. You definitely had some forward velocity, Lieutenant, because I tracked you all the way. I made you *think* you had lost me by deliberately breaking my radar lock on you.'

I stared at him, dumbfounded. Fortunately, Steffens was too much of a gentleman to allow me to wallow for too long. But what he said next was hardly reassuring.

'Let me tell you, Lieutenant, that if I can do this, then so can the Yugoslavs. Be careful over there. They are good fliers.'

I looked at Shaggy and he looked at me. Neither of us needed to say anything. The way forward was crystal clear. We needed to keep practising, then go up against the MiGs again at the end of the week.

But worse was to come. Fifteen minutes later, the minibus took us over to the British ops building on the other side of the airfield. There we ran into Mel. He looked like he'd seen a ghost. 'I've just had the *Ark* on the phone,' he said tersely. 'They want us back on board tomorrow morning.'

It hit me like a sledgehammer in the face. 'Can't we delay for a few days? There are still a bunch of things we need to do here, boss.'

He shook his head. 'No, they want us back. Quickly. Things are hotting up over there. It's just a matter of time before the whole place goes ballistic. And when it does, I think it's safe to say we're going to be in the middle of it.'

# CHAPTER 5

Our immediate presence in the Adriatic was requested because of a worsening of the situation on the ground. Having settled its dispute with the UN over who would control air strikes against the warring parties in Bosnia, NATO seemed to be moving inexorably towards the use of force in the former Yugoslavia. There would be no more opportunities to practise against the MiG-29. From now on, it was dedicated mission time.

As we flew out of Deci and rejoined the *Ark* as she steamed around the south-eastern corner of Sicily, there was a real sense that things were coming to a head. A new commander of UNPROFOR had been appointed, a Brit by the name of General Sir Michael Rose. Rose was an ex-SAS commander, a no-nonsense guy who was reputed to abhor the kind of mealy-mouthed dithering that had characterised the UN's operations to date.

The big problem was the UN's mounting inability to deliver humanitarian aid to the places where it was really needed, mainly as a result of the heavy shelling by the Bosnian Serbs – and in some cases, the Bosnian Croats – of the convoy routes. Thousands of Muslims were said to be in danger of starving to death. The worst affected areas were the siege cities of Bihac, Maglaj, Gorazde, Zepce and the Muslim capital, Sarajevo. In early January, 1,500 shells were fired into Sarajevo by the Serbs on a single day.

Even though I was headed for this hell-hole, my reaction to

these statistics was not very different from anyone else's. It was a curious thing, but I still felt a great sense of detachment from what was happening. I watched the TV like everyone else, and of course I was appalled by what I saw, but it all still seemed a very long way away. The tragedy that was being acted out daily on the Bosnian stage was in every sense a crime against humanity, but then again, so were events in Rwanda, the Caucasus and Kurdistan. As a human being, I knew that Britain was right to intervene in the Balkans. But on a personal level, I felt no more engaged now than I had before we sailed. It all felt terribly unreal.

The military threat was a different matter. Intelligence estimates said there were 10,000 to 12,000 Bosnian Serb troops concentrated around Sarajevo. These forces were known to be equipped with more than fifty tanks, 200 to 300 artillery pieces or large-calibre mortars, plenty of anti-aircraft artillery (AAA) weapons and man-portable air defence systems – the dreaded MANPADS weapons – too numerous to count.

On our second day on station, I took off with Deke for what was euphemistically termed an 'orientation flight' of the Bosnian theatre of operations. As I did so, I tried to focus on the 170 aircraft from six NATO nations that had been assembled in support of the UN humanitarian operation and to think as little as possible about the Bosnian Serbs' air defence capabilities. While NATO aircraft were illuminated on a regular basis by the Serbs' air defence radars, and occasionally shot at, none had, as yet, been brought down.

So, I tried to reason as I streaked above the Balkan countryside on my orientation flight, taking in all the CAP points under the direction of a NATO AWACS command and control aircraft, why should Deke or I be the unlucky ones on this occasion? Blind faith in statistics and the law of probabilities seems to have worked, since Deke and I made it back to the carrier without incident.

While the strategy for avoiding the Serbs' AAA and MAN-PADS systems was to remain above 10,000ft – although this, we were told, was not a cast-iron guarantee of safety – there was less to be done about some of the Serbs' more sophisticated SAM systems.

On paper, the big weapon was the Soviet-developed SA-2 Guideline, the kind that had shot down Gary Powers' U-2 over

Russia in 1960. However, because these were installed at fixed locations, NATO intelligence had plotted (or, at least, it thought it had) all the SA-2 sites in and around Bosnia, enabling us in turn to plot them on our maps and fly around them.

Far more worrying was the SA-6 Gainful, a big missile mounted three abreast on a tank chassis. The SA-6 had a speed of Mach 3, an engagement range of 24km and an engagement altitude of 50,000ft. And while the SA-6 wasn't as mobile as the MANPADS, the very fact it could be moved at all meant you could never be quite sure where it might be positioned on any given day. At all times, there was at least one NATO reconnaissance aircraft in the air over Bosnia scanning the ground with powerful sensors for interesting vehicle movements. Any redeployment of SA-6 batteries ranked way up the list of surveillance targets.

But the Serbs, who'd been tutored well by their friends the Russians, were more than capable of pulling off the odd little deception. Occasionally, SA-6s went missing. And on the days when there were rogue SA-6s adrift in the Bosnian hinterland, it wasn't any pilot's idea of fun to be flying.

Imagine my delight, then, a week after my orientation flight, when Mel informed Mowgli and me that we'd been tasked with a mission to go and photograph all the known SA-6 sites in Bosnia, the specific intention being to determine which of them were 'active' and which weren't.

There were several definitions of what actually constituted an active SAM site, though right now they all seemed pretty academic. The Serbs were quite capable of setting up dummy batteries, substituting real SA-6s for wooden mock-ups. Or sometimes they would set up individual SA-6 batteries minus their 'radar heads' – their radar guidance systems. This meant they were simply out there to deter us from flying over a particular area, since a missile without its guidance system is technically useless. Another ploy in this game of high-tech spoof was to dispatch radar heads and SA-6 launchers to a given site, but neglect to load any missiles.

To a high-flying NATO reconnaissance aircraft, distinguishing active sites from those that were there simply to deter was not easy. It was our job, therefore, to fill in the intelligence gaps by flying down the throat of these sites and taking pictures at medium altitude with our F-95 camera systems.

After offering silent thanks to Smitty, our man in the CAOC in Vicenza, who'd clearly fought hard to have this plum mission assigned to us, Mowgli, Oz and I got down to the serious business of plotting the sortie.

Oz participated in this exericise, too, because it was standard practice to get three aircraft into the air for a two-ship sortie. If all was OK with our two aircraft five minutes into the flight, Oz would turn round and land back on the ship, leaving Mowgli and me to push on à deux into Bosnian airspace. I asked Oz if he'd like to swap places with me but, a little selfishly, I thought, he declined.

After we were handed the target numbers and their lat and long locations, we went to work on plotting the mission. Our task was to photograph eight SA-6 batteries concentrated in four locations: Bihac, Tuzla, Sarajevo and Banja Luka. Of these, the priority was the site at Banja Luka, where 'unusual' activity had been reported by NATO pilots the previous day. We decided that the best course of action was to tackle Sarajevo first, then Tuzla, followed by Banja Luka and Bihac. This would give us a counterclockwise route in and out of Bosnia and just about enough fuel at the end of it to find the carrier again.

Following our briefing from the intelligence officer, a retired army major who we found just a tad too casual about the threat for our liking ('We're not too sure where such-and-such a missile system is at the moment, but keep your fingers crossed and you should be OK'), I took Mowgli and Oz through the sortie brief. Because we had a lot of targets to photograph, I reminded them that the need to conserve film was a necessity, as was accuracy.

In the era of the smart weapon, real-time satellite surveillance and stealth, it was somewhat galling to have to remind my colleagues that the best way to ensure accuracy with the F-95 camera system was to line up the target with a sight known as the 'sighting group' drawn in Chinagraph on the inside of the canopy soon after take-off. The camera sits at 20 degrees nose-down on the right-hand side of the aircraft just behind the radar. The trick is to roll the aircraft 20 degrees to port and mark the horizon with a line, then to draw a vertical line opposite your shoulder. In straight and level flight, where the lines cross is where the camera is pointing.

'So make sure you draw the sighting group properly,' I concluded, 'and, Oz, try not to roll right as you did the other day – we're not in the southern hemisphere now.'

Oz did a passable Taz of Tasmania impersonation, growling and muttering as he made notes. I wrapped the whole thing up by reminding them to be in the aircraft ready to go at 1450, in time for take-off at 1500. The time then, as we went into the mark, was minute two-zero – 2.20pm on Civvy Street. 'Any questions?' I said, glancing briefly at Oz and Mowgli before picking up my things and heading for the door.

Oz called me back. 'Which way do I roll again?'

Dickhead.

After a nervous team pee, we returned to the briefing room to find Chris, the squadron gofer, struggling through the door with our kit. I pulled on my 'speed jeans', anti-g trousers, over my flying suit and clipped on leg restraints. These attached to lanyards on the seat which, in the event of an ejection, snapped the legs into the seat for a clean exit from the aircraft. By a clean exit, I mean not having your legs amputated below the knee by the instrument panel on the way out.

Next came the combat survival waistcoat, or CSW, a vest much like those anglers or professional photographers wear, stuffed with pockets for carrying all the things we'd ever be likely to need if we banged out over hostile territory. Top of the list was the PRC-112 personal radio with transmit facility and an emergency locator beacon. Both of these channels were encrypted, allowing us to transmit freely without the bad guys hearing us – in theory, at least.

Another useful electronic gizmo was a hand-held GPS set which enabled us to plot our position to the nearest 50 metres or so. It also computed our position from something called 'bullseye', a coded location somewhere in the vicinity known only to people on the NATO staff with 'need to know'. If we were required to transmit our position, we always relayed our range and bearing from the bullseye off the GPS. To those who knew where bullseye was, calculating our true position then became a simple piece of trigonometry.

At least one of the CSW's pockets housed a pretty comprehensive medical kit, complete with extra-strong painkillers, bandages, catgut, needles and razor blades. In the course of my couple of days' combat survival instruction, one of the pieces of advice that had stuck in my mind was how to slit your wrists efficiently – along the artery, not across it – if things really went tits up.

Other goodies contained in the CSW included a silk handkerchief with a map of Bosnia printed on it; a heliograph for sending signals by the reflected light of the sun; a pack of Camel cigarettes – the hardest currency in the world; £500 worth of deutschmarks for payment and bribes behind the lines; and a 'blood chit' printed in fifteen different languages promising the bearer a shedload of cash if he delivered the pilot in his charge to a UN representative. There was also a holster for a Walther PPK and two extra clips of ammunition with ten rounds apiece. The weapons had to be drawn from a locked box in the briefing room, while the bullets came from ship's stores. Chris, the gofer, had already taken care of the ammo situation. Beasty was responsible for issuing the weapons.

As duty officer, Beasty was having a mad old time co-ordinating the final details of the launch with Flyco. He was sitting in a corner of the room, telephone jammed between ear and shoulder, wrestling at the same time with the lock on the gun box. At last he managed to prise it open and hand over the weapons.

I caught his eye as I signed for them, tapping my watch to indicate that we were ready to go. In the eyes of the irascible Beast, this was a dangerous if not insane provocation, but we needed the 'outbrief' before making our way up to the aircraft, and the duty officer was the only guy who could give it.

Five minutes before we were due on deck, Beasty got off the phone and talked us through it. The outbrief is basically a checklist covering weather status, ship's position and a tally of our personal kit. When he's happy that we're happy, the duty officer lets us go, but not before he's 'sanitised' us for the flight. This entails watching us as we get rid of all personal items and objects lest we fall into the hands of the enemy, whoever that happens to be. If I'd picked up anything from our threat lectures, pretty much anyone and everyone on the ground had a reason for slitting our throats.

Photos, letters, keepsakes, you name it; it all had to be left behind before we could fly. We even had to remove our name tags and rank insignia. Mine wouldn't have been much use to anyone, but I removed it anyway and handed it to the Beast.

'Here,' I told him, pressing the Velcro patch into his hand, 'I'm sure you could make better use of this than me.' The name on the tag read 'Lt Manuel Hung'.

Beasty gave it a cursory glance, then chucked it over his shoulder. 'Right. Scenario,' he growled, getting back to business. 'You've been shot down near one of the hot spots and the Bosnian Serbs pick you up. What are you going to tell them?' His eyes swept past me and landed on Phil Mould. 'Mowgli?'

'Name, rank, number and date of birth,' Mowgli spat out, as if this were the real thing.

A look of disappointment passed across the Beast's face. He would have made an excellent interrogation officer, but he would have been just as at home on the receiving end.

The outbrief concluded, he wished us Godspeed and booted us upstairs in the direction of the aircraft.

There is so much to do in the cockpit of a modern fighter aircraft that you have next to no time to think about the horrors that lie in wait for you on a live sortie. Thank God. A niggling concern, however, is getting a 'switch-pigs': screwing the mission through a duff switch selection. The cockpit of a jet fighter is such a complex place that it can happen. We minimise the risks by doing rigorous cockpit checks. But now, as we crossed the Bosnian coastline, I prayed I didn't screw up.

'Bookshelf, this is Vixen Two-Three and Two-Four, as fragged for Mission Echo Two-Five,' I told the AB Triple-C as we entered its workspace. There were three EC-130 Airborne Command Control and Communications platforms based at Aviano Air Force Base in Italy, and one of them was always on duty just off the Bosnian coastline. It acted as an aerial command post and relay service for NATO aircraft over the Balkans. 'As fragged' meant that our aircraft were carrying the weapons as detailed on the roster in the AB Triple-C: two Sidewinders for self-defence and the F-95 camera for recce.

'Vixen Two-Three and Two-Four,' a Dutch-sounding controller came back, 'you're cleared into theatre via Route Three, mission as briefed. On passing Gate Three, contact Magic on TAD Seventeen.'

A minute later we reached the gate and I contacted the AWACS on the required frequency. If these guys did their job properly, they'd watch our six o'clock all the way in and out of Bosnia for enemy air activity, leaving us to concentrate on the reconnaissance mission. A Yank controller on the aircraft informed us we were clear to proceed on Mission E25. The next time we needed to check in (emergencies apart) was when we left Bosnian airspace around forty-five minutes later. From now on, the watchword was speed.

I boosted the throttle and watched the speed increase to 500 knots, only marginally off the Sea Harrier's top whack of 600. This gave Mowgli, as my wingman, some spare knots to manoeuvre. To my dismay, the cloudbase had already dropped down to 14,000ft, forcing us down to around 12,000ft to remain visual. I checked my mirror and saw Mowgli dropping back into his fighting position – 500ft higher and tucked into my four o'clock. Although Mowgli would be taking pictures, too, his principal job was to ride shotgun for me, keeping his eyes peeled for SAM launches.

The co-ordinates of the targets are all plugged into the GPS that is lashed to the coaming. The GPS was a godsend, since it was so much more accurate than the Sea Harrier's standard navigation system, the NAVHARS. The GPS gave us 50m accuracy or better, enabling us to wait until the very last minute before we popped down to photograph the target. It also gave us a countdown to time on target, a neat little facility which, apart from anything else, allowed us to prepare mentally for the ordeal to come. The NAVHARS, which calculates position from the air-data computer, can manage only 3- or 4-mile accuracy over an hour-long sortie.

Three miles from the target I dropped down to 5,000ft and throttled up to give me speed over the target as I took the shots. I was now deep in the heart of the MANPADS missile envelope and all of a sudden 500 knots felt slow. I looked in my mirror and was relieved to see Mowgli sticking to me like glue. When I looked up again, there it was: a scarred patch of land, five dug-out revetments linked by a road system – the classic layout for an SA-6 site. It looked exactly like its depiction in the threat manual.

I threw on the required angle of bank and lined up as much of the SAM site as I could with the Chinagraph cross-hairs on the inside of the canopy. And then I was shooting overhead and turning on to the next heading. One down, seven to go.

As I turned I caught a glimpse of Sarajevo itself, dead ahead in the middle distance. It looked like the pictures I'd seen in tourist brochures before Yugoslavia had gone for a ball of chalk: the bowl of the mountains, the patchwork forestation, the quaint houses with their terracotta roof tiles and the minarets reaching up from the mosques. It all looked so ordinary – until I got closer. Then I could see that at least half of the houses didn't have roofs and that what I had previously taken to be parks were bomb sites, dotted with shell craters and oozing water from shattered pipes. But for all its horrors, it could still have been a model; a diorama at a museum. Cocooned in my flight suit, speed jeans, CSW, lightweight survival jacket and helmet, with the environmental control system regulating the temperature in the cockpit, I felt no more involved in the destiny of Sarajevo than I did in the wellbeing of, say, Bristol. All I could think of was the fact that there were people with surface-to-air missiles down there and that they were quite capable of shooting me down.

The time on target to Tuzla, the second site, sped towards zero on the GPS and, before I knew it, I'd dropped down again and shot another load of film. This time I could see only two of the three SA-6 sites I'd been briefed on. And, as with Sarajevo, it was impossible to make out any detail. That would be something for the photo-interpreters to worry about later.

I banked towards Banja Luka, already feeling better about the mission. Mowgli was still in my mirror, high and to my right,

Two 801 Sea Harriers fly past *Ark Royal*.

The 801 Squadron pilots. Left to right: Gazza, Deke, Oz, Shaggy, Mel, Henry (Splot), me, Mowgli and Beasty.

Me aboard the *Ark Royal* (*left*) and with 801 Squadron (*below*).

Running checks on a laser-guided bomb (*right*).

The flight-deck officer prepares to give the green flag to launch a Sea Harrier (*below*).

A MiG-29, similar to those used by the Serbs in Bosnia.

Two of 801 Squadron's Sea Harrier FRS1s flying in formation.

A surface-to-air missile site near Banja Luka.

Tanks and artillery south of Sarajevo.

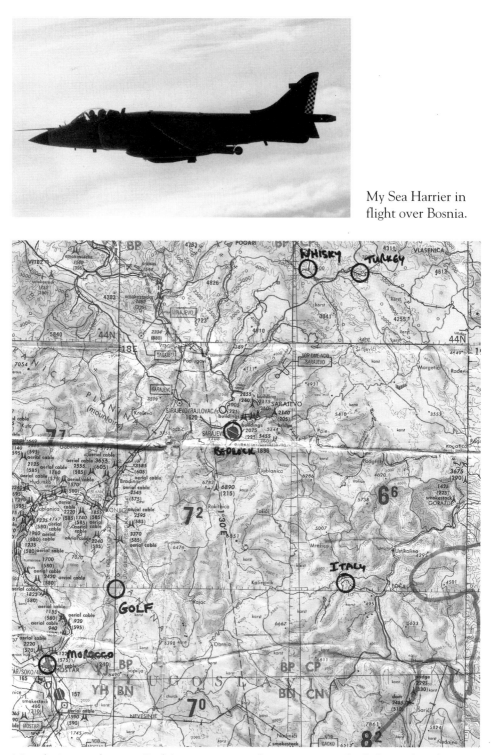

My Sea Harrier in flight over Bosnia.

My pilot's map showing 'Italy', my target on the mission on which I was shot down.

My Sea Harrier taking off on its final flight.

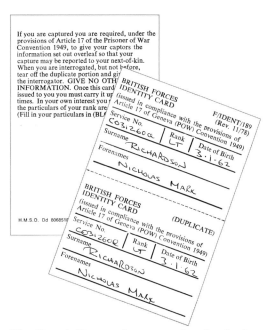

◆ **ENGINE EMERGENCIES**

**WARNING:** Immediate ejection may be the only option. During engine relight, attempt where possible to remain inside relight envelope

**BIRDSTRIKE/RICOCHET/
MECHANICAL DAMAGE/ENGINE SURGE**

(Loud bang or bangs and fluctuating RPM – Falling RPM, with steady or rising JPT (15 sec light) – Loss of thrust – Growling noise)

**IN FLIGHT**

*In event of severe engine malfunction in hover –* **EJECT**

*If time critical:*
Limiters ... ... Trip
*If thrust not restored:*
MFS ... ... ON

**DO NOT JEOPARDISE EJECTION OPTION**

*If time permits* ... ... Monitor for surge

*If surged or flamed out:*

| ENGINE RELIGHT DRILL |
|---|

Throttle ... ... HP cock off (2 sec min)
MFS ... ... ON
Throttle ... ... Idle (below 0·9M/20,000 ft)
Flaps ... ... Mid
Stores ... ... Jettison as required
Relight button ... Press and hold (if auto-ignition suspect)
Increase throttle slowly to minimum RPM
Monitor IGV, if incorrect, carry out **IGV FAILURE** drill (Card 25)
Relight indicated by RPM/JPT recovery to normal

*If engine surges again, or if no light-up*
Throttle ... ... HP cock off
LP cock ... ... Confirm ON
Fuel pumps ... ... Confirm ON
Prop ... ... ... Confirm ON
Wait 30 secs if possible — attempt further relight

*If Thrust NOT restored –* **EJECT IN TIME** ◆

My pilot's reference cards showing the emergency procedures for the aircraft.

If you are captured you are required, under the provisions of Article 17 of the Prisoner of War Convention 1949, to give your captors the information set out overleaf so that your capture may be reported to your next-of-kin. When you are interrogated, but not before, tear off the duplicate portion and give to the interrogator. GIVE NO OTHER INFORMATION. Once this card is issued to you you must carry it up at all times. In your own interest you should the particulars of your rank are (Fill in your particulars in BL

H.M.S.O. Dd 806851F

**BRITISH FORCES IDENTITY CARD**
(issued in compliance with the provisions of Article 17 of Geneva (POW) Convention 1949)

F/IDENT/189 (Rev. 11/78)

Service No. CO312601a
Surname RICHARDSON | Rank LT | Date of Birth 3.1.62
Forenames NICHOLAS MARK

**BRITISH FORCES IDENTITY CARD**
(issued in compliance with the provisions of Article 17 of Geneva (POW) Convention 1949)

(DUPLICATE)

Service No. CO312601a
Surname RICHARDSON | Rank LT | Date of Birth 3.1.62
Forenames NICHOLAS MARK

The British Forces identity card with which we were issued before undertaking a mission. In the event of capture, we were instructed to tear off the bottom half and give it to our interrogator.

Oz Phillips comes in to land on the deck of the *Ark Royal* alone (*above*), having seen my aircraft shot down. His expression as he descends from the cockpit betrays the strain and distress of the experience (*right*).

CILENTO ON CONNERY
The hidden violence
in a stormy marriage
— Pages 37, 38, 39

# The Mail

APRIL 17, 1994

ON SUNDAY

65p

## Pilot 'safe' after Serb attack

# BRITISH HARRIER DOWNED

By AMRA BASIC
in Sarajevo
and KIM WILLSHER
in London

THE Bosnian crisis reached a new flashpoint yesterday when a British plane was shot down and Serb tanks began the destruction of the UN 'safe haven' city Gorazde.

The Royal Navy Sea Harrier, from the Ark Royal in the Adriatic, was crippled while flying over the Bosnian Muslim city on a two-plane bombing mission aimed at defending the city hospital which was under fire from Serb tanks.

Eyewitnesses reported by ham radio that the plane exploded and fell from the sky after it was hit, but the pilot Lt Nick Richardson ejected safely and was later rescued unhurt.

Defence Secretary Malcolm Rifkind said last night: 'The Harriers were called in by the UN because of an artillery attack in which a hospital appeared to have been targeted. In

HIT: The Sea Harrier exploded, but its pilot ejected to safety

these circumstances close air support was called for.'

The captain of the carrier Ark Royal, Terry Loughran said the Sea Harriers had identified a Serb tank on their first run and had returned to destroy it when one of the planes was hit by a missile.'

### Scratches

A Nato spokesman confirmed later that Lt Richardson, a married man in his thirties from Somerset, had been picked up by an Italian-based UN helicopter which homed in on his radio rescue transmission from the Muslim village where he had landed. He had suffered 'only scratches'. Amazingly he had phoned home from the village to reassure his family.

Last night Downing Street officials were in touch with senior aides of President Bill Clinton who then called on the Russians to use 'maximum pressure' on the Serbs for an immediate ceasefire.

The Harrier was the first Nato plane to be shot down since the organisation's involvement in the Bosnian war.

The UN had given the Bosnian Serbs until 3 pm yesterday to stop shelling the town or face air strikes. The Sea Harrier was shot down at approximately 3.52 pm British time.

Lt Richardson and the other pilot, Lt 'Oz' Phillips, took off from the Ark Royal when the news came through

*Continued on Page 5*

The shootdown hits the headlines at home.

The milk float in which I was taken to Oskar's house.

The sleeping area I shared with the UNMOs at the bank. This photograph was taken before I was there, and shows it in a rather better condition than I remember it.

The canteen at the bank, again pictured some time earlier. The tablecloths and floral displays had certainly gone by the board by the time I arrived.

The SAS briefing room upstairs, whose existence I was unaware of until my last day.

Scenes of devastation in Gorazde. The tall, white building in the centre is the hotel where we had our observation post.

The River Drina, which we had to cross at breakneck speed to avoid Serb snipers as we rushed Craig to the hospital.

The SAS guys, Ahmed and me at the landing site, pictured by a thermal-imaging camera in the Puma helicopter which was about to evacuate us at last.

Relieved but exhausted, minutes after reaching safety in Sarajevo. Standing, left to right: Sean, Phil, Ant, Adrian and Simon, with Ahmed and myself in front.

Mel welcomes me back aboard the *Ark Royal*.

Oz, Wings and Terry Loughran toast my safe return on the Admiral's bridge. I'm still wearing the flight suit kindly lent to me by a Spanish Mirage pilot.

Then it's off to celebrate with the squadron, including Chris the gofer, Oz and Henry on the left; Shaggy, standing behind me, and Beasty, in the foreground on the right.

The reunion with my SAS mates, who paid a brief visit to the *Ark Royal* on their way back to Bosnia for another tour of duty. Left to right: Simon, Phil, Ant, me, Adrian and Sean.

With the rest of 801 Squadron after my return to the ship.

From: Admiral Sir Hugo White, KCB CBE

COMMANDER-IN-CHIEF FLEET
NORTHWOOD, MIDDLESEX
HA6 3HP
Telephone: 0923 83 7265
Fax: 0923 83 7131

20.4.94

Dear Nick,

I returned from leave yesterday and heard more detail about your and Oz Phillips' epic action over Bosnia. I would like you both to know that I and all my staff here at Northwood are full of admiration for your bravery and resolution in the face of obvious risks. You acted in the finest traditions of the Fleet Air Arm and Royal Navy. Thank you and very well done.

Yours sincerely, Hugo White

Just one of the letters I received on my return home.

vapour trails whistling off his wingtips as he followed me in the turn. The cloud was eating into our height envelope again, forcing us ever lower, but this didn't concern me unduly. We were halfway through the sortie, and I could already taste the tang of salt spray in my mouth as I slid back the canopy and jumped down on to the deck of the *Ark*. Once Banja Luka, the only location reputed to have a 'live' SA-6 site, was out of the way, I'd feel even happier.

I jinked around a column of grey steam vapour reaching down from the cloud base and saw the third site. Then I banked to the right and started to roll the cameras.

All of sudden – *wow-wow-wow* – the warning alarm on my raw gear screamed in my ears and an ugly green warning light started pulsing on the RWR. For a second or two, it was as if I was participating in somebody else's bad dream: the noise of the alarm, the flashing letters 'SA-6'. I still don't understand why it seemed as if it wasn't happening to me. Then instinct took over. I whipped my hand on to the nozzle lever, punched chaff and flares into the slipstream and rolled hard left to try to break the lock.

'Vixen Two-Three's locked!' I half screamed, half grunted, rolling with the g-forces.

'Vixen Two-Three, tail is clear!' Mowgli shot back.

We called Magic and informed our American AWACS controller that we were leaving the Bosnian theme park for the time being. I'd photographed five of the eight sites. The other three would have to wait for another time.

Mowgli and I were in the squadron briefing room, shooting the shit about the mission to anyone who felt inclined to listen to our hair-on-fire tale. We were happy to have been blooded and even happier to be alive to tell the story.

A bunch of pilots and goofers were gathered around, eager to listen. The only exception was Henry Mitchell, who was sitting in one of the chairs reading a paper with a scowl on his face. When our yarn was exhausted, I asked Henry what was up. It was not as bad as I thought: his cummerbund was ready for collection, which meant the dreaded visit to the Choghi tailor. He also needed to collect a dress shirt from stores on Nine Deck, which is about as far as you can descend on the ship. He'd been putting it off all day, but the moment of truth was now upon him.

'Tell you what,' I said. 'I'll go for you. I'll collect your shirt, Henry. And I'll even get your cummerbund from Wong.'

Henry looked at me as if I was mad, but I could see gratitude on his face, too. It was not only the distance that was off-putting: a meeting with the Choghi tailor itself was an unforgettable experience. 'You will?'

'I'm having some sandals made anyway, and young Chris here said he wanted a pair of boots,' I explained. 'The cobbler's right round the corner from the tailor, so there you go, problem solved. And after that last bloody sortie, I'm going to put in a special order for some custom-made brown trousers.'

Henry's face cracked into a smile. 'Thanks,' he said. 'And good luck.'

The truth was, I needed an injection of reality, pleasant or otherwise, to get my feet back on the ground after the rigours of the sortie. A visit to the cobbler's and the Choghi tailor would be the perfect tonic.

I yelled across the room to Chris, the gofer, who had been begging me for days for directions to the cobbler's and to stores. I hadn't given them to him because the route was almost impossible to explain and, well, I felt kind of responsible for his welfare. A solo trip to Nine Deck, where stores are located, should never be attempted on your first voyage. It's so far from the deck that on your own you might never find your way back up to the light. And Mr Wong and his mate Mr Chow, the cobbler, who were on Four Deck, had unpredictable natures and would have consumed an innocent like Chris in seconds, then spat out the pieces. The kid needed a wingman, and I was happy to oblige.

To get there from the briefing room, you first have to make your way to the walkway that links the port and starboard sides at the front of the ship. From there, it's a straight descent all the way down to the bilges. To access all the lower decks, you need to go down to Five Deck, which runs adjacent to the waterline. Getting to Five Deck is a relatively civilised affair, but after that your problems begin. From Five Deck down to Nine Deck, it's kidney hatches all the way, one above the other. Beyond Seven Deck, there are no stairs, only ladders.

When you have to negotiate a kidney hatch, which measures about 2ft by 18ins and is pinched in the middle (hence the name), you understand why there is an obesity limit in the Navy. If you are fatter than you should be, you could easily end up getting wedged in the hatch – a nightmarish scenario if the ship happens to be sinking at the time. And negotiating the kidney hatch and the ladders on the other side requires assault-course-type training.

Long before we got to the kidney hatches, we passed through Three Deck. Three Deck in this part of the ship is not pleasant. Before you go on down to Four Deck, you are hit by a truly dire smell: bitter, stale and vaguely visceral, an abysmal bouquet only marginally tempered by a soapy, chemical whiff of something approaching bleach.

I thought for a moment that Chris was going to chunder, but somehow he managed to restrain himself. 'God, what the hell is that?' he managed, his Adam's apple bobbing like a yo-yo.

'That,' I said, 'is the ship's laundry.'

The ship's laundry service, like the tailor's and the cobbler's, is a franchise owned and operated by Chinese. How this deal between franchise-owner and the Navy is arrived at I have no idea, but it is a naval tradition that has gone on for years and exists on almost every ship. It must also represent an extremely lucrative line of business, as anyone with a rudimentary grasp of maths could see. Every couple of days, I'd send a batch of clothes to the laundry at three or four quid a throw. There are approximately 1,000 people on an Invincible-class ship and most, I imagine, would avail themselves of the laundry service. Multiply this by the number of days of a voyage that could last six months or more, and you're talking a small fortune. In idle moments, I have imagined gangs of ferocious Triads fighting for the rights to this franchise, and perhaps this is not a million miles from the truth.

'No need to wash your own knicks ever again,' I told Chris as we pressed on towards Eight Deck. 'Just bring 'em down here and it's all done by magic.'

As we pressed on down, we entered a different world. There is

no natural light, of course, and the air is only just breathable, cir-
culated and recirculated as it has to be by giant fans to reach the
furthest-flung parts of the vessel.

At long last we reached stores and picked up Henry's shirt. Then
we ascended towards Four Deck to get to the tailor's and the cobbler's, situated towards the aft of the ship, passing cabins stacked
floor-to-ceiling with bunks and receiving hostile glances from oil-
smudged faces barely visible in the gloom. I found myself marking
the direction we'd come by the *Playboy* centrefolds pinned up at
the corridor intersections. I didn't have a ball of wool, so it was the
next best thing.

Just when Chris must have thought this was going to go on for
ever I paused outside an anonymous-looking cabin and pushed at
the half-open door, only to find it was jammed ajar by something
semi-solid on the other side – a pile of trousers, as it turned out.
With a heave and a shove, Chris and I managed to squeeze through
the gap and entered Wong's world.

The tiny cabin, no more than 6ft by 8ft, was packed floor-to-ceiling with cloth, half-finished uniforms and off-cuts. Against the
left-hand wall was a desk, its work surface lit by a dim lamp.
Beyond the beam of the lamp, I could just make out the tiny figure
of a bespectacled man, his face 3 inches from an intricate piece of
stitching. Even though we were almost on top of him, Mr Wong
gave no hint that he'd registered our presence, but this was all part
of the routine. Permanently deluged under a never-ending backlog
of work, the last thing Mr Wong needed was more custom.

I coughed several times, to get his attention, and eventually got
a reaction.

'No order today! No can do! You come back some other time,
maybe!' Mr Wong barked, without so much as a glance in our
direction.

Had I been ordering something for myself that day, I could have
knocked this ritual on the head very quickly with the mention of
money. But I had no need to resort to such underhand tactics. I
told Mr Wong I was here to collect Lieutenant Commander
Mitchell's black and white 801 Squadron cummerbund, not to
order.

Mr Wong looked up and said in perfect, unaccented English. 'That'll be £30, please.'

'Mr Wong, he's already paid.' I showed him Henry's receipt.

Mr Wong cast his peepers over the slip of paper and eventually gave a nod and a cluck of annoyance. A minute later, after searching through another enormous pile of clothes, he produced the cummerbund.

Chris stepped out from behind me and cleared his throat. 'Mr Wong, I'd like to order myself a pair of your special black mess boots, please.'

Mr Wong stared at him with a look of ill-concealed disdain.

'Stupid boy,' I said, feigning a clip to Chris's ear. 'This is a tailor's, not the cobbler's. We're going there next.'

For a nanosecond, as I caught Mr Wong's eye, we were united in a common bond of understanding.

Fifty yards and another maze of turns later, we reached another door. Beyond it lay a square chamber with a massive air-conditioning fan set in one of the walls. Beside this whirling contraption lay a second door, more of a hatch, really. I opened it up and pulled it back.

Inside, you could scarcely see a thing. There was a light of sorts, but here, too, it was very dim; the kind of illumination you get from one or two lit candles. There was an overpowering smell of leather – so strong, in fact, that it threatened to give me a migraine on the spot. The dimensions of the place were smaller than your average allotment shed: 6ft wide, 4ft deep and 5ft high.

In between a mound of what looked like raw, untreated hide and a heap of footwear in various stages of completion was a man beating away at a shoe. Because of the noise of the fan, which was 3 feet from Mr Chow's head, it was impossible to hear his hammer blows.

In a drill that had clearly been established at some central Chinese school of customer relations, Mr Chow ignored us for as long as he dared before finally glancing our way.

'Mr Chow!' I yelled, attempting to form a megaphone from my cupped hands, 'I've come to pick up my sandals.'

Mr Chow reached into the shoe mountain and pulled out a pair of sandals. He threw them at my feet.

'No!' I shouted. 'These are too small. Look, my feet are twice the size.'

Mr Chow delved back into the pile of shoes. When I was satisfied I'd got the right pair, I told him that Chris needed some boots pronto, a pair like the ones he'd made for me three years earlier.

Mr Chow sized Chris up from head to toe and yelled: 'You shame shize you friend?'

I intervened before he made mincemeat of the boy. 'No, you need to measure him.'

'OK, OK,' Mr Chow grumbled, and produced a pen and a piece of paper.

Thirty seconds later, Chris stepped off the paper to reveal two wobbly-looking outlines of his feet.

'OK,' Mr Chow barked. 'Ready for you in two week.'

Outside, I thought Chris was going to burst into tears.

'You have to trust me on this,' I said as I began navigating my way back via the Playmates of the Month. 'The guy is an expert. Somehow – don't ask me how – they'll end up fitting you like a glove.'

Chris said nothing as we climbed up towards the waterline. It would be several weeks, in fact, before he spoke to me again.

On 5 February, the Serbs lobbed a mortar bomb into a crowded marketplace in Sarajevo. Sixty-eight people died and more than 100 were wounded. In the ensuing mood of shock and outrage, General Rose grabbed the initiative with both hands and arranged a ceasefire in the city. Four days later, NATO issued an ultimatum against the Bosnian Serbs. Unless heavy weapons were withdrawn to a 20km radius outside the capital or grouped under NATO control, air strikes would be launched against them. Emboldened by the efforts of their allies, the Russians, to overturn the UN's authority to launch air strikes, the Serbs continued to prevaricate. As the 19 February deadline for the removal of the weapons approached, we found ourselves scrambled over the Balkans with bombs on our weapons pylons, certain that the call to drop them would come at any moment.

At the last minute, the Serbs backed down and removed their

guns, but elsewhere in the shattered province, they pressed home their attacks against the Muslims with renewed vigour. Even though the Muslim enclaves had been declared 'safe havens' by the UN, punitive action against the Serbs was still not taken. Perhaps, optimists suggested, this was because the international community had its eye on other, more encouraging developments at the time.

On 23 February, the Muslims and the Croats signed their own peace deal, agreeing to the creation of the so-called Muslim–Croat Federation. Only the Serbs remained resolutely opposed to any settlement, an attitude that only appeared to harden after 28 February, when a clutch of US Air Force F-16s shot down four Serb fighter bombers that had launched attacks on a Muslim ammunition factory in the Mostar area. After this, we were told, NATO was regarded by the Serbs with the level of hostility previously reserved for the Muslims.

Soon after this incident, Mel and I were on a 'roving CAP' sortie over central Bosnia, looking for airborne threats and carrying a couple of 1,000lb freefall bombs just in case, when Magic, the AWACS in our vicinity, suddenly ordered us to snap north.

'Unidentified contact bears three-five-zero. Forty miles. Battle pair, 20,000 feet, heading south. Mission identify.'

'Roger, Vixen Two-Zero,' Mel confirmed, 'mission identify.'

The boss, as ever, was calm and unflustered. It was the AWACS' next transmission that suddenly elevated this mission above all the others we'd been assigned.

'Roger. If identified as hostile, clear engage.'

In the space of an instant, I was transported back more than a month to the clear skies above Deci. Two of us against two of them. Only this time it was for real.

As we came north, I radioed the boss. 'Vixen Two-Zero. Check intentions?'

'We are to identify. I'll go eyeball, you go shooter.'

Mel's short précis of our intercept plan indicated that we were to go head-to-head with the bogeys in battle formation, 2 miles apart. Mel would be close enough to effect a visual identification as he closed on them, allowing me to snap in from the right and pull a shot on the beam if they turned out to be hostile.

If they didn't get us with their medium-range missiles first.

The AWACS counted us in. 'Bogeys, three-five-zero, 35.'

I checked the RWR, just in case the alarm on my raw gear had gone unserviceable. Nothing. But this was cold comfort. The Germans had shown themselves to be more than adept at masking their intentions during our encounter over Deci. Who was to say, if these were MiG-29s, that the Serbs were any less proficient?

With that thought in mind, I made a quick transmission to Mel, sticking to the established shorthand. 'Boss, if we get locked-up by MiG-29s, I'll spike, you drag.'

Mel, sounding a little taut for the first time, came back: 'Yeah. Good work.'

'Vixens, bogeys three-five-zero, 30 miles,' Magic said, counting us down.

Again I cast my mind back to the Deci engagement. If I didn't hit the notch dead-on this time, Mel and I were toast.

Magic again: 'Vixens, bogeys three-four-five, 25.'

I shot a glance at the RWR. If they're going to take a shot with their medium-range missiles, I thought, any moment now, the fucker is going to light up like a pinball machine. But the RWR stayed free of threat data and there was not so much as a nick-nick-nick in my earphones.

Mel and I pressed deeper and deeper into the no-escape zone of the bogeys' medium-range missile envelope. Then, suddenly, at 5 miles, Mel yelled that he'd seen them.

'Vixen Two-Zero, tally! Two MiG-21s!'

'Vixen Two-One, tally!' I responded, putting the Sea Harrier into a hard bank to port as I snapped in to take a shot at them from the beam.

My fingers worked like crazy to prime the missile. I put the system into super-scan mode and heard the growl of the seeker as it picked up the first of the bogeys' heat signatures nose-on. I looked up to see if I could spot the son of a bitch, but against the patch-work of fields and mountains below, picking out a couple of small, fast-moving targets was next to impossible.

But then, to my surprise, I did see something. For a moment I thought the aircraft was Mel's, but as my eyes stayed with it, I could make out its orientation: it was coming my way. And then I saw the second one.

The seeker tone built to a crescendo. On the HUD, the diamond told me the target was fully locked. My thumb hovered above the firing button.

And then, for the briefest of moments, I saw the target framed against a clear patch of sky. Etched in silhouette, I could see that it wasn't a MiG at all.

'Vixens, knock it off, knock it off!' I screamed. 'Miss i/d. Aircraft identified friendly!'

Mel, as calm as you like, merely said: 'Confirmed friendly. Jaguar.'

The two aircraft shot past us, apparently oblivious of how close they had come to being shot down. As I watched them go, I cursed Mel and I cursed the bloody Crabs, the latter, not for the first time. As was the wont of the RAF, they'd more than likely steamed into theatre without speaking to the right people or getting the correct clearances. Magic, spotting an unidentified pair of blips coming our way, had no doubt come to the conclusion that they were legitimate targets.

'Roger Vixens,' the AWACS controller chimed in. 'Haul off and resume roving CAP.'

When I landed back on deck forty minutes later and climbed down from the aircraft, it hit me. I'd come within a stone's throw of shooting down one of our own aircraft. I felt drained, weak and a little sick. A member of the groundcrew must have noticed me looking wobbly, because he came over to give me a hand.

'We almost had a severe embarrassment.' I told him what had happened.

'We almost had a severe bloody embarrassment here, too, sir,' he replied, looking at me pointedly.

'What do you mean?'

He hesitated for a moment. 'You blew Wren Alexander off the back of the ship just before you took off. She decided to walk behind the aircraft while you were doing your engine accels. It's all right, though, sir. No need to feel bad. She landed in the nets, luckily for her. Don't 'spect she'll do that again in a hurry.'

I was stunned. I remembered seeing a bit of a kerfuffle behind the aircraft as I'd done the 'accels', the series of tests that times the engine's run-up to full power. It's a procedure that requires concentration, so I hadn't been too focused on events outside the cockpit. I'd thought that the flap at the back of the aircraft was indicative of some kind of mechanical problem. However, when I'd looked at the yellowcoat, he'd given me the thumbs-up. Now I realised that he'd been telling me Wren Alexander was OK. Blimey. Blowing a Wren off-deck and being a split-second from blowing the RAF out of the sky, all within the space of an hour. I congratulated myself. A hell of a day's work, Richardson.

Mel and I dispatched a full report to the CAOC, leaving it to others to decide where the blame for this would-be 'friendly-fire' incident lay. If we ever got to hear about the results of the inquiry at all, we knew it wouldn't be for months.

After showering and changing, I popped down to the NAAFI on Five Deck and bought a large box of Milk Tray. Along the way, I bumped into several bagmen and pingers who were delighted to have the opportunity to rib me about Wren Alexander. The thrust of their accusation was that I'd been looking to cut down on my divisional workload and had done it deliberately. Bagmen and pingers tend to judge you by their own sick standards.

I negotiated one kidney hatch and dropped down on to Six Deck. Because you have to be pretty fit to be in the Navy, the sick bays on most ships tend to be empty most of the time – unless, of course, you happen to find yourself in a full-blown war. As a result, ship's doctors are a frustrated breed. They are usually to be found sitting around hoping against hope for an interesting outbreak of some exotic disease, or cursing their misfortune to be working in an age when yellow fever and scurvy are little more than entries in a medical encyclopaedia. So if you're not careful, you can walk into sick bay with 'flu symptoms and end up having your leg amputated because some overzealous surgeon's got a bit knife-happy.

Stepping into the ward, I saw several scab-lifters, as we call them, reaching for their bone saws. I quickly asked where I could find Wren Alexander. Masking his disappointment, one of the doctors gestured to a bed at the back of the ward. I was lucky to get off so lightly. The opportunity to practise surgical procedure on a pilot, of all specimens, must have been as exciting for these people as a trip to the cemetery was for Burke and Hare.

Wren Alexander looked up from her book. She appeared a little shaken, and there were a few cuts and bruises on her face, but the smile told me she was otherwise OK. I approached her with my hands in the air and my tail between my legs.

'It was my fault, sir. I should've checked with the yellowcoat before I went behind the aircraft. Stupid, really. I could kill myself.'

'Hey,' I said, gesturing to the vultures in the white coats. 'Don't do that. They'd have a field day with your body.'

She smiled and thanked me for the chocolates.

I sat down on a chair beside the bed. 'How are you feeling?' I asked.

'The only things wrong with me are a bruised ego and a bruised bum, sir.'

'When I said you should throw yourself into your work, Wren Alexander, I didn't mean you to interpret my remarks quite so literally,' I attempted.

She laughed politely. We talked about a lot of things. On the political front, it all looked quite encouraging. The deal between the Muslims and the Bosnian Croats was seen as a tremendous step towards peace, and the strong rumour below decks was that we would be heading home before too long.

After her visit to my cabin, I fully expected Wren Alexander to embrace this possibility with enthusiasm, but if anything she looked disappointed. I almost asked her if there'd been some change on the home front – a rift with her boyfriend or some other domestic development that had led her to view the job differently. But then I got it. Ten weeks on station and Wren Alexander was a part of the team; one of the boys. It was gratifying to see.

'What about you, sir?' she asked. 'I hear you've got a new son.'

I told her about Kristian, who was now out of hospital and safely home with Yvonne and the other children. Winter was moving into spring; it would be the perfect time to be getting home. We had already been on station for the best part of ten weeks, and if the good progress that had been made with the Muslims and Croats could now be extended to the Bosnian Serbs, I could see us flying back soon. Two weeks into April, three at the most. Either way, I was sure it'd all be over by Easter.

A few days later, I turned down an opportunity to transfer to another unit. In late March, my two-year stint with the squadron was up, and a place was being kept open for me as a flying instructor at RAF Valley in north Wales. It was a tailor-made opportunity to get back home to Yvonne and the kids. But I knew Mel was anxious for me to stay on. After some heavy soul-searching, I told him that I would see the deployment through to its conclusion.

# CHAPTER 6

In early April, Shaggy flew into a place that is feared by all Sea Harrier pilots, a place known simply as the Dark Side. This was the first of two rare and unusual events in the squadron's history to occur in the same month.

It started as a practice anti-ship mission against the US Navy's big carrier in the Adriatic, the USS *Saratoga*. I was up in Flyco overseeing the launch of the aircraft. A night take-off, though a regular occurrence, is hairy enough, but when you're simulating a couple of Sea Eagle anti-ship missiles strapped to your wings (by carrying a huge pair of drop tanks), things are never routine.

As usual, there were a load of goofers in Flyco, sipping their coffees and soaking up the ambience. Tonight, for some reason, it felt particularly claustrophobic, and I was a little spooked. I turned to Wings, the commander air, and asked whether we could thin out a few people. He agreed, and the ship's dentist, senior doctor and the padre were invited to seek alternative recreation.

The only non-operational person now left in Flyco was Snowy – Paul Snow, the ship's senior engineer – who'd never seen a night launch before and had asked me days earlier whether he could attend. Because I liked Snowy and knew he wouldn't be any trouble, I said he could stay, and Wings concurred.

I looked out of the window. Three Sea Harriers were just discernible at the end of the ship. Henry, Beasty and Shaggy were in the cockpits, their visors bathed in the red glow of the HUD's nocturnal filter, carrying out their pre-flight checks. At night, the lights on the superstructure are turned way down, creating an effect akin to moonlight. The whole picture is somewhat eerie.

'What's it like, a night launch?' Snowy asked, his hands cupped around his coffee mug.

'Same as day, only it's dark,' I attempted.

'Bullshit.'

I laughed. 'Right. There's nothing quite like a night sortie, Snowy.'

It was difficult to explain to a non-flyer, but at night, when you're in the cockpit, every point of reference seems different. A minute to launch and I could hear any abnormal click, whirr or ping of the aircraft as it thrummed on deck ready for the signal from Flyco. At night, my senses seemed to go into a rarefied, supersensitive mode. For example, there's an air-conditioning system in the cockpit that by day I never, ever notice. Yet in the dark, a second or two after I've slammed to full power, this system makes a belching sound that's so loud and unexpected it seems as if the engine is about to explode. If you're not ready for it, it can be quite off-putting.

When you release the brake, a string of lights leading up to the ramp exit rushes at you with the intensity of the warp-speed special effects in a *Star Trek* movie. You always try to hit the ramp as the bow of the ship is lifting, but at night it's impossible to tell which way the deck is pitching, and you rely on the rise and fall of the attitude indicator on the HUD.

As you launch off the ramp and pull back on the nozzle lever, dropping the jet pipes 35 degrees to help punch you into the sky, everything goes black. The light of the ship is behind you and there is nothing except an inky void to the front and sides of the cockpit. Because the ramp is inclined at 12 degrees, instinct tells you you're pitching up massively, but you're not. It's simply an illusion. Nonetheless, there is an overwhelming temptation to push down on the stick. Fight it, you tell your senses, or you'll fly straight into the sea.

For five seconds, the aircraft relies on ballistic energy to carry it forward. Only when it is up to 150 knots and starting to fly like a plane should, with air moving over its wings and creating lift, do the sensations start to become recognisable again. But even now, you're not quite out of the woods, because as you push the nozzle lever forward, adjusting the thrust of the jet backwards again, the nose drops. In the pitch black, it feels as if you're diving towards the water, when in fact all you're doing is levelling out. Trust in your instruments and you'll be all right. Do what your senses tell you to do and you're a dead man.

Just before the first aircraft took off, its red nose lamp lined up with the deck lights pointing towards ramp exit, I told Snowy what had happened to Henry a couple of years back when, on launching, he'd yanked the throttle lever to idle instead of dropping the nozzle lever back 35 degrees. The Sea Harrier had plummeted off the bow of the ship and, watching from Flyco, we all thought he'd had it. But Henry rapidly saw the error of his ways and rammed the throttle to the stops. All we saw was this mountain of spray as the aircraft clawed itself up from the waves. It had dropped to within 5 feet of them.

It's the night. I can guarantee it wouldn't have happened in day-light. After dark, shit just seems to happen.

Having seen the aircraft safely off the ramp, Snowy and I headed down to the aircrew feeder on Two Deck. The food we pilots get in this privileged *cantina* is outstanding and Snowy was quick to take advantage of it. We were both tucking into our nosh when sud-denly an announcement came over the buzzbox.

'801 duty pilot to Flyco at the rush.'

The delivery was so deadpan that half of me was tempted to ignore it. But 'at the rush' signified that somebody was in trouble. I crammed the remnants of my bacon buttie into my mouth and started to leg it back up to Flyco with Snowy in tow.

'What's wrong ?' he panted.

'Haven't a clue,' I gasped, but my watch told me that somebody must have aborted the sortie; and that meant trouble.

When a pilot levels off at 200ft and he is half a mile behind a car-rier at night, you might imagine he'd see a huge, brightly lit floating island standing out like the lights of Las Vegas, welcoming you in. But nothing could be further from the truth. It feels as if you're inside a black-painted goldfish bowl with a tiny pinpoint of light somewhere up ahead in the distance. That's the carrier. Slow down too soon and you end up in the hover with no momentum to carry you towards the ship. Approach too fast and you overshoot the ship and end up in a black hole with no point of reference at all – no light, no indication of where the sea is, nothing. If the stars are out, you at least know which way is up, but I've been on night sorties when I've mistaken the lights of fishing boats for stars, and vice versa. As with take-off, the important point when landing is to watch your instruments and obey them to the letter. Do what your senses tell you and you'll hit the sea or the carrier – or maybe both.

As I walked into Flyco, you could cut the atmosphere with a knife. 'Wings, what's the snag?' I asked.

The commander air was looking out of Flyco's angled window, gazing aft. 'It's Shaggy,' he replied, slightly too calmly for my liking. 'He's lost his HUD.'

This was bleak news. Because it is imperative that you follow your instruments at night, without that strip of glass on the coaming on which vital flight data is displayed, your capacity for landing the aircraft safely is gravely impaired. The critical moment comes when you translate from airborne to jetborne flight; when you're balancing on the thrust generated by the Pegasus. This, as I've explained, takes you through a dangerous speed band of from 120 down to 40 knots. Even when you're safely in the hover alongside, the pitching deck means the party is far from over.

The slide over and above the deck is best executed at 100ft, 50 feet higher than the deck itself. If the HUD's down, the only means of gauging your height is the head-down radar altimeter, which is conveniently situated on the lower left side of the cockpit, just where you don't want to be looking at a time like this.

If you can see anything when you look out of the cockpit, you might just catch the ghostly outline of the ship as she pitches and heaves in the swell off to your right. This is highly disorientating, as you think that it's you that's moving, not the ship. Correct what you perceive as this drift and you can end up ploughing, inverted, into the ocean. Execute the slide-over manoeuvre without reference to your true height – information that you can only get from the head-down display – and you can slam into the side of the carrier.

Worse still, you cannot practise for this eventuality: there is no simulator that can duplicate all the conditions. Only when I thought of this did it dawn on me that Shaggy had probably only landed on at night four or five times before. Without his HUD, the boy was in for a hard night's work.

I picked up a headset, joined Wings by the window and started to talk to him. The trick is to keep it tight and remain ultra-calm yourself. The last thing Shaggy needed to hear was any trace of anxiety in my voice. I opened the bidding by saying just two words to him – 'Slightly low' – and then watched to see what happened.

Half a mile behind the carrier, I saw the landing and navigation lights of Shaggy's aircraft pull a little higher into the blackness. It was a good start, but we had a long way to go.

'Correcting nicely,' I told him. Shaggy climbed a little higher. 'On the roger,' I said. He was back on glideslope.

I could tell he was rattled. His approach to the carrier was quite erratic, requiring constant corrective input from me. After what seemed an age, he managed to manoeuvre alongside the ship. I could see him a couple of hundred feet off the port side, his aircraft a barely discernible grey outline against the night sky. The Sea Harrier was oscillating slightly, up and down, left and right, which told me that Shaggy was trying to hold her steady by following the motion of the deck, which was pitching and heaving as it always does in a swell.

'Deck pitching slightly, rolling slightly,' I said, maintaining what I hoped was a cool, calm tempo.

The Sea Harrier continued to wobble off the left-hand side of the ship. Inside, I was thinking, 'Jesus Christ, Shaggy, you're going to kill yourself, and quite likely a bunch of us, too,' but somehow I managed to keep a rein on my emotions, and my voice. 'Don't follow the deck,' I told him softly.

Shaggy made his move towards the ship. The Sea Harrier is so sensitive to the touch at this moment, balancing as it is on four columns of thrust, that all you have to do is think the aircraft in the direction you want it to go and it'll head there. Shaggy must have banged the stick over, because suddenly it moved at breakneck speed over the deck.

I tried to warn him. 'Too fast!'

But Shaggy kept on going, shooting sideways across the deck, past the superstructure and into the Dark Side – the portion of airspace to the right of the carrier where there is no light at all. On the left-hand side, you can at least pick up the outline of the ship, thanks to the low-lit illumination on the deck. On the right there is no illumination of any kind. Once you enter this black hole, there is nothing you can do about it. If you attempt to move back to the deck, you'll more than likely plough straight into the invisible superstructure. Remaining where you are is not an option, because without a HUD you don't know whether you're straight and level or pointing towards the sea or the sky. You're in impenetrable blackness, hovering on your nerves, and there's no one who can help you.

Snowy, Wings and I said nothing. Because I couldn't see Shaggy there was nothing I could say or do that would make any difference. I had a fleeting vision of the flight-deck crew running helter-skelter for cover as the jet shot over their heads and then, like everyone else, I simply braced myself for the explosion.

Instead there was a roar behind the superstructure and Shaggy reappeared out of the darkness. Somehow, he managed to get the jet into a semi-stable hover and then, without a moment's delay, thumped it down on the deck.

'Bloody hell,' Snowy said, when we all started breathing again, 'how did he get away with that one?'

I said nothing. I had heard of pilots flying into the Dark Side, but this was the first time I had seen it happen. It was the kind of thing that wouldn't have occurred at the beginning of a voyage. I was more convinced than ever that it was time we had our marching orders and headed home.

The following day, any hope of a quick return to England was dashed when the Serbs launched an all-out offensive against the besieged Muslim town of Gorazde. For days the shells rained down with no sign of any intervention by the UN, even though Gorazde was one of the so-called 'safe havens' mandated to receive UN protection.

Finally, on 10 April, after numerous warnings from General Rose to the Serbs' HQ in Pale – warnings that had no effect at all on the bombardment – two US Air Force F-16s were ordered to attack Serb forces around the town. Two targets were engaged, a Serb Army command post and a tank; both were destroyed.

The Serb assault faltered for a while, but soon resumed. Throughout it all, the squadron flew regularly into Bosnian airspace, ready to intervene in whatever form was necessary. Six days after the NATO jets attacked, Oz and I were cruising over Sarajevo on a practice close air support (CAS) mission, when a crackle in my headset signalled I had a message inbound from Magic, our AWACS controller. We were told to proceed on the orders of Chariot towards the south-east and contact Fortune on the TAD Three frequency.

It was the directive from Chariot, the CAOC at Vicenza, that had really caught my attention. The call sign Fortune had been given to British forward air controllers in Bosnia. Chariot was telling Oz and me to make contact with one of them. The tone of the message made it quite clear that this had nothing to do with the CAS exercise: that it was quite likely this was the real thing. I was gripped by a combination of excitement and fear. But the great thing about Bosnia, a country about the same size as Wales, was that it did not give you much time to think. If I held my current speed, I'd be over the heart of the Serb offensive in less than three minutes.

I reached for the bundle of OS maps tucked under my left thigh, not for the first time cursing the fact that the Sea Harrier had no autopilot, and extracted the main map. Adjusting the throttle, I then wedged the main map into the coaming above the instrument panel ready for when I needed it, and reached down with my other hand for the thick green notebook that was tucked under my right leg, all the while concentrating on keeping the aircraft steady.

I opened up the 'green brain' at the page that contained the authentication codes the FAC had to give me to prove his identity. With so many different nationals involved in the UN operation in Bosnia, it would have been all too easy for a Serb to have masqueraded as a friendly FAC, sending hoax signals to NATO aircraft instructing them to bomb Muslim or even UN positions. Only when I was satisfied that the FAC was genuine could I take his 'nine-line brief', the instruction that would pinpoint exactly where my bombs were meant to fall.

'Vixen Two-Three to TAD Three,' I announced as soon as I was ready.

I received an immediate acknowledgement from the French FAC I'd been working with over Sarajevo. 'Roger. Vixen Two-Three to TAD Three.' He paused before adding in a Jean-Paul Gaultier accent: 'And good luck.'

Now to make contact with the British FAC.

*'Fortune Zero-Five, this is Vixen Two-Three.'*

*There was a brief pause, then a voice burst in my ears: 'Vixen Two-Three, this is Fortune Zero-Five. You're loud and clear.'*

I flicked to the next page of my green brain. It was filled with a jumble of random letters arranged in a grid. There was no time for pissing about. I needed to authenticate this guy fast. He sounded kosher enough, but rules were rules. Knowing my luck, this could have been the one Serb in Bosnia trained to mimic a Cockney. If I was going to drop bombs in the vicinity of a town crammed with civilians, I wanted to do it by the book.

'Fortune Zero-Five,' I said, articulating the words as clearly as I could in a hurtling, vibrating 10-ton tin can, 'authenticate Alpha Charlie.'

To verify who he was, all the FAC had to do was give me the correct letter from his grid, which was identical to mine. It was simple enough. And because we practised the procedure incessantly, I knew it would be second nature to him.

But there was an interminable pause. Over the open mike, I could hear what at first I took to be some kind of irregular jamming signal, like a series of thumps. It took me a second or two to realise that it was the sound of Serb shell explosions being broadcast live from Gorazde.

'This is Fortune Zero-Five,' the voice came back at last. 'I authenticate . . . Zulu.'

'Fortune Zero-Five,' I said, trying to keep the exasperation out of my voice, 'that is incorrect.' I cast a rapid glance at the green brain and picked out another letter. Let's try again.

'Authenticate X-ray Yankee.'

'*We haven't got time for this shite, mate!*' *the voice on the ground yelled in between two more artillery bursts.* '*We're getting bloody shelled here!*'

Another second ticked by. Through the HUD I could now see the smoke between the ground and the cloudbase ahead of me. Gorazde. I was almost on top of the place and still trying to reason with a dyslexic.

'Authenticate X-ray Yankee,' I insisted.

In the agonising pause that followed, as the airspeed indicator clipped 440 knots, I was gripping the top of the stick with its myriad switching systems as if I was trying to strangle the thing.

At last, the crackle in my headset, and: 'Bravo. It's Bravo.'

I almost did a victory roll. Bravo, the letter B. Bingo.

I readied myself for the initial instruction of the nine-line brief, but it never came. Instead there were several more bursts of shell-fire.

'*We know there's a tank or two above the ridgeline to the north of Gorazde. That's what you're gonna take out, mate. All right?*'

This time I never queried the breach of procedure. The bloke wanted to dispense with the nine-line brief and do this using buddy language, that was fine by me.

*I grabbed the map and scoured the topography. A moment later I found it, a sharp divide between two alpine faces running north–south about 10 miles north of the besieged Muslim enclave. I was now down to only 8,000ft, right in the heart of the MANPADS and Triple-A envelope.*

*I shot over Gorazde, banking the Sea Harrier to the left. Columns of smoke were rising from the houses below, but in the still air it could have been wood smoke. It was not what I imagined at all. From my vantage-point, there was little discernible damage.*

When the ridgeline veered towards me I saw how densely forested it was. I peered past the plexiglass, and for a few seconds the ridgeline undulated and coiled below my aircraft, and then it was gone. *I was out over the mountains again and pulling into a 'dumb-bell' manoeuvre that would bring me back again, this time from another direction.*

No close air support pilot likes to fly over a target more than once. Each pass makes the job of the ground air defence batteries easier. By varying the direction of approach, the pilot does retain some element of surprise but, as advantages go, it's a tenuous one.

*As I hauled back on the stick, feeling the gs wrenching at my oxygen mask and sucking my guts into my boots, my brain tried to review every nook and cranny of the densely wooded topography I'd just seen.*

Nothing. Not one damned manmade thing had passed before my eyes.

'Vixen Two-Four, spot anything?' I asked Oz.

My wingman was 500 yards behind me and a little off to the right. I was 500 feet below the base of the clouds, Oz a little higher, watching out for me.

*'Negative.'*

*I heard the disappointment in his voice. The FAC must have caught it, too.*

Though silent during the first pass, now that I was approaching the ridgeline again he was back on air.

*'We're pretty bloody sure there are two tanks down there, mate. Do you see 'em?'*

*The ridgeline loomed large in the HUD again. I banked the aircraft and peered hard past the canopy glare. My eyes watered with the effort.*

But as we shot out over the trees and pulled away to the north, I'd still seen absolutely nothing that remotely resembled a tank.

*'Come on,' the FAC yelled, incredulous, 'you must have seen 'em.'*

I pulled round again and went into another dumb-bell. I had to give it one last try.

This time, I pressed a little lower. I scanned the terrain as we tore towards the ridgeline. The trees formed an unbroken green canopy over the mountains. Then, as we rocketed overhead, I saw flashes of pale earth and grey granite beneath the branches.

A second passed, then another. I could almost hear the FAC's breath in my ears. And then, suddenly, and quite unexpectedly, a plume of smoke broke through the trees. Instinctively, I made a minute course correction towards it. As I shot overhead, I glimpsed the unmistakable outline of an olive-green main battle tank. The smoke had been from its exhaust as it manoeuvred into a new position.

'*Tally!*' I yelled. '*Two T-55s.*'

'*Tally!*' the wingman responded. He'd seen them, too.

'*That's your target,*' the FAC announced drily.

We started pulling round. I needed to talk to Vicenza.

'Chariot, this is Vixen Two-Three.'

The voice of the AWACS airborne command post came back instantaneously.

'Vixen Two-Three, this is Magic. Go ahead.'

'Two T-55s positively identified on ridgeline north of Italy. Am I cleared to engage?'

'Affirmative,' the air controller said. 'You're cleared hot.'

Hot? A war was going down in the heart of Europe and NATO was using incorrect terminology. 'Cleared hot' was the authorisation for bomb release during simulated practice missions. If I was going to start the Third World War, I wanted to be positive I had the full blessing of NATO's command authorities. For that I had to be 'cleared live'.

'Er, Magic, please confirm from Chariot that I am cleared live.'

A couple of seconds later the air controller was back again without a hint of contrition in his voice. 'Affirm from Chariot. You're cleared live.'

I went back into the drill, selecting the centre weapon pylon by means of a switch in front of my left knee. Then I found the rotary knob next to it and twisted it clockwise to arm the 1,000lb bomb. I was in the middle of this routine when I heard Oz's yell.

'*Flares!*'

I punched the flares button. There was no time to take evasive action. If a missile had locked on to me, I prayed that my flares, somewhere in the slipstream behind me, had done the trick and seduced it away from me.

Nothing happened, so I got on with the job.

The voice of the FAC boomed loud and clear into my headset.

'*Come on, man. We're getting shelled to shit down here. Do some-thing, for Christ's sake!*'

I switched the HUD to ground-attack mode and selected ASB3, the weapons-delivery mode we'd practised long and hard to perfect in Deci. I lined up above the ridgeline, focused on the target over my left shoulder and rolled the Sea Harrier into a dive.

The two tanks slid neatly into the middle of the HUD. I pressed the 'accept' button, waiting for the radar to range the distance between me and the tanks. I held the aircraft in the dive for as long as I dared, squeezing the accept button until I thought my thumb would fall off. But the diamond symbol that had flashed up with unfailing regularity in Deci – and everywhere else I'd ever called for it – failed on the one occasion I really needed it. I hauled back on the stick and pulled into a 5g, 30-degree climb.

'Vixen Two-Three, off dry,' I announced bitterly, my voice dis-torted by the aircraft's pull against gravity. 'No ASB3 lock.'

Procedure deemed it suicide to make a second attack run, but the FAC's pleas made it impossible to play things by the book now. So we went round again. But the same thing happened.

'Oz,' I said, 'I've got no ASB3 lock. You have the lead to dive.'

We pulled back around once more, coming in from the west, and I watched him go.

'Vixen Two-Four . . . in live.'

His Sea Harrier rolled over into its dive while I stayed aloft and scanned for SAMs. My vigil ended with a message from Oz.

'Vixen Two-Four, I'm off dry. No AS bombs lock.'

'For Christ's sake!' the FAC shouted. 'What the hell's going on up there?'

I checked my fuel gauges and pulled the Sea Harrier back round, determined to have one last go. I approached from the north and went into the dive. Once again, the tanks lined up perfectly in my sights. And once again I failed to get an ASB3 lock. I eased back on the stick. It was no use, I told myself. It just wasn't my day.

It was then that the missile hit me.

The blast was so violent that for a fraction of a second, it knocked me out. When I came to, I found myself hanging from my straps, struggling to make sense of what I could see. The lights on my instrument panel were ablaze. I felt an overwhelming urge to laugh. In all my practice sessions on the simulator, my instructors had given me a worst-case scenario in which two, perhaps three things had gone wrong at once, but never for an emergency that lit every light on the coaming simultaneously.

I had a massive engine fire. The instruments had gone off the clock; the jet-pipe temperature, normally set at 500 to 600 degrees, was registering over 1,000.

I gave the aircraft full left aileron and it righted immediately. I throttled back to idle to see if I could get the jet-pipe temperature down, but it made no difference. I had no choice but to shut down the engine in the hope that the rush of air through the turbine, coupled with a burst of the extinguisher, would snuff out the blaze. Then I'd try for a relight and, if that worked, get the hell out of there.

Less than ten seconds after the impact Oz burst through on my headset.

'Nick, you've got a real bad fire, man! Eject, eject!'

I should have reached down and pulled the seat handle there and then, but half of my brain was now mesmerised by images from my past. Strange, I thought, but your life really does flash before your eyes when you're in the shit. Just outside this window of calm, I heard a small voice telling me that if I ejected now, I'd land in the midst of the very people I'd just been trying to bomb.

With the fireball now clearly reflected in my rear-view mirror, I turned the stricken aircraft to the west. When I could no longer bear the heat through the fire wall behind me and had had enough of this game of chicken with planet earth, I reached down for the black-and-yellow ejection handle, closed my eyes, pressed my head back against the top-box on the seat and pulled.

A half-second ticked by, long enough for me to wonder if this was how it would all end for me: strapped to an aircraft from which my only deliverance would be a violent explosion as the fuel tanks blew.

And then I was hit by a massive force from beneath my seat.

My head felt as if it was being driven through my body, finishing up somewhere between my boots. My last conscious sensation was a sharp pain in my chin. Then I blacked out.

I was woken by another blow, so strong it drove the air from my lungs. I opened my eyes, gasping for breath, sure that I'd hit the ground. But I was still 2,000 feet up. The second jolt had been my parachute snapping open.

As I twisted beneath my 'chute, I glimpsed the plane off to the west, still airborne and trailing a long plume of fire and smoke. My relief quickly evaporated as I looked down. Between my feet the forest rose to meet me. I heard explosions and machine-gun fire.

You poor, dumb bastard, I said to myself. You're coming down in the heart of the combat zone.

I came down in a gap between the trees but hit the ground hard. I attempted to roll, as I'd been taught to do, but the landing punched the wind out of me and all my training turned to rat shit. After the initial shock of the impact, I lay there, my breath coming in short, sharp stabs. I felt strangely peaceful. I stared up at what I could see of the sky through the branches, mesmerised by the sun, a dull, flat disc behind the patchy overcast.

Keeping my head very still, I scanned my surroundings. They looked just like a stretch of the chase at home where Yvonne and I took the kids at weekends.

Some movement on the edge of my vision made me turn. A red squirrel was skipping along a branch 10 feet from my head. Funny how the damned things are under threat in England, yet clearly thriving here, I thought. The squirrel looked at me but evidently wasn't impressed, because it carried on along the branch, unperturbed by the intrusion.

Then it reached a curtain of dayglo orange and stopped short.

I don't know which of us found the sight of my parachute more surprising. It brought back all the trauma of the ejection – the crushing g-forces, the smell of cordite, the roar and the stillness – in a second of vivid replay. The squirrel stood up on its haunches, as if confronted by a predator, then scuttled into the dense branches at the top of the tree.

The silence of the forest returned and for a moment it was almost overwhelming. Then I tipped my head back and laughed. I'm not sure why, to this day – adrenalin, I guess, does funny things to the system when administered in big enough doses – but I laughed like I'd never laughed before, clutching my sides, the tears running down my face.

When I came to my senses again, I realised I was talking to myself. 'Well, Richardson, you've fucking gone and done it this time,' I said.

I stood up, a little shocked at how wobbly I felt on my pins, and dusted myself down, still muttering to myself like an old drunk.

I stuffed my helmet, g-pants and LSJ into a hollowed-out tree. Amazingly, this is exactly what the survival guide tells you to look for when trying to find somewhere to hide your gear. This advice had caused some merriment on the course – I mean, hollowed-out trees aren't always quite so handy when you drop down from the sky behind enemy lines. I made a mental note to tell the boys when I got back to the ship. Oz, Deke and Beasty would piss themselves laughing.

That was when it really hit me.

I'd been shot down behind enemy lines. Shot down. A cascade of information from all the intel briefs on the ship tumbled through my brain, but the only stuff I could latch on to was what the Serbs had threatened to do to pilots like me if they ever captured us.

I tried to move the parachute, but it was stuck in the branches. I had no idea whether I'd fallen on Muslim- or Serb-held territory. The clouds had rolled back in again now, but my brief glimpse of the sun had allowed me to get my bearings. I fumbled for the Walther PPK that was tucked into a holster in my survival vest. I had twenty rounds. Twenty rounds to protect myself against people who were reputed to skin their enemies like rabbits, or burn them alive, or impale them on stakes, just for the hell of it.

I listened for the sound of a NATO jet, anything that might reassure me that I was not forgotten down here. But the white noise that had filled my head after the ejection had been replaced with an eerie silence. For the first time, I felt cold, really cold, and I began to shiver uncontrollably.

I heard a noise. At first, it sounded like it was a part of the forest; the crack of a bough breaking or a stone bowling down a rock face. But it quickly steadied into something very definitely produced by humans.

Shots. First one, then another, then several. Before long it sounded as if Serb troops were raking the hillside below with bullets.

Panic seeped in. This wasn't happening. It couldn't be happening. Where could I go? Who could I turn to? I swept the trees, terrified suddenly that I was a second away from the rasp of a hand on my forehead, the yank as my head was pulled back, the slice of the knife as it cut across my windpipe.

I hadn't got halfway through my 360-degree surveillance of the forest when my nerves snapped completely. With legs like lead, I turned and ran in the only direction that made any sense: south, away from the shooting.

Several times I stumbled and fell. When this happened I hauled myself back up again and started to hit my legs, whispering hoarse messages of encouragement and cajolement at them as if they were nothing to do with me, stragglers in a race in which I was merely an observer. I kept heading south, remembering that this was the direction in which I had been flying when the missile had struck. The Serbs were to the north, that was for certain. Who or what was to the south I had no idea, but for the moment south was the only option.

Climbing a steep bank, I fell again and this time I did not get up. I don't know how long I lay with my face pressed against the pine needles, listening to the shellfire and the occasional crack of bullets. The next thing I remember is the sound of voices punctuating the distant noise of battle. Slowly, I lifted my face from the dirt and pulled myself to the top of the ridge.

Peering over a tree root, I saw them almost immediately through the trees: a group of five or six men around 200 yards away. I couldn't make them out in much detail, but there was a lot of shouting and pointing going on. It was obvious they were looking for me.

I ducked down behind the root, slithered back the way I had come and ran. I hadn't been going more than a couple of minutes when I heard more shouting. It was hard to be precise about the direction – the fight for breath and the rush of blood in my ears made it difficult to hear anything – but I knew it hadn't come from behind me.

Hunched low, I crept forward, head up. My skin prickling with anticipation, I saw through the trees, less than 100 yards away, a man holding a shotgun. I dropped into a squat.

The blood was pounding so hard in my temples that I thought I might black out. I forced my hand up to the holster that contained my PPK. It was shaking so badly that it took me a moment to find the gun.

As my fingers tightened around the grip, I continued to watch the soldier. The barrel of his gun moved restlessly, left to right, left to right, as if he was using it to sweep the ground. As my eyes held him, a second man swam into view against the trees, and then another, and then a fourth. Only one, so far as I could tell, was wearing military uniform. The rest were in flat caps and shirtsleeves. That some of them appeared to be civilians didn't make me feel any better: if this was a Serb hunting party, it didn't make a blind bit of difference whether they were armed with AK-47s or pitchforks. I recalled stories of what English farmers had done to Luftwaffe pilots who'd parachuted into the Kent countryside during the Blitz.

I turned round, listening for the approach of the first group I had seen. I was completely surrounded.

I pulled out the Walther and stared at it. I thought of Yvonne and the children and my first and last memory of Kristian, tiny in his incubator, his chest rising and falling in barely discernible movements. I felt the hot sting of tears behind my eyes and then anger – anger like I'd never known before. What the fuck was I doing here? This wasn't my war. These people hated each other. They'd hated each other for generations. What the hell difference were we ever going to make with our ships, aircraft and bombs? What did we think we were playing at?

A fragment of the conversation in which I'd tried to reason with Wren Alexander about the need for NATO and the UN to act decisively in the Balkans returned to me. It was all a bunch of horse shit. There was no good reason for our being here, none at all. Not only did these people hate each other, but most of them fucking hated us. So, why was I giving up my life for them?

I put my head in my hands and squeezed hard to stop myself from crying out in my pain and rage. When I opened my eyes again, I saw movement through the trees ahead. I stopped squeezing and blinked to focus. It was a child of maybe nine or ten years old. I blinked again and saw another. It was an intensely surreal moment, but a positive one. I began to think a little more clearly. If there were children in among the soldiers out there looking for me, then surely they weren't going to shoot me like a dog. Not now. Not with kids in their midst. As I watched the search party moving through the trees ahead, a sense of calm descended on me for the first time since my ejection.

I wasn't dead yet, I told myself.

I put the Walther back into my vest harness and started to creep towards a tree a couple of yards to my right. When I reached it, I sat down with my back against the trunk, my knees in the air and my hands in my lap.

I hadn't been there more than thirty seconds when the man in the combat jacket turned to his right and saw me. He stopped in mid-step and held his position, like a deer that has become aware it has been spotted by a hunter.

I sat there watching him, not moving a muscle. He returned my stare, unblinking, for what passed like a minute, though was probably only a few seconds. Then, ever so slowly, he raised his hand and clicked his fingers.

Even across the 200 yards that separated us, it sounded like a pistol shot. The rest of his group stopped dead. They looked at him and he pointed. Then they looked at me. Very slowly, guns raised, they turned and started to walk towards me.

I held my breath. The guy with the shotgun was 20 yards away when he motioned for me to get down. I did as I was told and lay face-down in the dirt. Unable to see the man as he stood over me, I braced myself for the shot. But when he put his hand on my shoulder and rolled me over, I saw that he was smiling.

There were ten of them, eight adults and two kids, and only one of them wore anything approaching a uniform. This was the guy in the combat jacket, which he was wearing over civilian clothes, who I took to be the leader of the group. His orders to the others seemed to go uncontested, although he was evidently not the oldest. I guessed he was probably in his mid-thirties, but his face was like a road map, the deep lines that criss-crossed it visible under grey, wiry stubble. His brown eyes, which darted around the forest like a frightened animal's, were almost hidden beneath a mop of brown, unkempt hair that looked as if it hadn't seen water in months.

As I stared into his face, none of these fleeting impressions seemed to count for very much. The only thing that really registered was the insignia on the shoulder of his combat jacket, which I recognised as BIH – Bosnian Army. To my enormous relief, there was no doubt I'd been found by Muslims and not by Serbs.

I scanned the rest of the group, anxious to make no sudden moves. They looked more like farmers than soldiers, and this, I realised later, was probably close to the truth. Some wore tatty old jackets, others wore hats and flat caps. Their trousers were dirt-stained and held up around the waist by pieces of string and cloth. To these make-do belts were strapped knives of various lengths and descriptions, which didn't look as if they'd seen action anywhere outside the kitchen. The heaviest piece of artillery they had between them was a shotgun, and I counted two of these: one in the possession of the guy in the combat jacket, the other in the hands of the bloke I'd seen first.

It was this man, who seemed older, calmer and more experienced than the BIH soldier (if that was what he was), who was the first to shake my hand. As he did so, he made a gesture which seemed to say it's OK, you're safe now, but it was difficult to be sure. None of them spoke any English. This was frustrating, as all I wanted to do, now that I knew I wasn't going to be executed on the spot, was to talk. More than anything else, I wanted to know if they knew that there were at least two Serbian T-55s less than thirty seconds' flight time from here.

'Do you know there are Serbs on the other side of the hill?' I said earnestly to the man who had shaken me by the hand.

He screwed up his eyes in confusion.

'The Serbs,' I repeated, enunciating the words slowly and loudly, and pointing in the direction of the crump-whump of the shellfire I could hear in the distance. 'Do you know how close they are to you?'

This elicited more blank looks, followed by bursts of animated discussion among the older members of the group. I think they were too polite to laugh, but the looks I got suggested that they thought I must have been a little touched by my ordeal. I wince at the memory now, because these people had been living among the enemy for years. It was like asking a defender of Stalingrad three months into the siege if he was aware there were Germans down the road.

But then the guy with the combat jacket tapped my new-found friend on the shoulder and spoke to him in a low, spirited whisper that conveyed a new sense of urgency about our situation. The next thing I knew I was pulled to my feet and being motioned to walk as fast as I could away from the area I had occupied since the ejection. I looked for the sun again, spotted it momentarily, and realised we were heading westwards, away from the Serbs I had seen on the ridge, which was good, but towards the sound of shell-fire, which filled me with a renewed sense of dread.

We spread out and walked for twenty minutes through the woods. It was apparent that they knew exactly where they were going and I tried to relax, but the feeling that we could be ambushed at any moment would not go away.

My new-found friend escorted me into even denser woodland, the forest floor crunching with every step that I took. After ten minutes of this – and maybe thirty minutes after the ejection itself – one of the other members of the group, a youth of around eighteen, sidled up to me. I quickly established that he wanted a cigarette and I reached into my survival vest for the pack of Camels I'd stuffed in there for precisely this moment, the moment no pilot ever thinks will come to him. But the pack was gone. Now I remembered that I'd run out of fags late one evening the previous week. I'd robbed my survival vest of the Camels and then forgotten to replace the damned things.

After watching me patting my survival waistcoat to no avail, the youth offered me one of his. It turned out to be some truly disgusting Yugo brand, stuffed full of black, evil-smelling tobacco. But, nevertheless, as smokes went, no cigarette had ever tasted so good.

In this more relaxed atmosphere the trees started to thin again and I spotted a clearing ahead. Soon we were in a small, steep-sided valley with a little stream running through it. Just hearing the trickle of water suddenly filled me with a raging thirst and I gestured that I wanted to stop and drink.

Ten years beforehand, I had participated in an escape-and-evasion (E&E) course run by the Royal Navy in the New Forest. During our ten days of instruction, we learned many things, one of which jumped into my head now: be careful of contaminated water. I was already squatting by the stream under the close observation of my friends when this vision of common sense came to me. I reached into my survival vest and produced several packets of sterilised water. To wary glances, I then began to offer them round. I have no idea what the Muslims thought this stuff was, but a couple of them sniffed the packets suspiciously and then handed them back to me. I pointed to the water and signed vigorously with my hands, saying, 'Good, good,' a couple of times, but this only confused them more, understandably, in the circumstances. In the end, even I saw how bonkers this was and, stuffing the sachets back in my vest, cupped my hands in the stream and drank.

It was while I was gulping down the water that a terrible thought came to me. What if my aircraft had crashed on a Muslim village and killed a bunch of women and children, maybe the very families of the people I was with now, while they had been out in the woods? The more I thought about it, the more the idea took root.

To convince myself that I wasn't on my way to my own lynching party as soon as these people reached semi-civilisation, I went into another mime session: turning my hand into an aircraft, making a vroom-crash sound and then pointing to them and falling over, as if dead. A stunned silence, followed by a dubious exchange of glances ensued. Then they went into another huddle to discuss what this could mean. I think I was a hair's breadth from being trussed up like a lunatic when my friend, the older member of the group, went 'Ahh!' and proceeded to pat me on the shoulder vigorously and shake his head, adding, 'OK, OK' a lot. I knew he had got the message when he pointed towards a hill ahead of us, indicating that the aircraft had crashed up there. Considering that this was where we were heading I was not filled with tremendous hope, but as my friend was smiling broadly as he went through this charade, I had to trust that everything was going to be all right.

It was as I thought of my aircraft that I remembered Oz. We had been low on fuel when the missile hit me. I knew Oz would have stuck around for a while after I'd been hit to try to get a bead on where I'd come down. Doing this for even a couple of minutes would have put him in severe danger of running out of fuel before he reached the ship. Then another overwhelming thought hit me: Christ, maybe he'd been shot down as well.

As we started to move away from the stream, I made a gesture to my friend that I wanted to reach into my survival vest and he nodded that this was OK. The bonhomie notwithstanding, I remained to be convinced that these guys weren't as trigger-happy as they appeared and was anxious to do nothing that might appear in any way threatening. Ever so slowly, I pulled my PRC-112 radio out of its pocket and began to screw in the antenna that fixes to the top. I flicked the switch from 'off' to 'guard' – the international distress frequency of 243.0 megahertz – and held my breath. After what seemed an eternity, the lights lit up in the correct sequence, which told me that the system was working all right. I thought about getting a fix on the GPS and reading off my 'bullseye' position – the coded co-ordinates that would allow someone back at headquarters to calculate my exact location – but thought better of it. Going on to the international distress frequency meant that anyone could pick up the call, including the Serbs, and the shorter my transmission time, the better. In these hills, it would be difficult for the Serbs to pinpoint my position using direction-finding (DF) gear, but I didn't want to take any more chances than I had to. The priority was to find out if Oz was OK and to let someone know that I was safe.

'Any station, this is Vixen Two-Three,' I said, dipping the transmit button and keeping my voice low.

I had grave doubts for some reason that the technology would work, but to my pleasant surprise, I was met with a response almost immediately.

'Vixen Two-Three, this is Thunder Zero One.'

The voice, a deep Texan drawl, painted a clear picture of the guy I was dealing with. I imagined a tobacco-chewing Yank wearing a 7th Cavalry hat and cowboy boots as he rode his tank-busting A-10 Thunderbolt II in the uncertain skies over the Balkans, looking for 'trade'.

'Vixen Two-Three, safe on ground,' I said. 'Where's Vixen Two-Four?'

The American must have been au fait with my situation, because he replied immediately: 'He's recovering to the ship.' And that was it, exchange over.

I switched off the set. In the hilly terrain in which I found myself, I was confident that if the Serbs did have DF gear, they wouldn't have got a fix on me.

We pressed on.

After another half an hour's walk through fields and ditches, copses and clearings, we came to a house on the edge of a tiny village. It was built into the side of the hill, chalet-style, half of it propped up by stilts.

As I was ushered up the front steps, I looked up and saw a man wearing a full-blown army uniform standing in the frame of the main door. I could see no insignia on him and the fear flashed through my head that he was a Serb; that the last hour had been nothing more than a sham and I'd been taken in by it. But the soldier, who must have seen some of this pass across my eyes, raised his hand and smiled reassuringly.

'Hi,' he said in near-perfect English. 'My name is Oskar. It's quite OK. You are in safe hands now.'

The house looked cosy enough from the outside, but something about it made me wary. Before I disappeared inside, I gave the hills and the sky a last, lingering look. The next nearest building was more than 200 metres away and appeared derelict and abandoned. By comparison with my immediate surroundings, the forest had seemed almost welcoming.

I was shown into a room with a large table in the middle. As the rescue party joined us, the four walls echoed with the clatter of feet on the bare floor. There was nothing on the walls except for a single map, which appeared to mark the position of friendly and hostile forces in the area with different-coloured pins. There was a preponderance of red on the chart, which I took to signify the overwhelming presence of the Serbs.

Oskar offered me a chair and I sat down. Then he disappeared into the next-door room. Chairs scraped across the floor as the search party joined me at the table. We stared at each other blankly for long, uncomfortable seconds and then the door opened again and Oskar reappeared, clutching a bottle and a plate. He set these down on the table and I saw the eyes of the rescue party widen appreciatively.

I knew that the bottle would contain slivovitz, the legendary local liquor. It was the other stuff I wasn't so sure about. It looked like something that had been thrown up by a domestic animal, then simmered for a couple of minutes just prior to being served.

Oskar saw me looking at it and smiled. 'Goat's cheese,' he said reassuringly. 'A local delicacy.' He gave me a knife and indicated I should dig in.

I cut off a piece and popped it into my mouth, holding his gaze as he watched me bite into it. It tasted strongly of ammonia and had an unpleasant chewy consistency, but somehow I managed to keep it down, smile and tell him I thought it was delicious. This became the signal for everyone else to dig in.

Mercifully, a shot of slivovitz removed the taste of this abomination, along with several layers of skin from my tongue.

I was just beginning to savour the ambience when the door flew open and another soldier walked in. He was dressed in combat fatigues, wore a cap emblazoned with a rank badge of sorts and had not one, but two gunbelts around his waist. His eyes, which were cold and very threatening, looked like they had seen a lot of close-quarter action; a lot of killing.

As he stepped into the room, a hush fell round the table. Oskar got to his feet and whispered something in the man's ear. The new guy grunted something back and glanced at me, then sat down in the chair at the head of the table. One of the farmers filled a glass with slivovitz and passed it to him. The bloke downed it in one, never taking his eyes off mine.

'This is Komandant Imamovic,' Oskar said, assuming a deferential tone. 'In conjunction with God's will, he has delivered us from the Serbs and with God's continued blessings he will expel them from Gorazde and from our country. He is not just our leader, but a great man. He wants you to know that you are welcome here.'

Though I doubted if Imamovic understood precisely what was being said, he certainly got the gist of it. As I watched him, he sat back and studied me, like a collector examining some rare artefact that has just come into his possession. I nodded my appreciation and he smiled back.

'Komandant Imamovic would like to know your name,' Oskar said.

'It's Richardson,' I replied. 'Lieutenant Nick Richardson, Royal Navy.'

There was another rapid-fire exchange between Oskar and Imamovic, then Oskar said: 'What was the purpose of your mission over Gorazde, Lieutenant?'

I was about to rattle off a reply when I remembered the last piece of advice I had received prior to taking off. In our outbrief, we'd been advised to stick to the Big Four if captured: name, rank, serial number and date of birth. It struck me then that this could be some incredibly elaborate ploy. The Serbs were meant to be good at deception and disinformation, weren't they? What if these guys were Serbs masquerading as Muslims? Maybe I was being tricked into providing information they'd otherwise only have to torture me for.

'Reconnaissance,' I replied, knowing I had to say something. If this kept up, I told myself, I'd need to modify my answers. I did not want to give Imamovic anything of military or intelligence significance.

The questions kept coming. How long had my ship been in the Adriatic? What was the name of my ship? How many people were on board? When was it due to sail back to England? I answered as simply as I could, taking care to provide Imamovic with nothing of any real tactical or strategic value. On the other hand, I didn't want to piss him off – whoever these people were, they seemed friendly enough for the time being.

As I indulged in this finely balanced game of Twenty Questions, my gaze kept returning to the map over Imamovic left shoulder. Surrounded as I was by Serbs, and held by a force whose intentions towards me I couldn't quite make out, I wondered how on earth the game progressed from here. Was I guest of these people, or their captive?

The next development served only to heighten my anxiety. After a further round of slivovitz, Imamovic got to his feet and made an impassioned speech, which Oskar proceeded to translate. As unbelievable as this sounded, the gist of it was the need to find my ejection seat so that it could be turned into a permanent memorial in the centre of Gorazde to the bravery of British fliers everywhere. Imamovic then came round the table, clapped me on the shoulder and urged me to follow him outside on to the balcony for a smoke.

A group of children were playing in the back yard just beneath the house. There were two who were so small they could barely walk and a handful of older ones, aged between four and eight. They were gathered around something they clearly did not want us to see, for they looked up guiltily and huddled tighter when Imamovic and Oskar tried to take a closer look.

While Oskar and I looked on, Imamovic descended the wooden steps, cigarette in mouth, and walked over to the tiny scrummage. He shooed at them like a butcher fanning flies off meat, but they would not move. He swiped again, this time with a little more success. But as one child was bowled away, another came and took its place.

Perhaps they persisted in this charade because they knew what Imamovic was capable of. I, on the other hand, was caught completely by surprise by the sudden appearance of an automatic in his hand. Imamovic pointed the weapon at the middle of the gathering. When the children saw it, a gap opened up to reveal what it was they had been shielding: a puppy, a tiny runt of a thing, probably no more than two weeks old. It was desperately thin and obviously very sick, because it was lying on its side, panting for breath. Now that I could see it, I could hear it yelping. It looked as if it was minutes away from death.

Imamovic cocked his weapon and pointed it at the dog's head. This elicited a collective wail from the children, who surged forward as one and regrouped in their protective circle around the puppy. A boy with a dirty face, no more than four years old, took a step forward, placing himself between the muzzle of the gun and the dog. The kid was snivelling, white tracks on his cheeks where the tears had spilled. He was begging Imamovic not to kill the dog. The komandant tapped him aside with the barrel and took another bead on the creature.

Another child stepped forward, a little girl, and placed herself in front of the weapon. She stood there staring at Imamovic with big, sad eyes. He thrust the gun forward. For a horrifying moment I thought he was going to do it. The children must have thought so, too, because the wailing grew to a crescendo.

I looked at Oskar, wondering if this was some sort of sick pantomime being put on for my benefit, but the interpreter merely carried on smoking his cigarette, leaning against the balcony, watching the whole thing with studied disinterest.

And then, as quickly as it had started, it was all over. Imamovic holstered the gun and turned back to the house. The children gathered up the puppy and ran off. As the komandant marched back up the steps, there was a jut to his jaw and a smirk on his lips, as if he felt he had just proved himself in some way.

We went back into the house. The country types who'd plucked me from the forest were slouching against the wall on the far side of the room. I thought that the interrogation was about to begin all over again, but instead another bottle was produced, the glasses passed around and the drinking began all over again.

One of the boys said something to Oskar and the rest of them burst out laughing. It must have been a pretty good joke, because it took a good long while for them to settle down. When the guffaws eventually subsided, I asked Oskar what was so funny.

'This man,' he said, gesturing with his glass to the swarthy type who'd made the remark, 'just now he reminded me what I told them when they set out to try to find you in the forest.'

'What was that?' I asked.

Oskar took a pull of slivovitz and stared into his glass for a moment. 'I said that if they found you before the Serbs, I'd let you sleep with my wife.' He added hastily: 'She is very beautiful, you understand.'

I gave him a lukewarm, neutral smile while I wrestled with the disturbing image of a well-built Slav, the kind of masculine interrogator-type of whom James Bond so frequently fell foul, bearing down on me, so to speak. It was difficult to know what else to do. If I didn't show some sort of approval, I'd probably cause him offence. If, on the other hand, I laughed heartily with the others, I figured there was a very real chance he might shoot me.

The drinking continued. The more boisterous it became, the more I was allowed to slide into the background. This was a relief, as I wanted to be alone with my thoughts. I had been on the ground barely four hours, but already it felt like a lifetime. I wondered what was happening on the ship and whether someone had told Yvonne. I consoled myself with the hope that the A-10 pilot had passed my message on to the relevant authorities and that, even now, the Yeovilton support network was doing its bit to ensure that the family was all right.

The frightening thing was this. Even if the Navy did know I was safely on the ground, I couldn't begin to see what they or anyone else could do about it. I was 125km inland and holed up within a tiny pocket of Muslim resistance fighters who could give in to the advancing Serbs at any moment. There was little chance of a helicopter rescue package – the threat density was too great. That left these people – Imamovic, Oskar and their buddies. But the longer I spent with them, the stronger the whiff of insanity that surrounded me became.

The drinking session had stopped just short of a riot. It looked as if they were anaesthetising themselves for the fight to come. When that showdown would be I didn't know, but I was along for the ride whether I liked it or not. I had no choice. Where these people went, I would have to go. It was an uncomfortable thought.

As the sun slipped behind the mountains and darkness fell, one final irony gave me cause to reach for the slivovitz bottle and drink a sorry toast to my rollercoaster of a day. I had trained for a contest with the Serbs' MiG-29s. But after some soul-searching, I knew that it could only have been a hand-held SAM – a MANPADS weapon – that had exploded beneath my aircraft.

I had the honour of becoming the first Navy pilot, possibly the first British pilot, ever to have been shot down by one.

This was the second of the rare and unusual events in the squadron's distinguished history to have occurred that month.

As I knocked back another shot of firewater, I noted the date. It was 16 April 1994.

# CHAPTER 7

Two hours after darkness fell, Oskar informed me it was time to move. I was to stay at his house, he said, until more permanent accommodation could be found for me. Minutes later, I was bundled down the steps and into a vehicle that resembled a milk float, with an armour-plated cabin and a throaty diesel for an engine. By the time I left, a sombre mood had befallen the drinking party. I got the impression that military action for Imamovic and his cronies was very close at hand; that what I had just witnessed was a farewell party, or even a wake.

I sat up in the cabin beside Oskar and his driver and we set off. The ride to the centre of Beric, one of the last hamlets outside Gorazde to resist the Serb onslaught, took just ten minutes. In the distance, the horizon flickered with the intermittent flashes of Serb artillery fire.

As the milk float rounded a bend, the dark shapes of once-trim houses loomed either side of us. In the muzzle flashes of the big guns, I could see roofs with holes in them, chimneys blown off and shell holes in walls. Then I became aware of a more solid source of light up ahead.

There was a large fire in the middle of the street. Forty or fifty people were standing around it, holding out their hands to the heat. They were bundled up against the cold, so many layers on them that it was impossible to tell the men from the women. No one looked up as we drove past and neither Oskar nor his driver said a word. Questions felt inappropriate, so I said nothing. But inside the questions tumbled. What were these people doing here? Why weren't they in hiding? Who was protecting them? I had never seen such total, uniform despair.

We drove on into the darkness again, pulling up a few minutes later outside a white-walled house. Oskar jumped from his seat and ushered me into an alley beside it. A door opened and a shaft of light spilled on to the ground by my feet. I looked up and saw a silhouette – a woman holding a child.

And then I remembered what Oskar had said at the HQ about his wife.

Before I was bundled into the house, I saw her in a moment of freeze-frame: 5ft 6, raven hair, dark eyes and olive skin. Her clothes were chic and fitted her well. She couldn't have been more different from the people I had just glimpsed around the bonfire. She was quite beautiful.

I stepped inside and she shook me by the hand. Her name was Admira. And this was Makhmud, she said, pride in her eyes as she looked at her infant son. The child stared at me, but his face registered no emotion at all. I found it unsettling and turned away.

The interior of the house was much like anything you'd find on the edges of Birmingham or Guildford or Leeds. It was carpeted and well-furnished, though oppressively dark. What light there was came from a single bulb in the middle of the sitting room. I could hear the fizz of the current as it fought the resistance in the wiring.

Oskar caught me staring at it and clapped me on the shoulder. Then he marched me through the kitchen and out to the back of the house. I lost sight of him in the darkness, but as my eyes acclimatised to the poor light, I found him squatting a short distance away. I could hear the ripple of fast-flowing water. As another flash of shellfire lit the horizon, I saw the glint of a stream by his feet.

'Look,' he said, gesturing with pride to something spanning the water. 'I make this myself, Nick.'

In front of him was a rudimentary turbine. Thanks to the spring run-off, it provided just enough electricity for a solitary bulb inside the house. This was an infinite improvement, he added, on candle-power and firelight.

We moved inside and he spoke quickly to his wife. Every now and again, their eyes would dart towards me. When the conversation was over, he scooped up the boy in his arms and gave him a kiss. Then he told me that he was going out and without further ado, he picked up his shotgun and stepped into the night.

Admira and I were left staring at each other. I tried to say something and so did she. I tried again, just as she did. We both laughed.

'My English . . . not so good,' she said.

I told her it was better than my Serbo-Croat. Then I asked where Oskar had gone. She pointed towards the hills behind the house, in the direction of the artillery fire. 'He must go into the forest. There are other men there.' She smiled self-consciously. 'They do what men do here. Maybe there will be some fighting. Maybe tonight they will just sit and talk and play cards.' She shrugged. 'I do not know. But he will be back. Inshallah. Oskar is clever. If it is God's will, he will return to protect us.'

I thought about the men I had left in the HQ and wondered if these were the people with whom Oskar was rendezvousing. If there was to be any kind of action, I reckoned they were just about drunk enough to kill each other, but not the enemy.

Admira pointed to a chair in the corner of the room. In the darkness, I hadn't noticed, but now I was aware that it was occupied.

'My mother,' she said, gesturing to a bundle in the chair. As I drew closer, the shape magically took the form of an old woman.

I shook her hand, feeling the rasp of her skin on mine. She said nothing and nor did I. Admira then led me back to a chair by the table in the middle of the room.

The child was sitting on the floor close by. He was dressed in shorts and a V-necked pullover. I guessed he was about five years old. His feet were bare, but otherwise he was like any kid his age: clean, tidy, healthy enough. Except for his eyes. In the gloom, they appeared quite black. I tried a smile and a wave, but got nothing in return. Not a flicker of a response. I thought of my own children, laughing and squealing as they tore round the house at 100mph as they did most of the time. And then I wondered at the horrors this boy must have seen to become like this.

Admira returned from the kitchen with a bowl of water and began to clean my chin. Only when she handed me a mirror did I see why I had so much blood on my flight suit. I had an inch-wide cut from the ejection, a wound that gave me a macabre version of Kirk Douglas's dimple. She bathed it with a wet cloth, then prepared the wound for dressing.

'Aren't you frightened?' I asked.

She glanced at me while she applied some gauze. 'Yes, sure.' She paused. 'We are all afraid. This is only natural.'

'Then why don't you and the boy move somewhere safer?'

'Because this is our home. We'd rather die here than leave it.'

The sting of something – it smelled like pure alcohol – made me want to flinch, but I didn't. 'What would the Serbs do if they came to this village, Admira?'

She held my gaze for a moment. 'If they do what they have done in other villages, then they would kill the men, rape the women and burn our houses down – with our children inside.' She gave a final press on the masking tape she'd used to secure the gauze to my chin. 'And they would kill you.'

She moved back into the kitchen.

I was left wondering how I would react if I were Oskar – or if, in some parallel universe, this were England, my village, the aggressor on my doorstep. Would I be flying and fighting in my Sea Harrier? Or would I be here, shotgun in hand, protecting my family from the enemy?

I distilled the choices this family faced. At some stage, escape must have been an option. But if they'd moved, they'd have traded everything they had for the misery of life on the run as refugees. Staying meant there was every chance they'd be massacred by the Serbs. Leaving meant life. But where was the pride in that? This place had probably been their home for generations.

How did this devil's alternative square with the picture of suburban normality I could still glimpse through half-closed eyes? I tried again to overlay an image of home on what I could see here, but the picture was too disturbing, so I let it go.

When I looked up, the boy was staring at the knee pad on the right leg of my flight suit. I plucked it from its pocket and held it out to him, together with my Chinagraph pencil. At first, he was reluctant to take it. But when I showed him how to doodle on the pad, wipe off the results and do it all over again, his eyes shone.

He approached me slowly, like a timid animal eager for some morsel of food in my hand yet hesitant to take it. When he did take the pad and pencil, he looked at me, smiled fleetingly, and withdrew to the corner of the room again. In the dim light, I watched as he made his first stabs with the crayon. Then he got the hang of it: drawing something, rubbing it off, starting again.

Admira brought me a cup of sweet tea and joined me at the table. We sat there, watching her son, with only the crump-whump of artillery fire outside to fill the vacuum of silence between us.

After some minutes, she asked me why the UN was doing so little to help them.

For a moment, I thought I had misheard her, but I saw the anger in her eyes.

'NATO is acting, Admira. But it's not easy. There are many voices to be heard before permission can be given to attack the Serbs.'

'You call a few bombs action? The town of Gorazde is dying. My people are dying. The Serbs are killing us while the world just sits on its hands. We need hope, Nick. If NATO does not give us hope, it could be bad for you.'

I turned to her. 'What do you mean?'

She did not flinch from my gaze. 'Maybe you see these people in the street when you come to the house. The people warming themselves by the fire? These people do not care any more if they live or die. How do you think they react if they know you are NATO pilot? Do you think they greet you as hero or try to kill you?'

'I'm not sure I understand. I was attacking a Serb tank when I got shot down. Six days ago, American jets blew up several Serb armoured vehicles outside Gorazde. That must count for something.'

Admira smiled and shook her head. 'Let me tell you why NATO attacked. Muslims have been dying for years and NATO planes do nothing. Six days ago, a UN soldier is wounded by Serbs in Gorazde. Only then does NATO attack. Yesterday, two UN soldiers were wounded in the town – British soldiers, Oskar told me. And today you come back with your planes and your bombs. Not for us. For revenge.'

It was only then that I remembered the FAC. God knows why I hadn't thought of him before. I can only attribute this lapse of memory to the rapid-fire succession of events that had befallen me since the missile hit the plane. Fortune Zero-Five, the forward air controller with whom I'd been liaising in my bid to bomb the two T-55s, had been British, a Cockney. FACs in this theatre of opera-tions came in only two forms: SBS and SAS. I was filled for a second with new hope. If there were SAS or SBS in the hills above Gorazde, then maybe I could make contact with them. Perhaps through this British UN contingent in Gorazde. I knew that to rush things, though, could be dangerous. My knowledge of the FAC was highly privileged. Maybe Oskar and his crew knew nothing of the presence of British special forces in the area. It was important for the moment I kept it that way. I managed to mask my excitement.

'Is that what you think?' I asked her. 'That the UN was only motivated by revenge for the death of one of its soldiers?'

'It does not matter what I think.' She nodded in the direction of the crowd outside. 'Perhaps, though, you are more valuable to them dead than you are alive.'

There was a cold blast as the front door flew open and Oskar tumbled into the room. He looked terrible. He was fighting for breath when he spoke to me.

'Nick, my friend,' he managed, 'it is time for us to go. I have got some men together, and a car. They are outside. We must get you to Gorazde.'

Gorazde? I tried to hide my feelings, but a wave of fear washed over me. Gorazde was supposed to be surrounded.

Oscar wiped a thin sheen of sweat from his brow. He glanced between me, his son and Admira. 'We must move through the Serb lines to get you there. When we make it to the town, there are friends there who will take care of you. Come. There is no time to lose. We must leave now.'

I followed him outside. I felt numb. Who were these friends? After what Admira had told me, I no longer knew who to trust. Maybe I was already being held as a hostage – as some bargaining chip for future NATO assistance – but I just didn't know it yet. There were other grimmer possibilities still – the mere thought of a trip into the woods conjured up a succession of stark images that did not bear thinking about.

As I stepped outside, I could hear the distant crack of small-arms fire echoing off the hillside. Oskar led me back down the alleyway to a dark, four-door saloon. Behind the windows, I could make out three faces: a driver and two men in the back. I got in beside them. Before I shut the door I looked up and saw Admira and the boy standing beside the car. Makhmud was perched on her hip, as he had been when I first laid eyes on them. He was holding something out to me. I peered through the darkness and recognised the pad and pencil.

I looked at her and I looked at him. 'Keep it,' I said, gesturing with my hands.

I shut the door and the engine purred into life. Then, ever so slowly, revs low, we eased into the darkness, lights doused.

Moving in the pitch black with no headlights along a road is one thing, but the driver soon climbed into the hills and turned off into a forest. I was scared shitless. We maintained a speed of around 30mph, ploughing down slopes and up sharp inclines, the engine screaming and whining under the strain.

It reminded me of ghost-train rides I'd taken as a kid. Shapes loomed out of nowhere and just when it seemed we would hit them, they veered away again. We always seemed to miss them by a hair's breadth. I wondered how much longer this could last.

The driver was either highly skilled or a complete lunatic. My only consolation was that he seemed to have done this before. Oskar said it was essential we move 'off-piste' because the Serbs had set up roadblocks on all the tracks. This fell into a category of knowledge that had 'need to know' stamped all over it. And I really didn't want to know.

What also worried me was the fact that none of these guys were what you'd call 'military'. Oskar, with his khaki-coloured shirt, was the closest to being a soldier; the others were dressed in civvies and looked as if they'd just got off a shift down on the farm. What the hell would happen if we ran into a Serb patrol? Could these guys begin to defend themselves with a shotgun and a couple of pistols against AK-47s and rocket-launchers?

As we bounced over the rocks and roots that made up the forest floor, my head hit the roof again. In hindsight, it would have been a blessing if I'd been knocked out. I found myself wondering about the consequences of a Serb attack on the car. Would the first thing I knew about it be the bullet that hit me in the face or chest?

A succession of morbid thoughts marched through my mind. When a bullet strikes, what does it feel like? If it hits you in the shoulder, does it remove the entire arm? Does it feel hot as it rips through skin and muscle? Or does it feel cold, like steel? If it strikes a limb, or shatters its way through bone, is that the only part of you that hurts, or does your whole body burn with the pain? These were questions I had never really had to face in a Sea Harrier.

I felt the panic mount. It twisted my guts and beat around inside my head until I thought I'd go crazy. I wanted to do what I had done in the forest: curl into a ball, lie back against a tree and pray for the nightmare to end.

My senses were overloaded. If I'd let them, they might have seized up altogether, leaving me mentally paralysed. I did not know from one moment to the next what was around the corner. It was a sensation from which there was no escape.

I did not understand why I was going to Gorazde. I did not really know why I had had to leave Oskar's. Inside his house, I could half forget where I was. Now I was heading through the Serb lines for a town that was the focal point of their offensive. But then I thought back to some of the intel briefings I'd had on board ship. The Serbian MO was to take the town first, then come back to tidy up the outlying hamlets. So maybe Oskar was right. In a country where nowhere was truly safe, maybe I was better off in a town that was having the shit shelled out of it.

In a Sea Harrier I'd felt several steps removed from death. If it came, the chances were I wouldn't know a thing about it. A missile in the fuel tanks and, boom, out go the lights. Here, I felt death of the most terrifying kind stalking me: a guy with his face in mine, twisting his bayonet in my guts, his hand clamped over my mouth.

Training, I realised, was a wonderful thing. It had taught me to cope; to manage my fear. But all the dangers I had ever experienced in the cockpit seemed trivial compared with what I faced here. It was as if all along I'd been engaged in something that had been no more hazardous than a super-realistic Nintendo game.

There was a grinding of the gears as we bumped our way down another steep incline and came to rest in a clearing. The driver switched off the engine and opened his door. Oskar clambered out of the passenger seat. The others followed suit, leaving me alone in the car. I held my breath and waited. Was this where it all ended?

The passenger door opened and one of my escorts stuck his head back into the car, leaned forward and pushed in the cigarette lighter. Seconds later, I saw his face in the glow of the tip of his cigarette. He looked at me and gestured for me to go outside with him. I found Oskar squatting down on the ground. My escort passed some cigarettes around and we sat there, the five of us, just smoking and listening.

The sensations in that place were so vivid that for a moment they conspired to choke me. The pungency of the tobacco, the smell of rotting vegetation, the stillness of the air, the stars through the branches. The cold and the silence. Every now and again, Oskar and his friends compared notes in low, hurried whispers. Judging by the tone of the conversation, they weren't all in agreement about what they were doing.

'The shelling has stopped, so we must stop,' Oskar explained to me. 'The Serbs are very close now. We must listen for them. And wait.'

I saw the problem. It was the first time I could remember that the guns had fallen silent. It was dinner time, Oskar told me. Nothing, it seemed, got between Johnny Serb and his food.

'Where are you taking me?' I asked him.

Oskar stubbed out his cigarette. 'There is a UN observation post in Gorazde. Already I have been on the telephone to them. They want you there, with them. Perhaps they will try to get you out by helicopter.'

I shook my head. 'I used to be a helicopter pilot. No way you'd want to risk a mission into Gorazde with so much anti-aircraft weaponry around.'

'That is where you are wrong, my friend,' Oskar said. 'The UN observers in Gorazde are British troops. Yesterday, two of them were badly injured in a Serb ambush. The UN organised a ceasefire to remove one of the injured men by helicopter. Maybe they can do the same for you.'

Before he had finished the sentence, there was a flash through the trees, followed by a boom and a rumble. The Serbs had clearly finished their dinner.

It was time to make a move, using the noise of the barrage to mask our progress through the wood. Oskar told me that there was a Serb patrol at large in this sector: one of their own patrols had spotted it earlier in the day. The difficulty was, they didn't know where it was now. So we just had to be careful and hope for the best.

We set off again, sticking to the tried and tested format: lights off, revs low, weaving in and out of the trees in the near non-existent light. I estimated that around forty-five minutes had passed since we'd left Oskar's house. I wondered how much more of this torture I would have to endure.

We stopped again. Oskar indicated that we should go one way, the driver the other. An argument ensued; low-key at first, it soon flared into something more passionate. The driver appeared to win the day and we started moving again. Our speed began to pick up, and through the trees I could now see the intermittent light of fires somewhere in the distance. Gorazde. We were almost there.

The first I knew of the trouble we were in was when the driver swore, we went into a hard right-hand turn and my head was thrown against the window. I opened my eyes and saw multiple flashes through the trees to our left. Then the windscreen shattered.

Beside me, one of Oskar's mates was struggling with the window handle and screaming for the guy on my right to hand him the shotgun. In the passenger seat, Oskar was already aiming his weapon at something I couldn't see. I screwed my eyes shut, but the muzzle flash was so bright it bloomed through my eyelids. The blast was deafening. I opened my eyes to see the driver punching a hole with his fist through what remained of the windscreen.

On the freezing cold slipstream, I heard shouting, the guttural bark of orders and instructions, then more firing. The guy on my left managed to get his window open and there was another bang as he loosed off a shot.

Then low-lying branches scraped across the roof as we careered between some firs. The trunks of the trees appeared so close that I thought we were going to get wedged tight. But the driver judged it to a tee and we shot through, the only casualty my friend on the left, who sustained several bad scratches on the back of his head and neck as he tried to hit the receding Serbs.

We had only driven a little way further on when Oskar started to laugh. He was rapidly joined by the driver and then by the two heavies in the back. It was so catching, even I joined in. And that was how we emerged from the forest: laughing our socks off, with Gorazde opening up before us.

The town was situated in a bowl, surrounded by forest, a portion of which we had just negotiated. Before the car careened down the next slope, I caught a fleeting image of the devastation that awaited me. The only lights in the town were from the dotted fires of burning buildings and the intermittent flash-bangs of artillery strikes.

No sooner had we left the trees behind than the car swerved on to a road and we beat it, hell for leather, towards the outskirts. As we hurtled down the deserted road, it struck me that in our encounter with the Serbs, I hadn't had time to be afraid.

Buildings loomed out of the darkness. We headed for one that was larger than the others, a four-storey concrete affair by the side of the road with very few windows. The driver swung into an alleyway beside it and parked up.

As I got out of the car, I was welcomed to Gorazde by a salvo of heavy artillery shells. The explosions boomed dangerously close by, illuminating the rooftops and sending reverberations through the air, rattling the masonry on either side of us.

Oskar took me by the arm and led me towards a side entrance. Wooden scaffolding had been erected around it, with boards hammered on to the poles, giving it a shed-like appearance. We opened a battered door and found ourselves face to face with a guard brandishing his AK-47. In the dim light of an oil lamp, which managed to illuminate half of his face, he reminded me of Blakey, the officious inspector in *On the Buses*. When he saw Oskar, he relaxed.

We carried on through, Oskar in front, me in the middle and the two heavies bringing up the rear. An inner door opened on to a passageway, dark except for a dim pool of light at the end. As we worked our way towards it, I began to trip over what felt like books – hundreds of them. Only when I reached the light could I actually see what they were: ledgers, some laid open, with careful, handwritten entries in black and red ink; others with cheques pinned to their pages. In another time, this place had been a bank.

I rounded the corner and the passageway opened up into what must have once been a half-decent canteen. There were about a dozen people in the room, some of them wearing combat gear, others dressed in civvies. The place was dominated by a long table, around which much of the group was congregated. Along the left-hand wall was a shelf, about waist-height, heaving with military kit – guns, rucksacks and radio gear. Adjoining it at right angles was a breakfast bar. A soldier with a haggard face, thick stubble and a mop of mousey hair was standing behind it, fixing himself a cup of tea. Behind him was a cooking area with a gas hob and a sink. Shelves had been fixed to much of the available wall space and these were lined with cans of food and other provisions.

Tracking round the room, I was shocked to see a guy on a stretcher, his face contorted in pain. He was being tended by a woman, who turned round, gave me the briefest of smiles and then went back to her work.

One of the soldiers at the table got up and greeted Oskar. They shook hands as if they'd known each other for years. Oskar spoke in English, as did his pal.

I studied the other man. He sounded like he was used to giving orders, not taking them, and his accent was clearly public school. He had a look of the Lord of the Jungle about him, with a mane of thick, sand-coloured hair, longer than the British Army's regulation length. After a few moments chatting to Oskar, he turned to me and smiled.

'Adrian Lloyd Jones,' he said, affably, holding his hand out. 'I guess I'm in charge here.'

'Nick Richardson,' I replied, a trifle gobsmacked by the surreal nature of the encounter, with its heady overtones of Stanley and Livingstone.

Lloyd Jones jabbed a thumb in the direction of the guy behind him, the bloke at the breakfast bar. 'You'll probably want to spend some time speaking with that guilty bastard over there. His name's Simon, but his call sign is Fortune Zero-Five. Between the two of you, I reckon you've got a lot to talk about.'

The other soldier looked up, gave me a self-conscious wave, then went back to his tea-making.

It took me a few moments to absorb this piece of news. I'd imagined the FAC up in the woods, heavily camouflaged and dug in under a pile of earth. I'd thought of him living off the land, evading the Serbs, emerging from cover only when NATO's planes came over seeking his guidance. I never thought for a minute that I'd find him behind a breakfast bar in a bank in the suburbs of a town.

The realisation washed over me in a wave of relief. Oskar hadn't just delivered me to any old British unit: I had made contact with the SAS.

From somewhere, a slivovitz bottle appeared and the room was soon filled with the low hubbub of conversation and the chink of glass on glass as stiff measures of the local brew were poured out and handed round. Adrian and Oskar proposed toasts to each other and then raised their glasses to a swift and happy conclusion to the war. Before we could drink to this, the room shook from the blast of a huge explosion, so close I thought the shell had struck the building itself. I swore, ducked and my drink went flying into my lap.

When I looked up again, I saw that no one else had reacted at all. I mopped at the spilled liquid, feeling pretty stupid. Fortunately, the slivovitz was so high-octane that within a few seconds it had evaporated anyway.

Simon, the FAC, who was sitting next to me, took a pull on his tea and eyed me sceptically.

'So, you were Fortune Zero-Five,' I said. I hadn't meant it to, but it came out a bit like an accusation.

'Look, mate, we had no idea there were any SAMs up there. If we had, I'd never have called the attack. Honest.'

'Hey,' I said. 'No offence meant. I should never have made that third pass.'

He took my hand and shook it. The relief on his face was evident.

A second blast shook the room. This time the only reaction was a flurry of hands coming up to cover the tops of glasses as plaster rained down from the ceiling.

I poured myself another drink and said nothing. If this was the way things were played around here, then I certainly didn't want to be any different.

Simon and I went on to talk about the attack, the shootdown and my escape. The T-55s, it turned out, had been part of a Serb push that had commenced the day before. It was in the initial hours of this assault that one of his colleagues, a guy called Fergie, had been severely injured. This was confirmation of what Admira had told me. Fergie had been shot in the head in a Serb ambush on his Land Rover. The vehicle bore the white markings and clear black lettering of the UN, but that hadn't stopped the Serbs.

Fergie had died on an operating table in Sarajevo. His mate, a lieutenant called Craig Keegan, who had also been injured in the attack, was the bloke here on the stretcher. His arm had been shattered by a bullet and he had lost a lot of blood, Simon told me, lowering his voice so that Keegan couldn't hear him. The guy, he added, was in a lot of trouble.

Looking at Keegan out of the corner of my eye, I wondered if he'd make it through the night. I watched as the woman who was tending him tapped the air bubbles out of a syringe and jabbed it into his good arm.

Another explosion rocked the building. When I opened my eyes, I saw Adrian making his way round the table, a sheet of paper in his hand.

'Here,' he said, handing it to me. 'This just came over the teleprinter. It's for you. It appears to be in some kind of code. Can't make it out. Maybe you can.'

I looked at him incredulously. A message for me? Who the hell knew I was here? I checked the piece of paper. In the header, I saw only two words that made any sense: *Ark Royal* The rest was gibberish. I peered a little closer and picked out the numbers 801 from a long string of numerics.

It was from the squadron.

Simon tried to read it over my shoulder. 'What does it say?'

'It's kind of hard to explain,' I mumbled after a first read-through. Following a day in which I'd banged out of an aircraft, struggled to avoid capture by the Serbs, enjoyed the hospitality of the Muslims and the SAS and had been shot at, I didn't quite have the wherewithal to run over all the nuances of squadron humour, in particular, its passion for *Blackadder*. The message, in bold type, read: 'FLASH IS NOT DEAD!'

A few pulls on my drink and I started to relax. After a couple more, I didn't even notice the artillery shells. I studied the assembled group more closely.

Apart from Adrian and Simon, there was one other guy who was clearly British and a soldier. It was hard to work out who was whom or did what, since no one was introduced to me and it seemed bad form to ask. Oskar and his mates were still at the end of the table, chatting away and drinking. Their presence prevented me from asking any questions. I figured that would have to wait until after they had left.

The third soldier was a thin-faced, fair-haired guy with an impish grin. He looked as if he'd barely left school. Simon and Adrian were clearly SAS: they couldn't have been anything else. But this other guy I couldn't be sure about. His name was Phil, and he was a Scot.

Next to Phil was a civvy in his early fifties. He had thinning hair on top, a bushy beard and a barrel chest, lending him a theatrical, Falstaffian appearance. He turned out to be Welsh and the philosopher type. On more than one occasion he expressed the view that he shouldn't have been in the town, and that this wasn't the UN's war any more. I tagged him as an UNMO, a UN military observer.

I would have had trouble placing the second UNMO if he hadn't come over and introduced himself. Robert Cronin was an ex-Royal Canadian Air Force pilot now in the service of the UN. He was wearing military fatigues, was about my age and build and had a lively sense of humour. In this unfamiliar environment I warmed to him instantly. Being aircrew, Bob had loads of questions, a lot of them about the missile strike on my plane. What was it like to be shot down? How was the ejection? We talked at length about it and it was good for me to get it out; a welcome release.

His words masked by the buzz of discussion in the room, Bob was able to fill in some of other gaps. He and Gareth, the Welsh UNMO, had been in Gorazde just prior to the launch of the Serb offensive on the town at the beginning of April. About a week after the attack began, they had been joined by Adrian Lloyd Jones' unit. This SAS team had been spirited into Gorazde on the orders of General Rose. It reported directly to him on the Serb advance and the Muslims' capacity to resist. They referred to themselves as UK liaison officers, or UKLO, Bob said. There were six of them, he said, including the injured Craig Keegan and Phil, the impish-looking Scotsman.

The situation was a mess, and no fucking mistake, Bob told me. I thought he was going to tell me why, but instead he just stared into his glass, studied the bottom for a good long beat, then raised it to mine. I'd chosen a hell of a bloody time to breeze in, he told me with a weary smile.

A blast of icy wind presaged the arrival of two more soldiers – the last two members of the UKLO team. These guys had SAS stamped on their foreheads. They were dirty and unshaven and looked as if they'd been fighting the Bosnian war singlehandedly against not only the Serbs, but the Muslims and the Croats as well. Then again, maybe they had. Each was carrying an SA-80 assault rifle fitted with a huge nightsight. Their fatigues bore no rank or insignia.

Lloyd Jones got up to greet them. It was then that I heard the lead guy of the pair say in a marked Liverpudlian accent: 'The fuckers are within a k of the town.'

The Muslims got the gist of this without any help from the trans-lators, because they rose from the end of the table as one and started for the door. Adrian clapped his hands and ordered 'you lot' – anyone who wasn't a part of his team – into the sleeping area next door. The party was over.

Oskar waved his two buddies out of the building, then turned to me. 'Well, Nick,' he said, 'I think you are in good hands now. The best, maybe. Between these men and General Rose, and with God's blessing, I hope you will make it out of here.' He smiled. 'If you ever come back, you know you will always be welcome in my home, in Beric.'

I shook his hand and thanked him for everything he had done. 'Come to England when the war is over,' I urged him. 'I'd like to introduce you to my family.'

He smiled, then turned to catch up with his friends.

I followed Bob into the sleeping area next to the canteen. This was accessed via a hole in the wall covered by a tatty hessian cur-tain. I pulled it back to reveal more shelves lined with cans of food. Beneath them, on the floor, were eight dirt-stained mat-tresses.

'What's with the mass exodus?' I asked Bob, jabbing a thumb at the SAS contingent next door.

He pulled a face. 'Fucking cloak-and-dagger stuff. Usually, when they bundle us out of there in a hurry it means that they're on the sat-net to someone important. It pisses me off sometimes, the way they treat us like second-class citizens. I mean, we're all in the same boat, aren't we?'

'I doubt if the Serbs would see it that way.'

He shrugged and seemed to calm down. 'Yeah. I guess we've all got a job to do.' He pointed to the blue beret tucked into one of his epaulettes. 'At least this thing offers us some protection. But if they ever got to find out who those guys were, that'd be it. Game over, man.'

He pointed to a mattress in the corner. 'Grab that one,' he advised me, "cos that thing is gonna be your home for the next few months – or the next few hours. Which, I guess, is all gonna depend on the Serbs.'

I digested the words slowly. Months? I hadn't given much thought to the length of time I might be holed up here, but if the siege tightened and the Muslims held out, maybe Bob's assessment might not be all that wide of the mark. The alternative was worse: waiting for the Serbs as they drove through the town, gutting the place, street by street, house by house.

Only now did the truth start to dawn on me. I was no safer here than I had been when I had landed in the forest. None of us was safe. It didn't matter how proficient the SAS were. There were only six of them – one of them so badly wounded that he didn't seem to know where he was – and upwards of 20,000 Serbs in the surrounding hills. The odds were appalling. This wasn't Princes Gate or the Falklands. We were talking five fit men against an army.

I closed my eyes and tried to picture my family, hoping that would give me strength, but I could no longer see their faces. Yvonne's face had become Admira's, and the kids all looked like Makhmud. I wished now that I had a photograph of them, something to hold close when no one else was looking. But in my eagerness to conform to NATO rules, I'd stripped myself of anything that might identify me if I was captured. I wondered when I would ever see them again.

There were three other people in the room I'd seen earlier but hadn't met. The first of these was the senior interpreter, a tall, gaunt Muslim with a cigarette perpetually stuck to his bottom lip. His name was Misha and he was, I guessed, in his late forties, though, as with everyone else hereabouts, it was impossible to be precise.

There was something almost fatherly about Misha. When he introduced himself to me, he asked whether I'd like to roll myself a cigarette using some of his precious tobacco. They had run out of ready-made cigarettes weeks before, and were reduced to rolling their own using hard, shiny lavatory paper. When I told him I was hopeless at this art, he took great pride in teaching me. By the end, though, I was still useless, so we agreed, laughing together, that I should stick to the SAS's Benson & Hedges. He fished into his pocket and gave me a rather ornate-looking metal cigarette-holder.

'Sooner or later, the Benson and Hedges will run out,' he told

me. 'Then you may have need of this. It will keep your cigarettes
from falling apart.'

I looked down at the reed-thin, abortion of a thing I had tried to
roll, its wisps of tobacco falling out of the end of the rough, crackly
paper. I saw what he meant and thanked him.

Besides Misha there was another interpreter, a slip of a girl who
could have been his daughter. Her name was Anna, and the poor
thing was absolutely terrified. She stuck like glue to Mary, the Irish
medic, whose calm and capable profiency in tending to Craig, the
injured SAS officer, drew the younger girl like a magnet.

Mary caught my eye and, remarking upon the cut on my chin,
was soon expertly cleaning up the wound, taking over from where
Admira had left off, and stitching it up. It hurt, but compared to
the injured soldier next door, I knew I had it easy, so I kept my
mouth shut.

Anna watched throughout. I warmed to her immediately, as
she had been the only other person in the canteen who had
flinched whenever a shell had exploded nearby. It turned out she
was Croatian, not Muslim, and this, I felt, gave us a lot more in
common than she'd probably ever have guessed. We were both
outsiders and, for different reasons, reviled as enemies by the
Serbs.

In the Muslims' eyes, we also shared a common bond. The
Croats and the Muslims had agreed to stop fighting and unite
under the Muslim-Croat Federation. But everyone knew the peace
deal was poised on a knife edge. If it broke down and reverted to
war, as is often the way with friendships that turn sour, the fighting
next time would most likely be even more vicious, if such a thing
were possible. I had no doubt that the Muslim community that had
worked with Anna in her guise as an interpreter for the SAS would
round on her at the slightest provocation. The outcome didn't
bear thinking about.

As for how I was perceived, Admira had spelled it out while I
had been in her house. For the moment, the Muslims were grateful
for what I had tried to do. I guess I was a symbol of hope. But
unless the UN acted again soon, unless NATO aircraft bombed a
few Serb tanks for real, I knew I would rapidly come to be seen as

the representative of a defunct, toothless organisation; one that had let them down from start to finish.

This realisation distilled my position. I was already on the Serbs' 'most wanted' list. But if the Muslims turned against me, then no matter which way I looked, I was as good as dead.

# CHAPTER 8

I pulled myself off the mattress at six, ran my fingers through my hair and stepped past the hessian curtain into the canteen. A train-load of thoughts had run through my head in the night, denying me sleep. My brain had passed the small hours crunching through the ins and outs of my situation. Never before had I been so utterly consigned to the hands of others, and it was an uncomfortable feeling. The only good thing about the previous few hours was that at some point the shelling had stopped and I hadn't even noticed it.

I rounded the corner and saw Adrian and the rest of the boys gathered around the sat-phone.

'Ah, Nick,' Adrian announced when he saw me, 'did you manage any shut-eye?'

I told him I hadn't; not a fucking wink.

He pointed to the breakfast bar. 'There's a brew on. Why don't you grab yourself a cup? Are you hungry?'

I hadn't had anything in the way of food since my plate of cheese at Imamovic's headquarters, but more than twelve hours on I wasn't in the mood for eating. The adrenalin had destroyed my appetite. My blood was coursing with so much of the stuff my hands and legs were shaking like a junkie's. If I'd tried to eat, I would have been sick. I told Adrian I'd settle for a cup of tea.

'When you're done over there, why don't you join us?' he said. 'I might have a job for you. Something to get you out and about.'

I smiled noncommittally and did as he suggested.

As I wandered back with my brew, I felt a familiar vibration shake the walls and the floor. Our respite from the Serbs' artillery could only have lasted a couple of hours.

'Ant and Simon are heading out to do a little reconnaissance,' Adrian said, pointing to a map of Gorazde on the table in front of him. 'There's an hotel a couple of hundred metres from here called the Gradina. It's about twelve storeys high and gives us a commanding view of the town and the surrounding hills. Be careful, though. The Serbs have snipers who know we've got an OP on the roof. Take your cue from Ant and Simon and you'll be OK.'

I had this feeling Lloyd Jones wasn't giving me the whole story. I remembered what Bob had said the night before about feeling excluded. I was grateful for the offer, but if I was to be a part of his planning, I needed a fuller picture.

'What's the position?' I asked him. 'About the Serb advance? Presumably, you must have got some guidance from Sarajevo.'

He looked at Ant, one of the blokes who'd breezed in during the booze-up the night before, and Simon and then at me. 'Intelligence is preparing itself for the big one,' he said, dropping his voice. 'The Serbs' final push. But we've heard this kind of talk before. That's why I need you on that roof. I want a first-hand report on the situation. Then we'll see how we're placed.'

Ten minutes later, Ant, Simon and I stepped past Blakey the guard and out into the street. I thought I had a pretty good idea of the lie of the land from the car journey, but I was wrong. The bank was in the middle of what appeared to be a huge building site. There was rubble everywhere, interspersed every so often with water-filled shell holes. At some point or other, the bank had fallen within range of the Serbs' guns. I wondered what it would take for it to be targeted again.

I stuck close to Ant, who led the way. In the pecking order of the SAS troop, I guessed that he probably ranked number three, after Adrian and Sean, the Scouse guy he'd been with the night before who had broken the news that the Serbs were within a kilometre of the town.

Anthony – Ant – was built like a brick khasi. He was also the silent, thoughtful type, the antithesis of the fast-talking Simon. Between them, I felt I was in good hands: Ant, the level-headed northerner, in front; Simon, the resourceful Cockney, bringing up the rear.

We reached the corner of a wreck that I could see had once been an attractive townhouse. The entire interior had been gutted by a direct hit from a shell. Ant pressed back against the wall and I followed his cue. Ducking low, we edged our way around it, finding some cover behind a chimney stack that had fallen on to the pavement.

Ahead of me, stretching left and right, was a long, wide boulevard littered with shell holes and chunks of masonry. While there were no cars around, not even wrecked ones, there were people, which surprised me.

From my vantage-point, I could see four civilians: a mother and a daughter cowering in an alleyway immediately across the street and two much older women, clad in traditional black Muslim garb, wandering along our side of the street towards us.

'If we stick to this side, we should be all right,' Ant told me. He turned to study the hills in the distance, double-checking, I knew, what the locals had already developed a sixth sense to detect: the depth of the sniper-free zone in the shadow of the buildings.

When the old women passed us, their eyes registered nothing. Gorazde had been under siege for months and I struggled to imagine what effect this must have had on the minds of its mainly female inhabitants, their menfolk either dead from the fighting or waiting to die in the front line above the town. And all that before the Serbs came to deliver the coup de grâce. As they shuffled by, Ant and Simon didn't give them a second look. They were 'friendlies', and in a tactical sense, I guess, this was all that mattered.

After another 100 metres, we rounded a corner and there was the Hotel Gradina, a big, ugly concrete and glass high-rise. We entered via the lobby and our feet crunched over glass, blast damage from a nearby shell-strike. The place was filled with the overpowering smell of human excrement.

Simon stood by the lift doors, his finger poised on the call button.

'Very funny,' muttered Ant as he made his way round the lift-shaft to the stairs. The place couldn't have had any electricity for months.

We started to climb the stairs. After three storeys, the diffuse light from the lobby gradually winked out and we were left to push on to the top in darkness. I could hear Ant somewhere in the stair-well above me and Simon a storey or two below, whistling lightly. Our progress was slow because the stairs were littered with rubbish, great big bags of the stuff.

When my foot brushed against one of these obstacles, I would gingerly feel my way forward, tracing its outline with my toe, and then step over it, hoping there was nothing on the other side that would make me trip and fall. It was only when one of the 'bags' moved that I realised they were people and that some of them – those who had not moved when I'd touched them – were very probably dead. There were no groups here, no families; just indi-viduals, people living and dying a storey apart from each other in the darkness.

It took us around fifteen minutes to reach the top. And in all that time, I never heard a sound from anyone other than Ant and Simon. When Ant opened the door to the roof and daylight washed into the stairwell again, I had never been quite so grateful to see it.

There was a 3ft wall around the edge of the roof and beyond this I caught a glimpse of rooftops and streets. Staying low, we made our way towards a pair of binoculars mounted on a tripod in the north-west corner. Simon and Ant started to point out the sights of the town. As for the people on the stairs, no mention was made of them. Like the women in the streets, it was as if they didn't exist. No threat; no tactical importance. The snipers, I was told, were 2km to the east, tucked into position somewhere on the lower slopes.

Snatching a glance at the houses below, I was reminded of my first glimpse of Sarajevo from the air. At least 30 per cent of the houses were burned out, their roofs missing. It was just like gazing down on to a partially constructed honeycomb. Every few seconds, I could hear the whump and whistle of shells being fired, then a bang and a low rumble as the rounds struck home. Columns of smoke hung in the air, their tops merging with the low clouds. Despite the official onset of spring, it felt cold enough for snow.

Shuffling round to the left, Ant and Simon indicated a mast high on a ridgeline to the north of the town. It was not far from there, they told me, that Fergie and Craig had been ambushed. Sean had actually been up on the tower, scouting with a pair of binos, and Ant in a Land Rover below when Craig came on the radio with the news that Fergie had been hit. In the chaos that surrounded the incident, word had it that the Serbs had broken through the Muslim lines and were heading hell for leather for the centre of the town, like the bloody barbarians at the gates of Rome.

Ant and Sean's first reaction had been to leg it, but after a quick regroup, and in the belief they could save Fergie, they turned back to look for him and Craig. Their journey into no-man's-land became a terrifying ordeal in itself.

After several hours' covert ingress, they were shown the place where the Land Rover had come off the road, but found no sign of their two colleagues. It turned out – though they did not find this out till later – that they had long been evacuated. Ant's radio had gone dead and so he and Sean had been unaware that Lloyd Jones had negotiated a ceasefire to allow the two injured men to be rescued from the front line.

Fergie had been airlifted to hospital in Sarajevo, but had died soon after he got there. Craig had refused to be flown out, electing to stay with Adrian and the rest of the boys in the town. Although Craig's decision had been made with the noblest of intentions, it was clear now that his condition was a lot more serious than anyone had first imagined. Everyone knew that he should have taken the helo ride with Fergie, though nothing was ever said about it. Adrian, who had used all of his powers of persuasion to negotiate the ceasefire for the helo evacuation, had exhausted his credit at the Serb headquarters in Pale. There would be no more casualty evacuation flights.

As we worked our way on round the rooftop, Ant pointed to the wreckage of a tank about 2km to the north-west. Through the binos, I could clearly see the scorchmarks up the hull. Simon, who had witnessed the vehicle's destruction, told me that it had been torched only after its crew had been overpowered by the locals. It turned out that the tank, a T-55 like the pair I'd tried to bomb on the ridgeline, had been jumped on by hundreds of civilians when it had made an attempt to break through the defences and carve a pathway into the town. After it had crushed a few townspeople under its tracks, the Muslims got their revenge. They dragged out the crew, chopped them into pieces, then threw the bits back into the tank and set fire to it. Most of the people who had taken part in this incident, Simon told me, had been women and children.

I asked him how this had made him feel.

'Can't say I fuckin' blame 'em really. If this were my neck of the woods, I'd be pretty pissed off, too. They're all right, the Muslims. A bit fuckin' whacko at times, but decent people, by and large. In my book, the Serbs had it coming to 'em.'

'I think you're wrong there, mate,' Ant said from behind the binos. 'I reckon they're all as bad as each other. I don't trust anyone here further than I can piss.' He took his eyes away from the binos and looked at us. 'When the shit really hits the fan, we'll end up just another set of targets to these bastards. You mark my words.'

He pointed towards a patch of waste ground a couple of hundred metres from the hotel. 'There's an anti-aircraft gun down there that the Muslims have been using against the Serbs' hillside positions. It's not as easy as it sounds using a triple-A cannon against ground targets, but this lot were so bloody useless, they couldn't have hit a battleship. So one day, I showed 'em how to use it in ground-to-ground mode. 'Course, they were grateful, especially when they started hammering the shit out of the Serbs. But I never showed 'em how to use it for what it were really meant for – shooting down bloody aircraft, 'cos pound to a foockin' penny, one of these days they'd have taken a pot at a NATO plane with it. That's how much I trust the bastards.'

He paused. 'Hang on a minute. What's all this?' He stuck his head above the parapet and pointed towards some high ground beyond the wreckage of the tank. 'There's some close-quarter fighting going on in those woods. Shit!'

'What's so special about that particular area?' I asked. Now Ant mentioned it, I could see some fires in the woods in the position he had indicated.

'That patch of ground is the only way in or out of here for the Muslims,' he replied. He made a sweeping gesture with his arms that took in most of the skyline. 'Basically, the Serbs are all around us, except for that little piece of land right there. And now there's a full-scale battle taking place on it. For once, I do believe Green Slime's got it right.'

'Green Slime?' I asked.

'Our name for the sleazos who provide us with intelligence,' Simon explained. 'Unreliable fuckin' breed.'

'Hold on,' I said. 'You mean to say there is a way out of here, after all.'

'More like *was* a way out of here,' Ant replied, peering through the binos again. 'Till now, the worst of the battle has been in the direction of the hospital over there.' He jabbed a thumb across the river behind us. 'But with this fresh round of fighting, I'd say the Serbs are poised to sew up the bloody—'

He never finished his sentence. A bullet thudded into the brick-work of the liftshaft, just above the door that led out on to the roof. The three of us ducked for cover as bits of concrete, masonry and plaster showered down around us. I had never been on the receiving end of a high-velocity round before, and it scared the living shit out of me. I heard the whistle and crack of the bullet only after it had exploded against the side of the building.

We were still lying prone when there was a crackle on Simon's radio. He rolled on to his back, fumbled inside his jacket pocket and produced the set.

It was Adrian. I could hear his voice over the shellfire.

'You'd better get back quick,' he told Simon. 'We've got a problem here.'

Simon signed off and Ant laughed and seethed at the same time.

'*You've* got a foockin' problem,' he said under his breath.

All I could think about was the fifteen minutes it would take us to renegotiate the stairwell and the bodies I would trip over before I reached the ground again.

It was Craig. When we got back to the bank, his condition had worsened appreciably and Mary the medic was calling the shots. He'd lost a lot of blood and nothing she could do would stem the flow. He needed urgent medical attention, she told Adrian, a whole lot more than she could do for him; and he needed it right away.

'That means a trip to the hospital,' Adrian told Ant. 'I need Simon to get back on to the roof of the Gradina. Take Misha as your translator and Phil and Nick as your two manhandlers.' He turned to me. 'That OK with you?'

'Fine,' I replied. 'I want to help in any way I can.'

'Good. As you probably know, the area where the hospital is in has seen some heavy shelling these past few days, but Craig's condition has pretty much forced my hand. It could get hairy down there. I need to warn you about that.'

'No problem,' I said, wondering who I was kidding. 'I want to go.'

Adrian took me by the arm and led me away from the group towards where Craig was stretched out on the floor. The injured officer had gone grey in the face. The only consolation was that he didn't seem to be in too much pain. His eyes were glazed, like a lizard's. They held me without seeming to register I was there.

'Listen, Nick, there's another reason I want you to get over to the hospital,' Adrian said, as soon as we were out of earshot of the others. 'You see that guy over there standing next to Misha?'

I turned and saw a young bloke in uniform with a mop of black curly hair. He was dressed in a combat jacket and clutching a Kalashnikov, but he looked as if he should have been at school.

'The kid? Who is he?'

'That's Ahmed,' Adrian explained. 'A local Bosnian lad. He spends quite a bit of time here, just hanging around, shooting the shit with the boys. I guess you could say he's become a bit of a groupie. But he's a decent enough kid and seems to know the area like the back of his hand. A right little Artful Dodger. Anything I need to know about the local situation, I ask Ahmed. And he's just indicated that there's a problem brewing.'

'What kind of a problem?'

'It seems as if the natives are getting a tad restless. They think that the UN and NATO have abandoned them. And who the fuck knows? Maybe they're right. But that's where I'm hoping you'll come in.'

I could see Lloyd Jones thinking on his feet. The bloke who had persuaded the Serbs to hold their fire while a UN helicopter had airlifted one of his injured men to Sarajevo had a diplomat's touch, and no mistake. I found myself warming to him, but wondered, too, where this conversation was heading.

'If they see you down at the hospital, word is very quickly going to get around that you're alive. I need you to be a symbol of hope to these people. Let them know that the world hasn't entirely forgotten about them. If this attitude of theirs is left to fester, it could get pretty bad for us.'

'Hey, listen, whatever it takes,' I assured him. 'Like I said, I want to help.'

He clapped me on the shoulder and thanked me.

'One other thing. What's good for the Muslims ain't going to work for the Serbs. If they do break through and get into the town, you're going to need to get out of that flight suit. We've got the blue beret, you haven't. Somehow, we're going to have to disguise you.'

'Any suggestions?'

He nodded. 'I've already spoken to Misha. He's got some clothes you can wear. He lives close to the hospital, so while you're over that way, make sure he delivers. It might just save your life.'

Five minutes later, Phil and I grabbed Craig by the armpits and manoeuvred him out of the door and into the street, where a jeep-type vehicle was already waiting. Where it came from I don't know – any kind of vehicle was an ultra-rare commodity in Gorazde. Lloyd Jones must have been working his magic again.

We manhandled Craig into the middle of the rear seat and propped him upright. Mary had given him another sedative shot for the journey. I don't think the poor guy knew what planet he was on; a small mercy, given his condition.

With Phil driving, Misha in the passenger seat and Ant and me in the back with Craig, we set off. As he accelerated away from the bank, Phil warned us to hold on tight. For pretty much the entire journey we were within range of the Serb snipers. The real danger area was the bridge over the River Drina. Only two days earlier, a five-year-old girl had been shot dead as she and her mother had attempted to scurry across it. Our best chance, Phil informed us, was to get the vehicle up to ramming speed as we hit the river – and then fly over the bridge.

I thought it was just a turn of phrase, but the Scotsman wasn't kidding. I caught sight of the speedo. It was nudging past 100kph.

Either side of us, once-proud buildings flashed by. Many had had their top floors blown clean off by the relentless bombardment. There were large craters, some of which gave Phil scant room for manoeuvre as we rocketed towards the bridge. Water mains had burst everywhere, leaving small lakes on either side of the road. From these, bits of cars and collapsed buildings jutted above the waterline at improbable angles.

'All right, hang on!' Phil yelled.

Up ahead, through the windscreen, I glimpsed the bridge. We hit the outer marker at about 150kph and took off. For a moment, I experienced weightlessness. Ant and I grabbed Craig and held on to him tight. Then we struck the ground with a vicious thud that sent a shower of sparks past the window.

When I looked up again, we were tearing around the edge of a large square. Once, I imagined, this had been one of the focal points of the town, a place where people would come and hang out, close to the river, on a lazy summer's evening. Now it was deserted. And I identified something else that made Gorazde so eerily different from other European provincial towns. There were no birds here. No birds at all. The war hadn't just destroyed the buildings, it had stripped the place of its soul as well.

As I got out of the car, a shell exploded close by. I felt its double shockwave on my skin. The journey from the bank had taken us 2km closer to the front line. Ant and I eased Craig out of the back of the car and started up the steps of the hospital, a long, low building on the edge of the square. As we did so, I counted the seconds to the next shell-strike. Watching Phil cover us into the building with sweeps of his SA-80 rammed home just how much closer to the Serbs we were.

A bloke with a leg and an arm missing was smoking a cigarette on the steps. I made eye contact with him and he raised his arm and gave me a thumbs-up. Did he know I was a NATO pilot? Was my flight suit that distinct?

My thoughts were interrupted by another deafening blast. Fifty-eight seconds. Less than a minute between salvos. Jesus. We banged our way through the double doors and stood in the hallway, peering down the three corridors that led off it and wondering which to take. From the far reaches of one of them, a scream rose and was quickly silenced, leaving us to contemplate its echo.

Misha started down the central corridor, a cigarette in his mouth, peering through the gloom, calling softly for someone, anyone. I was still tracking the glow of his cigarette when a door opened to our left and a doctor wearing a shabby white coat appeared. He seemed to know immediately who we were and beckoned for us to follow him.

We made our way along the ward from which he had appeared. As I glanced into the rooms leading off it, it was mainly children that I saw, or perhaps it is only the children that I remember now. There were burns and wounds on torsos, faces and limbs the like of which no news bulletins had ever prepared me for. I couldn't help thinking of the last time I had been in a hospital, staring at the tiny form of Kristian in his incubator. Three and a half months ago. It seemed like a lifetime.

At the end of the corridor we turned into an anteroom, where another doctor and a nurse were waiting. Someone – Adrian, I guess – must have called ahead to let them know we were coming. A television was on in the corner, tuned somewhat surreally to what looked like the Balkan counterpart of *It's a Knockout*. Apart from a few chairs and a beaten-up old table, the room was quite bare. A pervasive stink of cigarette smoke masked other more malodorous smells I had first detected in the corridor.

The second doctor and the nurse led Craig away to be operated on, leaving us with the first medic.

'Tell the doctor this is the NATO pilot who was shot down yesterday,' Ant told Misha. 'Tell him. It's important.'

Misha yabbered something and the doctor turned to me. He

gave me a smile and pumped my hand warmly, then started to examine the cut on my chin. He made such a fuss about it that I got quite embarrassed and tried to wave him away. But the bloke wouldn't have any of it and led me into an adjoining surgery, where he carried out a closer inspection of the wound and Mary's stitching.

After the kids I had seen in the wards, I felt like a complete fraud for taking up this guy's time. I was uncomfortable, too, with the role that Lloyd Jones was carving out for me. As far I was concerned, my association with NATO wasn't something to be overly proud about – certainly not here, amid the dead and dying of the town. The way I saw it, all NATO had succeeded in doing was dropping a couple of bombs on a handful of Serb tanks and then buggering off.

Eventually, thank God, the guy pronounced himself satisfied with the state of the cut and left it alone. This was a blessing, as looking around me at the bloodstains on the bed and the dirt engrained in the shelves, I figured I was better off the way I was. The only bandages I could see were used ones, piled up in a corner on the floor, ready, I presumed, to be taken away for boiling and to be used again.

I rejoined the others in the waiting room as a shell blast, much closer than any previous explosion, shook the building. For several seconds afterwards, in distant parts of the hospital, I could hear the sound of glass shattering. Then the screams started all over again.

To mask the noise, the doctor switched TV channels and turned up the sound. *It's a Knockout* was replaced by what looked like a war movie – a shot of a heavy gun being loaded and readied for firing. It was only after a dishevelled-looking soldier had pulled the lanyard and the weapon had exploded into life that I registered the CNN logo in the corner of the picture and the caption beside it: Gorazde.

The doctor mumbled something and lit a cigarette. A second later, the shell struck. Again, at the extremity of my hearing, I caught the tinkle of glass and the sound of screaming. Two seconds later, I heard the rumble of the same explosion on the TV. The doctor shook his head and chuckled to himself, then reached into a drawer in the desk he was leaning on and produced a bottle of slivovitz, pouring himself a good stiff finger.

Behind him, a nurse in a white uniform stained brown at the front and the sides began to tidy a cabinet that had nothing in it but three half-full medicine bottles. I watched, mesmerised, as she brought one of the bottles out, wiped it with a damp cloth, and then put it back on the shelf. She did this with the other two, then started again. Each time she repeated the procedure, the shakes in her hands got worse.

I looked at Phil, but he appeared to be oblivious of anyone else in the room. He divided his attention between the TV and admiring what he found on the top of a Bic biro, which he'd just pulled out of one of his ears.

*Boom!* The howitzer on the TV belched flame from its muzzle, prompting the nurse to flinch with such force that she dropped one of the bottles. It smashed on the floor at the precise moment that the shell struck, 100 or so metres away. When she bent down to clear up the mess and I caught sight of her face, I could see that her cheeks were wet with tears.

This last explosion, closer than the others, prompted Phil to get on his hand-held radio and call Adrian. From the tone of the conversation, I could tell that the tactical picture had worsened appreciably since we'd left the bank. When he signed off, the Scotsman pulled Misha over and told him to ask the doctor how long Craig would need to remain in the hospital after the operation. The doctor, who seemed a lot more interested in the quantity of drink left in the bottom of his glass than in Craig's fate under the knife, mumbled something which Misha duly translated: several days.

A spirited argument then ensued between Adrian, back at the bank, and the doctor, with Phil and Misha acting as go-betweens. Phil insisted on getting Craig out in the shortest possible time, and every so often would report back to Adrian on the radio with the doctor's latest compromise. Over the course of an intense twenty-minute negotiating session, what started off as a two-day recuperation period was eventually whittled down to just two hours. It was only after the discussion had ended that Phil pulled me to one side and told me what had induced Adrian to drive such a hard bargain. Simon, conducting a lone vigil on top of the bank, could see that the Serbs were poised to advance on several fronts around the town. But the area where they looked most like breaking through was here, just a couple of klicks from the hospital.

Two hours suddenly seemed like an eternity.

Phil reminded me about the directive from Adrian to get myself kitted out with some civvy clothes. And so it was, five minutes later, that I found myself tucked in behind him and Misha, heading out of the hospital for God knows where, the relentless beat of Serb artillery in my ears and grainy images of street-fighting from old newsreels of Stalingrad and Moscow in my mind's eye.

Subconsciously, I must have started to count the seconds between the shell-strikes again. When I became aware of it, I noted that in the short space of time we had been inside the hospital the average interval between detonations had dropped from around a minute to just thirty seconds.

We reached Misha's apartment after a fifteen-minute dash through the town that at one point took us close to the banks of the river. The open area next to the Drina was an unhealthy place to be on account of the Serbs' snipers, a small army of whom kept this sector constantly in their sights. I did not feel safe again – and in a very loose, comparative sense – until I was marching up the stairs to Misha's third-floor flat. As in the Hotel Gradina, there were people living in the stairwells and in the long, central corridors of the block, although the darkness made it impossible to tell how many. With so many houses destroyed and so few people on the streets, it must have been the same story in all the apartment blocks in Gorazde.

Misha rapped on his front door and moments later there was a rattling of bolts and chains. When the door opened, we were greeted by a small, timid-looking woman and two children, a boy aged about four and a girl a couple of years older, who stared at Phil and me suspiciously from behind the folds of their mother's skirt. Misha never introduced us. We simply followed him through the kitchen and into the sitting room, where he invited us to sit on a battered sofa. The flat was warm but dark, the only light that spilled into this world of greys and browns coming from the small, taped-over windows.

Misha flopped down on a chair by a table in the middle of the room and barked something at his wife, out of sight behind a curtain she'd drawn between the sitting room and kitchen. He turned to us and announced that tea would be served. I could see that, in some way or other, the whole show was designed to impress us.

Presently, the tea arrived, hot and sweet, according to the local taste. As we sipped at it, Misha remembered the clothes and rattled off a further set of orders to his wife, who reappeared shortly with a two-piece suit on a hanger.

It was not what I had expected.

'Misha, I couldn't possibly take this . . .' I began. My flight suit was one thing, but the thought of stumbling around town dodging shell-strikes in an undersized grey pin-stripe was ridiculous. From the modesty of the surroundings, I knew, too, that this would be his only suit and it was this, finally, that prevented me from accepting it. I told him all I really needed was an old pair of trousers and a shirt, something to change into quickly if the need arose. Misha nodded and soon a pair of brown trousers and a flimsy-looking shirt appeared. Like the suit, there was no way they would have fitted me, but I took them anyway to avoid any further risk of offending him.

Misha sat back with the self-satisfied look of a man who had discharged his responsibilities and rolled a couple of cigarettes. He gave one to me and kept the other for himself. In the corner of the room stood the children, the whites of their wide little eyes visible through the gloom. Misha's wife kept out of sight behind the curtain.

Before the war, this would have been pretty much the extent of Misha's life: a dingy flat and a dead marriage, with a smoke with his mates down at the local café at lunchtime to relieve the boredom. But with the arrival of the UN in Bosnia, interpreting, alongside gun-running, had become the boom industry of the conflict, and now Misha was an interpreter.

In the short space of time I had been on the ground, I had seen two slices of Bosnian life up close: Oskar and Admira's, and now Misha's. The two couldn't have been more different. Perhaps it said something about the savagery of the war itself. Bosnia was a place where East met West and where echoes of mediaevalism were still audible in the late twentieth century.

Our tea finished, we got up and made to leave. As we retraced our steps to the front door, I tried to thank Misha's wife for her hospitality, but she retreated into the shadows with her children and the words died in my throat.

Clutching my bundle of clothes, I stuck close to Phil and Misha as we ran from building to building to avoid the snipers on the way back. When we finally reached the hospital, Ant told us that they'd operated on Craig and he was due to be wheeled out of theatre in around twenty minutes. All we could do until then was sit and wait. Not in any hurry to go back into the waiting room to watch myself being shelled to death on the TV, I went out to the corridor for a smoke. Phil must have had similar misgivings about the entertainment on offer, because he joined me.

'What's a nice guy like you doing in a place like this, then?' I asked in a lull between the shelling.

Phil smiled. 'Search me. The whole thing was Rose's bloody idea. When the Serbs launched their offensive last month, the general wanted to get people he knew he could trust into the town to give him reliable reports about the situation on the ground. Rose is ex-Regiment, so we got the short straw. We were already in-theatre, acting as the guy's eyes and ears in other parts of Bosnia. So, in answer to your question, I guess you could say we were in the wrong place at the wrong time.'

The look on his face told me that Phil wasn't altogether upset to be here. It was the kind of shindig, I supposed, that people like him joined the SAS for.

It transpired that Adrian, Phil and the rest of the boys had been allowed by the Serbs to enter the town during a lull in the fighting, only to have the sector go ballistic on them the following day. As far as the Muslims and the Serbs – or anyone else, for that matter – were concerned, they were UK liaison officers, or UKLOs, attached to the UN. But when the first NATO jets had appeared with bombs under their wings, and were guided to their targets by FACs within Gorazde, the Serbs must have quickly realised just who it was they'd let in. There was little doubt in the minds of the boys that the ambush on the Land Rover that had seen one of their men killed and another gravely wounded was a premeditated act of revenge.

There was a sudden commotion behind us. I turned to see Craig being carried into the waiting room on a stretcher with what looked like a piece of scaffolding protruding from his upper body.

Phil dashed back into the waiting room and got on to the radio to Adrian. While we'd been outside, another argument had broken out between Ant and the doctors over Craig's recuperation. It seemed as if, in the space of time Craig had been out for the count, the medics had had second thoughts about releasing him – and looking at the state of his arm, I wasn't surprised. There were two bolts through the upper part and one below the elbow with rods between them to keep the whole thing straight. Beneath the metalwork, I could see the crude stitching that kept his flesh together.

The pain it must have caused was apparent as he started to come round. When he opened his eyes, Craig immediately started to shout and lash out. Ant and Phil tried to restrain him, but it was clear that the injured man had no idea who they were or where he was. Only after persistent attempts to get the message across did Craig finally sink back on his stretcher and accept his condition. The doctors stared at Ant and Phil with open looks of I-told-you-so hostility.

Phil got off the radio and called Ant into a corner of the room for a confab. Thirty seconds later, they walked back to where the doctors were standing over Craig and brazened it out.

'Right, that's it, mate,' Ant said, staring into Craig's glazed eyes. 'We're fucking off out of here.'

The doctors could do nothing. Misha, Phil, Ant and I each took a corner of the stretcher and together we manhandled the injured man back to our vehicle at the base of the hospital steps. While I could see it would be dangerous to leave Craig to the unpredictable mercies of the shelling, I still thought, all things considered, that he was probably better off with what meagre care the doctors could offer than he was with us at the bank. But I kept my opinions to myself. For the moment, it was enough simply to be on the move again. If we stayed still for too long, I was convinced, we were itching for a direct hit from a Serb shell. There was no logic to this, of course, but the feeling followed me wherever I went.

When we reached the bank, Mary the medic took one look at Craig and went apoplectic.

'Dear God!' she yelled as we set the stretcher down on the floor behind the table. 'Look at his bandages. He's still bleeding like a stuck pig! You should have left him at the hospital.'

'That was not an option,' Adrian Lloyd Jones said tersely, getting up from his position by the radio.

Mary moved across the room to confront him. 'Don't you understand?' she told him, barely able to conceal her rage. 'Unless this man receives urgent medical attention, he is going to die.'

Lloyd Jones did not reply immediately. He looked, I thought, a very different man from the one I had met last night.

'There have been some developments of which you are possibly unaware, Mary,' he responded at length without sarcasm or rancour. 'In the past two hours, the Serbs have begun the last stage of their push to take the town. And if the reports coming in from Sarajevo are correct, the hospital will be in the first sector to fall.'

Her hand came up to her mouth. 'Oh, God,' was all that she said after a long pause. 'What are we going to do?'

Lloyd Jones' face betrayed no emotion. 'Nothing. There's nothing any of us can do, except sit tight. Sit tight and wait for directions from Sarajevo.'

Looking back, Adrian Lloyd Jones must have had an instinct for the storm that was about to break. But, like everything else, he kept it close to his chest.

For the first time since I had been in Gorazde, all the members of our disparate group were co-located in the bank. Mary and Anna attended to Craig's needs as best they were able, administering painkillers and doing what they could to staunch the flow of blood. Bob Cronin, the Canadian UNMO, and Gareth, his Welsh oppo, were in the rest area next to the canteen arguing over when the best time to have left Gorazde would have been – a discussion that was way too academic now for me to want to join it. Misha sat quietly at the table rolling a cigarette.

After Adrian had broken the news that the Serbs were advancing on all fronts to take the town, an uneasy period of calm had descended on our group. I was too wrapped up in thoughts of the front line, of Oskar and Admira, of the hospital and Misha's family, not to mention our own fate, to consider the significance of the things that the SAS were *not* doing at that moment. Things that, with hindsight, offered clues to the knowledge that Lloyd Jones had in his possession at the time. One of these deliberate omissions, I realise now, was not having someone at the OP on top of the Hotel Gradina to report back on the fighting: where it was occurring and where it was heading.

Lloyd Jones sat by the radio, a cup of tea in one hand, his head in the other, as he monitored the static mush filtering through the speaker. Ant and Phil were both cleaning their weapons. Simon was crouched in a corner, repacking his FAC kit into an SAS-issue Bergen rucksack. Sean was leaning against the wall by the door, sipping a coffee and polishing the lens of his rifle's thermal-imaging night-sight.

They must have known what was about to happen.

The first sign of trouble came twenty minutes after our return from the hospital, when there was the sound of a scuffle from the entranceway. Blakey, the Muslim guard, ran into the canteen and yelled something in a babble of Serbo-Croat punctuated by snatches of incomprehensible pidgin English. Sean and Phil ran down the corridor clutching their weapons to see for themselves. They were followed by Blakey, brandishing his AK-47.

Angry shouts carried along the corridor. Amid a wall of shrill, unfamiliar voices, I caught the remonstrations of Sean and Phil. Then came the noise of wood splintering, followed by the bang of the door slamming shut and the scrape of a flurry of bolts locking home. Sean and Phil were back in the canteen, struggling for breath. It was the urbane Liverpudlian sergeant who broke the news to Lloyd Jones.

'They're trying to get in,' he said in a tone that made it clear that even he didn't quite believe what his eyes were telling him.

'Who, for Christ's sake?' Lloyd Jones shot back.

'The Muslims, boss. They've smashed down the guard house and now they're trying to get into the bank itself.'

'OK, then let's make sure the place is properly secure,' said Lloyd Jones calmly. 'Simon, get upstairs and check the main entrance. If anyone tries to get in, you know what to do. Ant, give Phil and Sean a hand shoring up the side entrance. Everybody else, into the sleeping area and stay there till I call you back.'

As we all moved to our respective positions, I caught one last exchange between Ant and Simon, a coda to the disagreement they had had on the roof of the Gradina.

'What did I foockin' tell you?' the big, bluff northerner shouted to his colleague, as Phil headed off to check the main entrance. 'I told you these foockers could change sides at the drop of a hat.'

In the sleeping area, Gareth, the group's self-appointed prophet of doom, was already telling Bob Cronin that it was all over. Our only chance, the Welsh UNMO reckoned, was to lay down our weapons and come out quietly. 'It's not our bloody war anyway, so we might as well—'

Whatever he said next I missed in an explosion of noise. The crowd was trying to break the door down – with what sounded like a battering-ram.

At least the building was semi-secure. But how long do steel bars hold? I blocked my ears in a bid to drown out the din of fists and boots hammering on the reinforced doors and windows, but I couldn't. There was nowhere in the building anyone could have gone to escape it. It was relentless. The situation had rapidly come to a head and there was no way out.

The last I saw of him, Lloyd Jones was hunched over the radio with a handset clamped to his ear. I knew he was on the horn to Sarajevo, though I couldn't see how Rose or anyone else could help us. The SAS are renowned for their ability to extract themselves from tough spots. But when you no longer know who your enemy is – and with the Muslims hammering on the doors of the bank, it was clear we'd now lost the trust of the very people we'd been sent to protect – even the SAS looked out of their league.

Gareth had shut up and, like everyone else, now merely stared dumbly at the curtain that divided our room from the corridor. Mary and Anna clung to each other for comfort. Misha had begun to pray.

Above the banging and shouting, I suddenly became aware of a new sound: the wails of young mothers and old women – the people who formed Gorazde's first and last line of resistance – as they exhorted their menfolk to storm the bank. They were ululating, the sound that Muslim women make from the back of their throats to express extreme pleasure or pain.

As soon as she heard this, Anna began pulling at her hair. I watched as her face transformed into a terrible mask of fear, riven with deep lines. Then she began to scream. The sound of it mingled for a moment with the noise outside. Then Mary slapped her across the face. The Croatian girl gawped at the medic, eyes wide with incomprehension, and burst into tears.

Yet the scream must have registered above the clamour, because there was a brief respite, the kind of hush that falls on a crowd of rescue workers searching for earthquake victims in the rubble of collapsed buildings. Then the racket started again, even louder, if anything, than before. Mary held Anna, rocking her back and forth as she continued to sob quietly.

I lay back, still trying to block out the noise. All I could think about was the Serb tank that had stalled on the outskirts of town. Would we share the fate of its crew? Would we, too, have our limbs ripped from our bodies as the crowd fell upon us? It was really at that moment, I think, that I resigned myself to death.

I said goodbye to Yvonne and then, one by one, to the kids. I even apologised to them for not having taken that posting to RAF Valley when it had been offered to me by Mel on ship. I knew the pain it would cause when Yvonne learned the truth: that none of this really ever needed to have happened.

And then it struck me. What a fucking stupid way to die.

I don't know how much time elapsed between then and the point when the battering stopped. It could have been a minute or it could have been an hour. When it did happen, none of us moved or said a word – for fear, I think, that the slightest sound could have set it all off again. We were still in this state of shock and disbelief when Lloyd Jones stuck his head round the curtain and called us back next door.

When I walked into the canteen, the boys were already seated at the table. Lloyd Jones invited us to do the same.

'There have been a couple of developments,' he announced drily, but behind the public-school stiff upper lip I could see the toll the past hour had taken of him. 'I've managed to persuade the mayor of Gorazde to come to a meeting here at the bank in twenty minutes. Sarajevo has called on the Serbs to agree to a two-hour ceasefire tomorrow at midday, and there's every hope that they'll play ball. When the mayor gets here, I'm going to tell him what's on offer: a two-hour cessation in the shelling to allow him to get the injured out of the hospital. He's called off the dogs because he wants to hear what we've got to say. After everything that's just happened, I don't have to tell you that we need to get the Muslims back on our side.'

At the other end of the table, Gareth got to his feet. Having heard his views in the sleeping area, I knew what he was about to say.

'If you guys lay down your weapons and we all walk out of here with our hands up, I have complete and utter faith that we will all come away from this place unharmed,' he said, his voice trembling with Welsh ardour. 'What this situation requires is for us to remain calm and—'

He was interrupted by a crash behind him as Simon pushed his chair back and smacked his SA-80 down on the table.

'I didn't join this outfit to lay down my fucking weapon to nobody,' he shouted. 'If we go out of here, we do it in a blaze of glory. Fuck the Muslims, and fuck the Serbs. My only faith is in this thing.' He picked up his assault rifle and waved it above his head. 'Anyone gets in the way, I'm going to fuckin' let 'em have it.'

Everyone just stared at him. Sean muttered something under his breath about uncalled-for Rambo behaviour, but otherwise nobody said a word. Simon took his place again, calm as you like, as if nothing had happened.

Partly to hide my shock, and partly because the vacuum of

silence needed to be filled, I asked Lloyd Jones what the second development had been.

The boss stared at the table for a beat. 'Whatever happens, from now on it looks as if we're on our own,' he replied at length. 'Sarajevo has ordered us to stay put. There's no magic ending to this story, no rescue plan in the works. They're talking about maybe getting a convoy in here in three or four days' time, but frankly, that kind of talk just goes to show how out of touch they are with the real situation on the ground. The Serbs have this place sewn up, and in three or four days' time it will all be over.' He rubbed his eyes wearily and added: 'I'm sorry to have to tell you, therefore, that it's all down to us now. We've been left to fend for ourselves.'

The Muslim delegation swept in on the dot of 6pm. It was led by the mayor, a stern, stocky man with a chubby face, who held his gaze straight, deliberately not looking at any of us, as he marched into the canteen. He was accompanied by five 'aides', three of whom wore Bosnian Army uniform and carried Kalashnikovs. One of these heavies removed the mayor's coat and ushered him obsequiously to a seat near the head of the table. The mayor straightened his ill-fitting suit and sat down, gesturing generously for us to do the same.

Before the meeting, Lloyd Jones had asked me to sit in as an observer. The degree to which things had changed since my visit to the hospital was manifest in the clothes that the SAS had asked me to wear. In the wake of the crowd incident my status as hero pilot had changed irrevocably, and it was now deemed essential for me to masquerade as a soldier – ironically, for my own safety. Over my flight suit I was wearing the combat jacket of their dead colleague, Fergie.

There was a clatter as the Muslim delegation sat down along the left-hand side of the table, placing their weapons in front of them. Directly opposite me, the SAS did the same. The two groups stared at each other with ill-concealed suspicion. The British soldiers, I noticed, had replaced their SA-80s with automatic pistols. Like western gunslingers at a game of poker, they had positioned them in full view of their adversaries. Only Lloyd Jones remained unarmed, taking his seat beside the mayor at the head of the table. I sat at the foot, next to Anna, who interpreted at that end. Misha sat alongside the SAS men, acting as Lloyd Jones' interpreter. Mary, Bob Cronin and Gareth remained out of view in the sleeping area.

The atmosphere was so charged that even Craig, lying in his customary place on the stretcher, was watching and listening, his eyes clear and alert.

Adrian got to his feet and started by thanking the mayor for calling off the crowd. When his right-hand man had finished translating, the mayor responded with a regal nod of the head, a gesture that made it very clear he wanted us to believe he had the power of life and death over us, which in all probability he did. With the tips of his fingers spread out on the edge of the table and his head bowed, Lloyd Jones fell quiet briefly. Then he drew himself up to his full height and stared directly into the mayor's eyes.

'I have to say, sir,' the SAS man said softly, 'that I do not understand why the people of Gorazde turned on us in the way they did. That the United Nations are in this town at all is because we are trying to help you. Surely your people can understand that.'

I watched the mayor's face as his aide whispered into his ear. As the SAS boss took his seat again, the mayor's expression darkened. His speech started as a low growl but rapidly descended into a table-thumping diatribe. 'The United Nations has abandoned Gorazde,' his interpreter announced. 'NATO has abandoned Gorazde. We have seen no NATO aircraft over the town for thirty-six hours, and the Serbs have chosen to attack as a direct result of this betrayal. We do not view the UN or NATO as an ally any more. That is why the people reacted in the way that they did.'

Lloyd Jones was unabashed. 'You have to understand that the weather these past two days has been pretty bad,' he replied. 'The fact that no NATO aircraft have been back to attack the Serbs has nothing to do with abandonment or betrayal. The jets need good weather, it's as simple as that. As soon as it clears, they will be back, ready to hit the aggressors again.'

The mayor scowled as he listened to the translation. Lloyd Jones pressed on.

'I asked you here, sir, because Sarajevo has come up with a plan that will allow you to evacuate your wounded from the hospital. We know how vulnerable the hospital has become. My men saw the shelling first-hand earlier today. But from twelve noon tomorrow, for a period of two hours, the Serbs have agreed to a ceasefire that will enable you to get the wounded out of there. It's a good offer, the best we can do until the weather clears.'

A snort issued from the mayor's throat. 'From the lack of support we have had from NATO and General Rose this last day and a half, why should we trust you any more? And why should we believe the Serbs, either?'

A muscle twitched at the side of Lloyd Jones' face. 'I have it on good authority that the Serbs will keep their word on this.' He paused. 'In fact, I give you my word that the Serbs will not violate this ceasefire.'

I couldn't help thinking, given the Serbs' propensity for duplicity, how brave or rash, depending on your view, this promise was.

The mayor's English must have been better than he was letting on. He leaned across the table and spat a handful of words back at Lloyd Jones. Even his interpreter seemed reluctant at first to translate them.

'Why should we trust you?' he said. 'How do we know that you are not working with our enemy?'

Lloyd Jones let the words sink in, then asked the mayor if he had ever heard of Liverpool.

The mayor, as wrong-footed apparently as the rest of us by this sudden change of tack, stumbled that he had.

'Then try to see this from our point of view,' Adrian told him levelly. 'Let's pretend for a moment that our positions are reversed. Let's pretend that this is Liverpool, a famous English city, and that an aggressor is on our doorstep, shelling the shit out of us. Then let's advance this scenario further. Let's say we appeal to you, the Bosnian Muslims, for assistance, because the people of Liverpool are dying and the city is about to be overrun. Would you come to our assistance? Would you?'

From the other end of the table, I saw the anger burning in his eyes.

The mayor, having listened to the text of this speech in his native Serbo-Croat, merely gave a contemptuous shrug.

'I'll take that as a fucking no, then, shall I?' Lloyd Jones said quietly.

Now the mayor looked up and held the officer's gaze.

I tried to signal to Adrian not to go down this path, but the SAS boss was already in full stride. Scarcely pausing to draw breath, he berated the mayor for daring to suggest that the British Army, the UN or NATO could possibly be in league with the Serbs and for questioning the motives and morality of the very people who had come to his town to help its people. Every other word of this impassioned speech was a 'shit' or a 'fuck', words that sounded so alien on Lloyd Jones' lips that they compounded the shock.

The mayor's translator went to work. I watched the Muslim party bristle and realised that our collective fate was sealed. For an uncomfortable moment, it looked as if the heavies with the guns were going to make a move for them. The SAS must have thought so, too, because, as one, they straightened, ready for action.

The mayor ended the stand-off by getting to his feet and clicking his fingers. Then he and his cronies filed out of the room.

No one said a word until long after the door had slammed shut. Lloyd Jones walked over to the sink and splashed some water over his face. Slowly, those around the table got to their feet. No one needed to be told what to do. The bank had just become the scene of our last stand. Doors needed to be guarded; locks secured; weapons checked.

I moved over to Lloyd Jones and, out of earshot of the others, said: 'Possibly not your best move, Adrian.'

He threw some water over his neck and, his face still over the sink, nodded ruefully. 'Yeah. I'm sorry. It's headquarters I don't understand. We were sent here to report dispassionately on the fighting in this sector, to inject some bloody reality into the wild claims being reported by both sides on the state of the siege. Well, it doesn't take a size 9 hat to work that out any more. The Serbs have always hated us, and now the Muslims do.' He turned to face me. 'The position is untenable. What the fuck do we do?'

'I think we ought to get out of here,' I said.

He didn't object, so I pressed on. 'You said it yourself. We're now caught between the Muslims and the Serbs. The Serbs are within a hair's breadth of taking the town and, if and when they do, they'll kill anyone they suspect of aiding and abetting their enemy, which means you, me and the rest of your troop, for sure, unless, of course, the Muslims beat them to it.'

From the look on his face, I knew I wasn't telling him anything he didn't already know.

'Headquarters doesn't get it because they're not here,' I went on. 'You've got to be here, on the ground, to see what a fucking mess this place is. There's nothing to be gained any more by sticking with it, Adrian. I think we should leave – and leave now. Before the Muslims get themselves organised and come back to finish us off.'

'All right,' he said, simply. 'How do we do it?'

'Get them to send a helicopter,' I told him. 'It'll be hairy, but I used to fly helos and I know it can be done.'

'OK. But Craig must have the option to come with us. I can't order him to stay here with the UNMOs. God knows what might happen to him.'

I agreed. There was no guarantee Craig would be up to the journey, but the decision had to be his, however much it impacted on the rest of us.

'You reckon it's OK for the UNMOs to stay?' I asked.

'They'll be all right. It's us soldiers they want.' He paused. 'Do you honestly believe they'll send a helicopter?'

'Yes,' I told him. 'Provided we make it easy for them.'

'How do we do that?'

'Come up with a suitable landing site. One that's far enough from the town to be away from the worst of the fighting, but close enough to give us a chance of making the RV.'

'Think you can do that?'

I nodded. 'All I need is a map.'

# CHAPTER 9

W orking against the clock, Simon and I pored over his map for possible landing sites for a helicopter big enough to remove an eight-man unit in a single lift. Eight men, because we would need a guide with good local knowledge if we were to stand any chance of weaving our way unseen through the Muslim and Serb lines.

Adrian already had somebody in mind for this: Ahmed, the young Muslim lad who spent so much of his time hanging around the bank. Ahmed was due to arrive in the next hour. When he turned up, Adrian would ask him outright if he wanted to break out with us. Since Ahmed was always saying he would give his eye teeth for a chance to leave, there was a better-than-even chance, Adrian thought, that he would agree. So Ahmed figured in our planning as the eighth man.

The landing site had to be a combination of many things. It needed to be in a clear, flat area, preferably in a valley, so that the noise of the helicopter's approach would be masked by the terrain. It needed to be away from the town, obviously, but not so far away that we would be unable to reach it during the hours of darkness – the only time a helo pilot would remotely consider undertaking such a dangerous mission. We reckoned that the optimum time to leave would be around ten o'clock, and that the pick-up would need to be around five, shortly before it got light. That would give us seven hours to cover as much territory as we could.

Normally, the distance wouldn't have presented too much of a problem, but there were several factors working against us. First we had to get past the Muslims, then slip through the Serb lines, and to cap it all, we would have a severely injured man in our midst, and Craig's disability would hamper our mobility big-time.

It took us around fifteen minutes to find somewhere that fitted the bill: a clearing in a forest on the floor of a secluded valley around six klicks from the bank. We deliberately picked a site within the narrow slice of territory to the north-west of the town that had been the last area to hold out against the Serb advance. This had been the patch of land I had had the good fortune to parachute into, home to Oskar and Admira and to the Muslims who had picked me up after the ejection. Having seen fighting in this sector from the roof of the Gradina that morning, we had no idea whether it was still in Muslim hands. But if it wasn't, we reckoned we might just be able to use the chaos to our advantage.

We reported our findings to Adrian. He listened to the logic of the idea and pronounced himself satisfied. It was now time to brief the rest of the team.

While the UNMOs, Misha, Mary and Anna still sheltered in the sleeping area, Adrian called the unit together and broached the plan of action.

'As you know,' he told them, keeping his voice low, 'the situation has got much worse over the past couple of hours. Furthermore, after our little meeting with the mayor and his gang, it isn't likely to improve any. In my opinion, therefore, it's time now for all the military personnel in the bank – you guys, me and Nick here – to get out of Gorazde while we still can. To that end, Nick and Simon have found a landing site around 6km from here. I haven't put it to Sarajevo yet, but with any luck they'll be able to send a helicopter to the LS and get us out tonight.' He paused briefly, then added: 'Any dissenters?'

No one made a sound.

'Good. Any questions?'

Phil stuck his hand up. 'Boss, we're moving from a relatively safe place – ha, ha – into a fucking battlefield. What kind of chance do we stand of making it out alive?'

'I don't know, Phil. But instinct tells me it's a hell of a lot more difficult to hit a moving target than one that's sitting still. Sarajevo has been mumbling about sending a convoy in to get Craig and us out, but that's baloney in my view. There's too much fighting out there and, in any case, both sides, the Serbs and the Muslims, are out of control. We don't have any more time to lose. If we go, we must go tonight.'

'What about Craig?' Ant asked.

'What about him?' Adrian shot back.

'Is he coming, boss?'

'I think that's a question you had better put to him.'

All eyes turned to the injured officer, who had pulled himself into a sitting position on the stretcher, his back against the wall. 'You are not leaving me behind and that is fucking that,' he stated with slow deliberation.

'I think that settles that, then,' Lloyd Jones said.

'What about the others?' Sean asked.

'The UNMOs, translators and medical staff will be all right. We're the guys with a price on our heads. To further protect them, it's essential that they don't learn of our intentions. That way, they can genuinely tell the Muslims after we're gone that they had no inkling of what we were planning.'

'All right,' Ant said, 'but how the fuck do we sneak out of the bank, boss? What do we do with the guard?'

Blakey. Shit. I hadn't thought about Blakey. The Muslim delegation might have gone, but Blakey was still in the guard house, sitting tight with his AK-47.

But clearly Lloyd Jones had been doing some thinking while Simon and I had been studying the map. 'We make out like we're heading out on routine patrol and we leave in two groups,' he said. 'If the guard stops us, we knock him out. Cold. Clinical. Easy.'

There were nods of agreement all round.

The meeting broke up and Lloyd Jones moved to the sat-net. He rubbed his hands and blew on them, like a safe-cracker might before getting his fingers dirty on a challenging combination lock, put on the headphones and called Sarajevo.

'We've had a meeting,' I heard him tell the liaison officer there.

'The pocket's collapsed. It's all over bar the shouting. It's time we got out of here, Harry. All of us here are agreed on that.'

There was a pause as he listened to the feedback.

'I am not using overemotional language, mate. It's the truth. The pocket has collapsed and, aside from the fact that this link is encrypted, frankly, I couldn't give a shit who might be listening in. If you lot were here, you'd see for yourself. It's no state secret. It's bloody obvious. The Serbs are entering the town and the Muslims have turned against us. The place is about to implode with us in it.'

Another pause.

'No, there's no point sitting tight and waiting for a convoy, Harry. By the time it reaches us, we'll all be dead. What do I suggest? We've got a helicopter landing site picked out about six klicks from our position here. I'd like Sarajevo to extract us tonight and from the following grid reference.'

He rattled off the co-ordinates and waited for a response. A couple of seconds later, he grunted an acknowledgement and signed off.

'They're going to get back to us,' he said, turning our way. 'They need to think about it.' He rubbed his eyes. 'Jesus. What a bunch of wankers. First they tell me not to use politically incorrect, overemotive terminology when talking about Gorazde's fate, then they suggest we might all like to sit around twiddling our thumbs while they send some lorries to come and get us. Is anyone actually clued up over there to what's happening in this place?'

There was a blast of cold air as the door to the outside world was opened by Phil, who was now on guard. A second or two later, in strolled Ahmed. The moment Adrian clapped eyes on him, the young Muslim was whipped into the furthest corner of the canteen and briefed on the situation. In less than a minute he had agreed to act as the group's guide.

This was good news, as Ahmed knew the terrain intimately.

While we waited for Sarajevo's response, several of the lads disappeared into a huddle and debated which equipment should come with us and which should stay behind. Sean, mindful that we all needed to be armed, came over and thrust Fergie's SA-80 into my hand.

'Do you know how to use this thing?' he asked.

I nodded. It had been a couple of years, but I had received instruction on using the SA-80. The only aspect of the weapon with which I was not familiar was the big night-sight that the SAS had brought in with them. But with so much going on, I figured this wasn't the time to inquire about minutiae. I'd check with one of the lads later.

'Are you all set, then?' Sean queried.

Yes, I told him. Except I was fucking starving. The thought of a 6-klick yomp through uncertain territory had reminded my stomach that I had not eaten now for over twenty-four hours. In view of this, Sean told me to get a 'baby's head' down me. A baby's head is military slang for a boil-in-the-tin meat pudding of which the SAS seemed to have an abundant supply. I did as I was told and got the kettle on.

There was a crackle on the sat-net, then a voice proclaiming our call sign, Alpha Two-One.

Adrian picked up the headset and microphone and held one of the earpieces to his head. Through the other, we could all hear the taut voice of the LO at the other end. We gathered round and listened.

'No dice, you're staying put,' the voice said. 'Sorry.'

'You're fucking joking!' Adrian told him. He paused, turning to us. 'They've rejected it. Can you believe that?'

'Don't let them do this, boss,' Ant urged him. 'Stick it to 'em.'

'Fucking right,' Phil agreed.

Lloyd Jones looked at me. I nodded. Put the boot in.

He picked up the mike again. 'Sarajevo, this is Alpha Two-One. You still there? It is imperative we leave tonight. None of us buy this, Harry. Come hell or high water, we are leaving tonight, with or without your assistance. That means, if necessary, we'll do a walk-out, the full 80 klicks to Sarajevo on foot.'

You could have heard a pin drop. I caught the dispassionate acknowledgement from Sarajevo: 'Roger, Alpha Two-One. Stand by.'

Pulling off the headset, Lloyd Jones turned and gave us a look, as if to say, now what?

And then a different voice came on line. 'Alpha Two-One, this is Sunray.'

Lloyd Jones straightened in his chair.

'Did he say Sunray?' I whispered to Phil.

'Yeah, mate. It's General Rose.'

Sitting bolt upright, Lloyd Jones clamped the headset back on and started to scribble notes on a pad. It was now impossible to hear anything over the speakers. We peered over his shoulder like cheating schoolboys in an attempt to read his writing.

'Roger,' the boss said at last. 'Alpha Two-One, over and out.'

There was an unnaturally long pause as Lloyd Jones switched the set to standby.

'Well?' I asked.

'You're not going to believe this,' he replied, 'but we've been ordered out.'

If we could have cheered, we would have. But to keep our plans from the UNMOs, medics and interpreters, all Adrian got back was a handful of grins.

But I could see that there was something still troubling the boss. I asked him what the problem was.

'The problem,' he said, 'is that there has been one significant change to our plans. The helicopter won't be coming to the LS that you and Simon found on the map. They've given us another set of co-ordinates. And I'm afraid to have to say it's going to be a bitch.'

The new landing site was twice as far away as the LS chosen by Simon and me, and with Craig in tow it seemed touch and go as to whether we'd make it. General Rose had not given Adrian any reason for the change of site. To me, it smacked of jobsworth – someone at headquarters who was determined to stamp his signature on our plans after we'd made it clear we were coming out of the pocket, shit or bust. In retrospect, there were probably good reasons for it to which we weren't privy. A site 12km from the town was undoubtedly more secluded than the one we had chosen and, given Sarajevo's access to threat information, maybe they knew something about our LS that we didn't. But it didn't alter the fact that, having budgeted on seven hours to get us to the original site, we now had to make an RV twice the distance away in the same length of time.

The difficulty over the next couple of hours would be maintaining the secrecy of our plans in front of the civilians. Because it was supper time, we had to allow Misha, Mary, Anna, Bob and Gareth back into the canteen. It was now past eight o'clock and our departure had been set for ten. This was around the time that a patrol usually left the bank for the Gradina to carry out a routine rooftop observation of the town. What Blakey would make of all eight of us trooping out of the bank at that time, I didn't know – none of us did – but nothing could be gained now by worrying about it. The next milestone in our plans was the pre-break-out brief, which was scheduled for the moment the five civilians went to bed.

Supper time ticked by agonisingly slowly. I was hungry, yet keyed up to the point where I felt physically sick. If it hadn't been for Sean's advice, I probably would have stayed off food for another twenty-four hours, but I forced down the meat pudding and headed upstairs for a smoke away from the innocent banter of the UNMOs, medics and Misha, which was beginning to grate on my nerves.

I had practised escape-and-evasion techniques with the Navy, but God only knew how I'd fare for real. I needed to be alone with my thoughts. Despite the dangers, my overriding fear was that it would be me who would let the side down if push came to shove.

Upstairs I found Sean and Anthony in whispered but spirited conversation. There was a feeling among the SAS that Bob Cronin, who had once been a pilot in the Royal Canadian Air Force, ought to be given the option to come with us, they told me. I agreed, because in the short space of time we'd been together I'd come to like Bob and felt bad at the prospect of leaving him behind without a word of explanation. It was decided that Sean would take Bob aside and explain the deal to him. Whether he came or not would then be up to him.

At 9.30pm the civilians started drifting off to bed. When they were out of the way, we filed upstairs for the brief, moving into a small office which I had not been in before. It was furnished with a table and seven chairs, and there were several mattresses on the floor with UK-issue sleeping bags on them. This cleared up a mystery for me. Throughout, Lloyd Jones and co. had given the appearance of never needing any sleep. Now I realised they'd had their own private den all along.

Lloyd Jones spread an OS map out on the table. 'You all know by now that we've had a new RV allocated by headquarters. It's not going to be easy, because the terrain between here and the helicopter LS verges on the mountainous. Normally, of course, we'd take the long route, find a way round the obstacles, but tonight that option mightn't be open to us.'

He pointed to the narrow patch of territory, extending northwest from the bank as a thin wedge shape on the map, where the Serbs were attempting to close the pocket. There were Serb forces to the left and right of the wedge with the Muslims in between. It would be largely down to Ahmed, with his superior knowledge of the territory and the tactical situation, to guide us through. As back-up, Simon would monitor our progress on the hand-held GPS, the sat-nav, to make sure we didn't drift off course.

Adrian turned to me. 'Every half-hour, I'll point out a prominent feature on the route with a click of the fingers. It could be a crossroads, or an isolated tree, or a bend in a stream. This will be passed down the line from person to person, so make sure you listen out for it. If for any reason we do get split up, we'll RV at the last designated feature. Got that?'

I nodded.

'OK. We're going to be moving in two groups of four. Ahmed will lead the first group, with me, Simon and Ant behind. We will depart the bank five minutes ahead of the second group, which will be led by Phil, with Craig, Nick and Sean bringing up the rear. We'll go out with our regular kit, nothing that should arouse any suspicion, but if the guard gets twitchy, don't dick around, Sean. Take him out.'

The senior NCO gave him a thumbs-up.

Lloyd Jones indicated a clearing in a wood on the edge of the town, around 500 metres from the bank. 'We'll RV here, cam up and then proceed in file formation to the helicopter LS. Everyone will keep a 10m separation from the next man to minimise the damage potential if we do get bounced. Ant, you carry the sat-net, and Simon, you take the aerial. We'll all carry our personal radios, but remember to keep the damned things turned off. Any questions?'

No one said anything.

'Sean, what news from the Canadian?'

'He's staying, boss. He reckoned, all things considered, he was better off here. He appreciated the offer, though. Said he'd destroy all our remaining equipment after we leave, so that's one thing less to worry about.'

Lloyd Jones turned to Craig. 'How are you feeling?'

The injured man raised his eyes. The officer was putting on a brave face, but I could see the pain behind them. 'Thanks to the drugs Mary's given me, surprisingly well, actually,' he said, forcing a smile. 'The biggest difficulty will be shielding my arm along the route. But don't worry. I'll be OK.'

Lloyd Jones checked his watch. 'Group One, be ready to leave in fifteen minutes,' he said. 'This is it. Let's go.'

We moved downstairs, ready for the off. At the allotted moment, Ahmed, Adrian, Simon and Ant got up from the table, picked up their weapons and, without a word to us, moved towards the door.

I braced myself for trouble. At the very least, I expected to hear a raucous shout from Blakey, or a heated exchange between him and Adrian, but after a minute of silence I figured they must have made it.

Four minutes later, Phil, Craig and Sean pulled themselves to their feet. As they moved towards the door, I patted my pockets to make sure I'd remembered everything and my hand touched something cold and metallic. When I pulled it out to see what it was, I found the cigarette-holder Misha had given me.

I still felt uneasy about leaving without a word to the civilians. Misha had been good to me. He deserved better. They all did. But there was nothing to be done about it.

I placed the holder on the table, end upwards. He would find it when he woke up.

What would have become of us by then?

There was a *pshhht* from the darkened passageway: Sean whistling to me to get into position by the door.

I took a last look around the canteen, pulled the collar of Fergie's combat jacket up around my ears and stepped into the guard house, hot on Craig's heels. Blakey's lean-to was lit from the inside by a single candle. Instinct told me that the trick to this moment was to keep my head down and go for it; not to stop even for a split second. But curiosity got the better of me. As Phil and Craig stepped into the street, I raised my eyes to see if I could see where Blakey was.

I trawled the gloom, but the lean-to was empty. I stepped on through the door, a momentary feeling of elation in my heart. Without Blakey to see us go, we would have a hell of a head-start.

But a hand grabbed my shoulder.

I stopped, and the shadowy images in the street briefly blurred from the rush of blood to my head.

I turned, and there was Blakey, standing behind the door, outside the lean-to. In the dim glow of the candlelight, only half of his face was visible as he looked me up and down.

'You!' He barked. 'You, pilot!'

My whole body tensed. I was a fraction of a second away from dropping my shoulders in resignation and turning back into the bank before another response kicked in. I held Blakey's gaze, yanked my shoulder out of his grasp and turned to follow the others. I half-expected the double click of a bullet sliding into the chamber of his AK-47 behind me, but all I heard was the crunch of grit underfoot as I kept walking. An alleyway opened up in front of me and I darted into it. I probed the shadows for a glimpse of Craig, but the darkness enveloped everything.

I kept going, too pumped up on my own adrenalin to stop, too shit scared to be able to function in anything other than a kind of automatic mode. As my eyes grew accustomed to the dark, I could make out a row of houses on the left and an expanse of waste ground to my right. The air was filled with the reek of cordite and the smoke from burning houses wafted on a light breeze to the suburbs from the centre of the town.

As I walked briskly, anxious to catch up with Craig, I noticed the glow of candlelight behind some of the boarded-up windows of the houses. Part of me felt drawn to these lights, knowing there were families here, a human warmth I hadn't felt for months. I pulled myself into a crouch and kept going, past the houses and into the woods that lay on the edge of the town. If I strained hard, I could now just hear Craig's footsteps in front, but a moment's lapse in concentration and I could lose my bearings altogether.

And then the trees thinned and I found myself in a clearing, where six bodies were visible in the light of the moon, which had reappeared from behind the clouds. Seconds later, Sean appeared. We had all made it to base camp.

I felt a tap on my shoulder, turned and saw Phil's face, inches from mine. 'Cam-stick,' he whispered, prodding me with the thing. 'Smear some on your fingers like this, then rub it into your face. When you're done, get someone to check you over, then do the same for them.'

As the group got to work, flashes of artillery fire lit the sky beyond the trees and the air reverberated with the aftershock of explosions. In my heightened state, it felt so damned good to be out of the bank that I momentarily lost sight of the dangers to come. I was brought back to reality by Simon, who tapped my neck to indicate where I had omitted to apply some cam-cream. Then he motioned for me to look him over. On my left, Ahmed and Adrian Lloyd Jones were engaged in an intense, low-volume discussion about the route.

'I know Muslims have position here, here and here,' Ahmed said. He pointed to the map that Lloyd Jones had folded to A4 size on his knee.

'We need to progress north-west, so let's go on this track here,' Lloyd Jones told him, gesturing to a path with his torch, a penlight model with a red filter. From where I was sitting, the Muslim positions looked close; no more than a kilometre away.

'And look,' Ahmed continued in his halting English, 'afterward, Serb lines go from here to here on this side and here to here on other side.'

'We'll worry about those later,' Lloyd Jones said. 'First things first. The important thing for now is that we stick to our bearings. Simon, how's the sat-nav behaving?'

'Steady as a rock.'

'Good, then let's keep moving. Time now is 2230. We have six and a half hours to make it to the RV.'

Lloyd Jones folded the map away and signalled Ahmed to lead him out. We stuck to the orbat – order of battle – for our departure from the bank, only now we merged the two groups into one. Ten seconds after Ahmed exited the clearing, Adrian went after him, followed by Simon and Ant. I felt the knots in my stomach tighten. There had been something safe and reassuring about our little clearing and my earlier exhilaration evaporated. From now on, ambush would be an ever-present danger.

For some reason, my mind drifted back to threat briefs we'd had on *Ark Royal*. I recalled the part about the millions of anti-personnel mines that had been dumped on Bosnia. My only consolation, from a personal standpoint, was that, being seventh in line in the orbat, it would be a damned poor piece of luck if I were the poor sod who stepped on one.

Craig got up to leave and I started counting. One thousand and one, thousand and two . . . At ten seconds, I got a tap on the shoulder from Sean.

A quick suck of the damp air and I was back into the forest. The moon had disappeared again, leaving an intermittent patchwork of stars as the only points of light in this dark and hostile world.

Five minutes after we left the wood behind, the ground began to rise. Our march from the clearing had been incident-free, except for one startling moment when the air behind me split in two as a burst of static belted out from Sean's radio. It went on just long enough for a voice – Phil's, I think – to half shout, half whisper in the gloom: 'Turn that fucking thing off!' I could only imagine the excruciating pain this had caused Sean, the ultimate professional, ten paces behind me.

The incline steepened rapidly and the ground was extremely wet underfoot. Before long, Phil, Craig and I found ourselves bunched together on an impossibly sheer mud face. I had no idea how high it would rise as it was so dark I could scarcely see my hand in front of my face. All I knew was that the bulk of the escape party was on the slope above me, with Sean bringing up the rear.

I knew I was in trouble when I dug my toecaps into the mush, hauled myself up a step and promptly slipped back another three. I was already exhausted. Now I felt physically sick. Sick from the exertion and sick from the stench of mud. It was so close to my face I could smell nothing else.

My arms and legs burned with the effort of climbing. My lungs felt as if they would explode. I took another step forward, only to find myself slithering back towards the bottom of the slope. Desperate to stop myself, I lunged out with my left hand. At first, I felt nothing but mud between my fingers; then I came into contact with an exposed plant root. I grabbed it, but my fingers were too cold to hang on. I shot down the slope as if it were sheet ice, landing in a heap at Sean's feet.

Wearily, I started the climb again by digging in the tips of my fingers and pulling myself up a few yards. Then my feet gained a little purchase on some stones and I was able to make more progress. But it was hard work, and I was soon racked by doubt. The route seemed madness to me, but – and this was the real source of my disquiet – the others appeared happy with it. If there was a problem, I convinced myself, I would have heard about it. I was forced to conclude that I was the only bloke who was in any difficulty here. And since I was sure that I'd still be stuck on this mud slide come daybreak, I felt that the only option open to me was to turn back, to take my chances with the Serbs, Blakey and the rest of them. To do anything else would be to risk bringing the whole escape party down with me.

It was best, I told myself, if I simply let go.

My brain was still coming to terms with this decision when I heard a sharp noise beside me: the reedy, suppressed cough of someone in pain. I lifted my cheek from the mud and turned. Through the gloom, I was dimly aware of a shape hugging the slope a few feet away. My initial impression was that it was lifeless, but then I caught a movement, a motion that was almost mechanical: the rhythmic swish of something cutting the air, the squelch of mud, then the scything movement again.

I caught a glint of metal. Only then did I realise that it was Craig. He was stuck in the mud, belly-down, hanging on with his good arm and clawing desperately with the metal frame of the other in an attempt to force his way up the hillside. Every so often, in the distant flash of a shell explosion, the dim light reflected off the contraption that held his arm together.

Somehow I managed to find the strength to manoeuvre myself on to the ground above him. I reached down, grabbed a handful of combat jacket and pulled as hard as I could.

'Come on, mate,' I offered, not quite sure who I was trying to convince, 'we'll make it.'

But he was like a dead weight. I hauled him up a few feet, but then, sickeningly, I felt us both sliding back again. Had it not been for Phil, who suddenly appeared from nowhere and grabbed us both, we'd have tumbled backwards into the night.

We could make little headway, however. It was all Phil and I could do just to hold Craig there. Again, my mind filled with the idea of turning back. If this was how I felt after an hour of breaking out, how on earth was I going to survive another six? Had it not been for Craig's courage – and the knowledge that his grit in the face of this obstacle was putting me to shame – my doubts would have got the better of me. What sealed it was a quip from Simon as he joined Phil and me and tried to haul the injured man up the slope.

''Ere, Nick, I don't know about you, mate, but I'm breathing through my arse.'

To know that the SAS were feeling the same pain was a powerful tonic. I determined then to plough on for as long as they did.

The moment of truth came sooner than any of us had imagined. Suddenly, there was a muffled cry of rage followed a split second later by a blur on the edge of my vision as Sean powered up the hill towards Lloyd Jones and Ahmed. As the rest of us lay panting in the mud, I could hear an intense argument going on in the dark a few metres above us. Several minutes later, when we finally caught up with them, we found Sean, Adrian, Ant and Ahmed in another huddle.

I could only guess at the monumental bollocking that Sean, the senior NCO, had given his immediate superior, but Lloyd Jones' voice, when he addressed us, sounded suitably chastened.

'I'm sorry, guys,' he whispered, 'but we're not going any further this way. We're going to take an easier route.'

Forty-five minutes after we had started to climb it, we had progressed barely 200 yards up the hill.

It was 11.42. Eighteen minutes to midnight. Five hours and eight minutes until the helicopter touched down at the landing site. Now I shared Sean's anger over the time we had wasted in the interests of sticking to the shortest possible route.

Maintaining the same height level, we headed left and started to work our way around the hill until we moved back on to our north-west bearing. Hugging one contour line made our passage much easier; a blessing, but one that immediately prompted a fresh raft of concerns: where were the Muslim positions? And how far to the Serb lines?

I was still on alert fifteen minutes later when I realised I'd lost sight of Craig. In open terrain, it had been possible – just – to maintain a visual bead on the guy in front, as long as you didn't drop more than ten paces behind him. I had grown used to the sight of Craig's back, but now it had vanished. Before there was time for the panic to rise, I heard the rustle of something or someone moving at speed through vegetation to my left, followed immediately by the sound of branches snapping. And then my feet slipped from under me and I was tumbling down a steep, slippery bank. Leaves and branches lashed at my face and shrubs cracked and broke under my weight. But no sooner had I braced myself for a drop through space than I hit something soft and heard a muffled cry of pain as I relocated Craig. It turned out that the entire group had slipped down the side of a 20ft bank and we were all now piled one upon the other in an undignified heap.

In the silent aftermath of this incident, just before everyone started to pick themselves up again, I heard the trickle of water nearby. We had ended up by a small stream.

A few yards away, the red light of Adrian's torch played over his map. A three-way discussion ensued among the three nav gurus over where this stream was and whether it could be exploited in our journey to the LSRV.

Having found it on the map and traced its path upstream,

Adrian, Simon and Ahmed agreed it would be useful to track it for a while, even though, at one point, it did pass dangerously close to the Muslim positions. The advantage of following the stream was that it took us along relatively level ground, allowing us to make up for the time we had lost on the hill.

By my estimation, we were now only five or ten minutes' walk from our first encounter with the Muslims.

We set off again, sticking to the right of the stream. The seconds ticked into minutes as I combed the shadows restlessly with the barrel of my rifle, wondering where the first shot would come from.

A succession of alarming thoughts ploughed through my head, but the one to which I always came back was the notion that right now, this very second, I was caught in the cross-hairs of a sniper's infra-red sights. Yet as we forged on, it seemed as if the countryside itself was dead; the silence so overwhelming that I found it hard to believe anyone could be watching us.

Where was everybody?

The tension broke only when we turned hard right, striking northwards up the hillside again. This time, fortunately, the slope was gradual, and we made good progress.

The mystery of the missing Muslim position did not become clear until ten minutes or so later, when we crested the ridge and saw the outline of a house. A few paces further on, more houses drifted into view. Somewhere in the distance a dog barked and quickly fell silent again. Something about the picture wasn't right.

And then we smelled it, the pungent odour of carbon. By the time we reached the perimeter of the village, it was clear that the entire settlement had been torched by the Serbs.

I had seen reports on the TV about ethnic cleansing, but had never imagined I would see it at this close range.

As we left the village behind, the smell of burning receded and a new realisation dawned. We had just crossed the new frontier between the Muslim and Serb positions. I checked my watch. It was 1.15am. We had three hours, forty-five minutes remaining on the clock and 8km to go.

It was achievable, provided we just kept moving.

*

The road petered into a path with a long, patchy hedgerow running beside it. The first sign of trouble was the sound of voices, but for a couple of seconds I didn't associate it with any kind of threat. I thought it was just Adrian and Ahmed arguing again over the route.

Then I heard the warnings coming down the line, low, urgent whistles – *fshht, fshht, fshht* – passed from one man to the next, and I knew we had a problem.

I was just wondering what the fuck to do when I saw Craig hurl himself over the hedge. I dived after him and landed with an uncomfortable thud on the rock-hard soil on the other side. How the hell did this man, who had seemed at death's door barely hours earlier, keep a lid on his pain?

I switched my attention back to the voices coming down the track. We had made so much noise crashing over the hedge that I found it hard to believe they hadn't heard us. But their discussion continued, growing louder by the moment. I saw them now, three silhouettes about 60 yards away, gun barrels clearly visible over their shoulders.

With the worst possible timing, the moon had reappeared from behind its cloud cover, casting what felt like a spotlight on our field. Picked out on the ground between me and the approaching soldiers were the first six members of the patrol, lying prone, their rifles trained into the hedge. All it would take was for one of the Serbs, if that's what they were, to look through the hedge, and they would see us.

If it came to a fight, I knew we had the edge, but it would put paid to all our escape plans. A gun battle here, in the ethnically cleansed wasteland we had just pushed through, would bring every Serb this side of Gorazde down on us at the speed of heat.

Ever so slowly, I lowered my right eye to the night-sight and peered through. I expected to see night turned into day, but the result was so piss-poor, I gave up. I just pointed the barrel and hoped for the best. There was a soft double click to my right as Phil cocked his weapon.

From my training briefs on the SA-80, I remembered that the gun was meant to be cocked quickly to ensure that the round moved nice and sweetly into the chamber. Anything less, and it had a tendency to jam. With the soldiers almost on top of us, I pulled the bolt back as quietly as I could and prayed that the thing had primed properly. And then I prayed I wouldn't have to pull the trigger at all.

I gritted my teeth and waited.

I saw three pairs of feet making their way along their path. The first was 20 yards away; less, maybe. Bang opposite the middle men of our group, Ant and Phil. I don't understand a word of Serbo-Croat, but there was an arrogance to the tone of the voices, a confidence, that to me made it abundantly clear that they were Serbs, not Muslims.

The feet kept coming. The conversation had stopped now. All I could hear was the traipse of boots on the wet, gravelly path and the light chink of metal as buckles and ammo clips chafed against other items of equipment.

And then the man at the back stopped.

I held my breath and kept my gaze fixed on his feet. They were about a yard and a half from my face. The toes of his boots were angled my way. I waited for him to unsling his rifle or rasp a command to his colleagues, but instead he hawked some phlegm from the back of his throat and spat it over the hedge. It landed with a clearly audible plop between me and Craig.

Ten minutes after the soldiers had disappeared, there was a rustle of movement to my left. Then Sean appeared and whispered that it was all right to get up and on our way again. He tapped me on the shoulder. 'That was a close one, eh, mate?'

Like it was all in a day's fucking work.

When I told him I'd had trouble with the night-sight, he took my rifle, had a squint down the barrel and whispered, 'Helps if you switch it on,' before passing it back to me.

There was no group confab before we saddled up and moved out again. We simply stuck to the right-hand side of the hedge and kept moving. We were now well into the north-west passageway leading out of Gorazde, with Serb lines either side of us. Before we'd left the bank, Ahmed had said there were still a number of islands of Muslim resistance in this sector, but the burned-out village had clearly taken him by surprise and I began to wonder if there were any Muslim troops at all this far from the town. In any event, the north-west corridor wasn't limitless: sooner or later we knew we would run into the end of the pocket, the main line of the Serb advance. Given the uncertainties of the tactical situation, I prayed that the helicopter landing site had not been overtaken by the Serb front line.

We pressed on and were soon plunged into darkness again as we continued to work our way around the hill and the moon slipped below the ridgeline. Presently we came to a fork in the trail. We took what we assumed was the continuation of the path we were on, the right-hand track, and kept going. For the next hour, we followed this trail, knowing that it would take us almost directly to the LSRV, because this was how it was shown on the map.

In retrospect, having Ahmed lead the group at this point was a mistake. The kid was out of his depth. The last time he'd strayed this distance from the town had been in the dim and distant past, long before the siege. And at night a landscape can look completely different anyway.

At close to four o'clock, when we should have been within sight of the LSRV but clearly weren't, Adrian called the party to a halt. As we all closed up, we found the boss in the middle of yet another heated discussion with Ahmed and Simon about the route. With one hour to go before the helicopter touched down, I was hearing things that made my blood run cold.

'How the hell did we come to be on this track?' Lloyd Jones was saying, his voice hissing with anger. 'It's pointing the wrong fucking way. It's heading north and the LSRV is to the south of here. Christ, maybe four, five klicks to the south.'

Ahmed said nothing. With his modest grasp of English, saying anything meaningful was probably beyond him, and it was academic now, anyway.

'Simon, why the fuck didn't the GPS give us some warning of this?'

With commendable courage, Simon told him the truth. 'Because I stuck it in my pocket, boss. I thought Ahmed knew what he was doing. It was my fuck-up. I'm sorry.'

No one said anything.

After the elation we'd felt after our close shave with the Serbs on the trail, a terrible realisation began to dawn on me. This thing was slipping away from us. It was now touch and go whether we'd make it to the LSRV.

But when he spoke again, Lloyd Jones had regained his composure. 'There's no point back-tracking,' he said. 'We don't have time to go back and pick up the original track. If we're going to make the RV, we're going to have to move cross-country. Sooner or later, we'll intercept the track and get back on course. Everyone agreed?'

We all made as if to move, but a voice called us back.

'I don't know, boss,' Sean said, sucking his teeth. 'Think about it. The faster we move, especially over unknown terrain, the more we expose ourselves to ambush.'

'What are you saying?' Adrian asked him.

'Maybe we should hole up for the night,' the experienced NCO told him. 'Maybe we should build a fucking LUP here, now, and then do the whole thing again tomorrow night.'

A hush fell on the group. I couldn't believe what I was hearing. An hour ago, we had been on track to make the LSRV and freedom. Now, with this talk of establishing a lying-up position, a type of hide I knew the SAS were past masters at constructing, all of that was being pulled from under our feet.

I couldn't stand the thought of another minute in that place; the prospect of twenty-four hours there made me want to put a bullet through my brain.

'I think we should keep the LUP as an option, but still make a go of it,' Lloyd Jones told him after a moment's thought. 'Anyone else disagrees, now's the time to say it.'

There was no dissent, so we picked ourselves up, cut left and headed south.

Simon, this time with the sat-nav firmly in his grasp, led the way, with Ahmed behind him, the rest of the orbat otherwise unchanged. What had started as a brisk walk now became a half-run, and before long I had worked myself into a muck sweat.

We negotiated a series of low hills and narrow valleys at the same unrelenting pace and soon intercepted the original path.

Twice Craig fell, and twice I crashed into him in the darkness. But on neither occasion did the injured officer say a word. With the ground this wet, it was often easier to climb than to descend, and it was usually on the descent that we lost our footing and the procession turned to rat shit.

Down or up, it all amounted to the same thing: pain and exhaustion to the point where our legs and lungs burned with the effort.

One thing forced me on: the thought of hearing the helicopter before we made it to the LSRV. We were so close now; around a kilometre, I estimated, from the pick-up point. We had made up spectacularly for our earlier mistake, covering almost 3km in twenty minutes. The question was, would it be enough?

At 0440 we hit the crest of another small hill and saw the valley in which the LSRV was nested stretching out before us. We ploughed on for another few hundred metres, but quickly found ourselves in dense wooded terrain, with trees ranged either side of us as far as the eye could see. We stopped and took stock. Around me, I could hear the sound of men catching their breath, a last respite before the final dash to the field that Sarajevo had earmarked for our extraction.

We had twenty minutes left on the clock. To me, it was just enough. But I hadn't counted on the SAS's overdeveloped sense for unacceptable risk. Unbeknown to me, Adrian had already made up his mind: we did not have enough time to carry out a recce of the LSRV, and without that, he could not sanction the extraction. The first I knew about this was when he jogged over to where I was bent double, catching my breath, and yanked me upright.

'I want you and Simon to comb this area for an alternative RV. We're not going to make it to the designated landing area. We're out of time, Nick. If we're still going to make it, we're going to have to grab the initiative here.'

'But the helicopter . . .' I protested. 'It could break cover at any moment.'

'You leave us to worry about that,' he said. 'You know what it takes to land a Puma or a Chinook in country like this, so find somewhere close. But for fuck's sake, do it quickly.'

*

Simon and I spread out, but keeping within sight of each other. Faced with so many trees, and with the ticking of the clock in my ear, panic seeped into my thinking. For much of the break-out I'd been a passenger, but now it was all down to me and Simon; that, anyway, was how it felt. All I could see was this damned wood; and in a little more than fifteen minutes the helicopter would be on top of us – or, rather, it wouldn't. It would be the best part of a kilometre away, with us nowhere in sight. The boat was about to sail and we were on the wrong fucking jetty.

I forced myself on. From my brief glimpse of the valley as we'd crested the last ridge I knew we were in a bowl, with the trees extending much of the way up the hillside towards the nearest peak. It seemed a waste of time looking for a landing zone on the upper slopes, and, in any case, the angle of incline was probably too steep for a helicopter to land. That left something lower down, towards the valley floor, as our only hope.

I cut a couple of hundred yards to the south and Simon followed me. We were committing all our resources to one area, but I guess he was thinking along the same lines. Or maybe he just didn't trust me bumbling around on my own. If there were Serbs an hour down the track, there were more than likely Serbs here, too.

I came round the southernmost edge of the wood and saw a field dotted with trees. It was better than the wood, but still quite unsuitable as a landing zone. At the end of the field, 150 yards away, was a hedge. Six minutes had elapsed since I'd left the main group. The helo would be here at any moment. I ran down to the end of the field and peered over the hedge.

The clearing on the other side was about 100 yards square. Size-wise, it was feasible. The problem was, it was on a slope. The gradient ran east–west, left to right, at an angle of around 10 degrees.

Simon pitched up and gave it the once-over.

'Shit,' he whispered, the disappointment in his voice verging on despair. 'He's never going to be able to touch down on that.'

'He doesn't have to,' I told Simon. 'He can hover with one wheel on. The rest of him can hang in the air.'

'But his rotor blades are going to hit the fucking ground.'

'No, they're not. It's close, but if he's any good, he'll make it.'

If it had been me, I'd have had a crack at it. But I wasn't the one sitting in a helicopter with NVGs strapped to my face, waiting for an SA-16 surface-to-air missile to fly from its launcher and latch on to my engine exhausts. Down here it was easy to be judgemental.

'Is that going to be good enough for the boss?' the SAS man asked.

'It's fucking well going to have to be. Look at the time. Beggars can't be choosers. This is the place. Let's go and tell the others.'

We found them close to where we had left them, huddling for cover behind a belt of low bushes. I told Adrian the score and he didn't hesitate. We all ran for it.

A minute later, we were rounding the edge of the wood, making for the spot, when a flickering light on the horizon caught my eye.

'What's that?' I asked Adrian.

He continued to study it as we jogged towards the hedge. 'It's the Serbs,' he said. 'They're burning their way through. They must have encountered some resistance up there. It means we're going to have to get out of here tonight. Come tomorrow, they're going to be all over this place.'

We hopped over the hedge and into the field. I looked at my watch. There were three minutes to go.

Now we had to listen for the helicopter and alert the pilot to the change of LSRV the moment we heard it. Both Simon and I had search-and-rescue radios, which were set to different frequencies to maximise the chance of one of us being heard by the helo pilot.

The seconds ticked down to five o'clock. All of us strained for the sound of engines and rotor blades.

But all we heard was the regular beat of explosions from Gorazde and the occasional crack of small-arms fire on the ridgeline.

At 5.10am, there was still no sign of the helicopter. It was so late, I couldn't help but think of the worst-case scenario. What if it had been shot down? What were our choices? We couldn't return to Gorazde – the Muslims would kill us, and that was before the Serbs finally overran the place. Nor could we stay here. I was wondering what that left when Adrian cursed under his breath and stood up. It was now 5.15.

'This is a load of crap,' he said. 'Simon, rig up the sat-net. I'm going to call Sarajevo.'

Simon slipped his Bergen off his back and started to unpack the radio, which was big, about the size of an impressive-looking stereo deck. Ant, meanwhile, set about assembling the antenna.

It took around fifteen minutes to set the thing up. The antenna, which screwed together like a tent pole, was about 25ft high. Normally held in place by guy ropes, it was now angled skyward by Phil and Ant as Simon prepared the radio.

Simon told Adrian that we might have only one shot at this. As a weight-saving measure, all the spare batteries had been left at the bank. The batteries in the sat-nav had been charged, but there was no way of telling how much juice was left in them. Sarajevo was 80km away as the crow flew and separated from us by high terrain. The only way we'd know for sure if the set had enough power to reach General Rose's headquarters was when – if – we got an answer back.

We watched over Simon's shoulder as he threw the switch.

A dim glow issued from the display panel. Simon looked up and nodded to the boss. Adrian took the handset and crouched low, cupping his hand over his mouth to shield his voice.

'Sunray, this is Alpha Two-One, over.'

Even though he held the handset close, I could hear the static crackling through the earpiece.

Nothing.

'Sunray, this is Alpha Two-One, over.'

It could almost have been a faint echo on the ether, but this time I heard: 'Alpha Two-One, this is Sunray, over.'

The voice on the other end sounded too casual for my liking. In my book, Adrian would have been well within his rights to have gone ballistic over the missing helicopter. But he didn't. He simply passed over the details of the new landing site.

'Alpha Two-One did not make original RV. Stand by to copy grid reference of new RV, over.'

Simon, who had already written it down, handed it to him.

'Helicopter required at grid reference four, three, five, seven, eight, two. Repeat, four, three, five, seven, eight, two. Over.'

Again, the faint echo back: 'Roger, Alpha Two-One, helicopter on its way, over.'

Adrian passed the handset back to Simon, who hung up.

I broke the stunned silence. 'What the fuck does that mean, "on its way"? The guy made it sound like he'd been waiting for us to call him. But that wasn't the arrangement. The helicopter was supposed to be here thirty minutes ago.'

Adrian was keeping his feelings in check. Or maybe he was always this cool under pressure. 'The important thing is it's on its way. Sarajevo's thirty minutes' flight time from here, if that. All we have to do now is sit tight and wait.'

I was still fuming. It wasn't over yet. We had the Serbs up in the hills a stone's throw from us and now a new enemy. In thirty minutes' time it would start to get light. As an ex-helo pilot myself, I wouldn't have risked a mission deep into hostile territory with the light coming up. When you're strapped into a machine that lumbers along at a top speed of 140 knots, darkness is the only thing between you and the enemy. If the helicopter wasn't here by 0600 hours, I knew it wouldn't be coming at all.

I wandered a few yards away from the group, leaving a flurry of activity behind me as Simon and Ant derigged the sat-net.

As I raised my eyes, I thought I saw the first light of dawn behind the ridgeline, but it was only the fires started by the Serbs; they were now raging out of control. I heard someone beside me, turned and saw Adrian. We both watched the fires in silence for a few minutes. My composure had returned, and with it, I saw things with a new clarity.

'They never sent the helicopter because they thought we weren't going to make it. That's the God's honest truth, isn't it, Adrian?'

He almost said something, but thought better of it and turned to join the rest of the group.

Adrian was right about one thing. There was nothing we could do but wait.

To minimise our chances of being spotted, we grouped ourselves in a small circle in the north-west corner of the field. And there we sat, our would-be landing site framed by the flames on the ridgeline and the intermittent shellfire that was still pummelling Gorazde. No one said anything. There was nothing left to say. All we could do was sit there and pray that the chopper turned up.

After another fifteen minutes, Adrian told Simon to make the final arrangements. The FAC, who had been sitting beside me, grabbed a handful of landing site markers and ran in a half-crouch towards the middle of the field. There he laid them out in a standard pattern to show the helo search-and-rescue pilot where to land and the angle of approach he should use.

Something on the ground next to me caught my eye. It was Simon's map and penlight. Ever since we had seen the fires, something dark and disturbing had been tugging at my thoughts, but I had been too busy to ponder what or why. Now the feeling swept over me again. Shielding the dull, red glow of the torch with my hand, I shone the penlight over the map, which was folded to display our sector. A quick glance and I located the field we were in and then the ridgeline above it.

Even before I read the name of the village that was being torched by the Serbs in front of our very eyes, I knew that it would be Beric.

My despair as I thought of Oskar, Admira and Makhmud was interrupted by the sound of a dull, low-frequency thud. I was still trying to get a bearing on it when the Puma broke cover between two hills on the other side of the valley. The pilot must have picked up the markers straight away, because the helicopter immediately veered towards us.

With its lights off, the Puma steadied and went into a hover. I saw it now as an indistinct outline against the stars, above and to the right of our position. It stayed there for ten seconds, then twenty. The downwash made my eyes smart. Beside me, Simon was yelling information on the angle and direction of slope into his radio.

'Come on, guys!' I found myself shouting over the howl of wind rush, engines, rotors and gears. 'You can do this!'

The helicopter began its final descent towards the ground. Even now, I was assailed by a battery of last-second doubts. Maybe Simon had been right. Maybe the incline was too steep. I could have sworn I could hear the tramp of feet as the Serbs, by now clued up as to what was going on, charged down the hillside towards us.

The Puma's nose gear touched the ground. Then, like a reluctant swimmer dipping a toe into ice-cold water, it pulled back up again.

We stayed in our huddle like frightened rabbits, trapped in the vortex of the sound footprint.

The helicopter seemed to take an age to set back towards the ground. But this time its nose wheels touched the slope and stayed there.

There is a standard procedure in a situation like this. Never run towards a helicopter during a night RV, as the rules say you'll get blown away by a burst of 7.62 from the gunner. You wait for one of the crew to come to you and carry out a positive identification before leading you back to the aircraft.

But no one came. The helo just hung there in its semi-hover, 30 yards from us. Freedom was so close, and yet we couldn't do a damned thing to reach out and grasp it.

A minute passed. And then for one of the group it became too much.

There was a flurry of movement close by as someone – I never did find out who – picked himself up and ran towards the Puma.

I tensed in expectation of a volley of shots, but they never came. Instead the individual was hauled in through the open cabin door by the scruff of his jacket.

From that instant, the rest of us needed no encouragement. We all got up and sprinted for the cabin door, crowding by the wheel as, one by one, we waited to get inside.

Craig and I were the last two on the ground. It seemed to take for ever to manhandle his dead weight on to the cabin floor. When we finally managed it, I grabbed the door frame and readied myself for one last effort. But before I could pull myself up, the Puma shot skyward and I stumbled backwards on to the ground.

The next thing I knew, I was staring at the belly of the helicopter and it was 50ft up. I started waving and shouting, but it made no difference. The helicopter continued to climb.

I braced myself for the moment when it nosed towards Sarajevo, but somebody must have done a head count, because slowly it stopped ascending and lowered towards the ground again.

The Puma was still 8ft off the ground when I jumped for it. Four pairs of hands reached down and caught me. And then they pulled me aboard.

I looked up and saw seven familiar faces outlined in the muted glow of the cabin lighting. There was a surge of power from the twin turboshaft engines in the roof and then a lurch as the helicopter banked towards the south.

And then we were cheering, all of us, at the top of our voices.

At long last, I was going home.

# EPILOGUE

As soon as the helicopter touched down in Sarajevo, every-thing seemed to happen at once. I was taken to see General Rose and we had a frank exchange of views over the way the oper-ation had been handled. As well as being a tough son of a bitch, Rose is a consummate diplomat and I sensed rather than heard his anger and frustration at how he had been prevented from han-dling Gorazde the way he'd have liked by the bureaucrats at the UN. It was Rose, too, who in a funny kind of way set me wonder-ing about my own role in the proceedings with the deadpan line: 'Five out of ten for results, Nick, but ten out of ten for effort.'

For the next few hours, however, I had no time to get overly bogged down in a rerun of my bombing mission over Gorazde or the reasons for the shoot-down. That would come later, when I was back on board ship.

Before flying out of Sarajevo to Split, where I was due to pick up a Royal Navy Sea King flight bound for the carrier, I went and paid my respects to the helicopter crew that had got us out of the pocket.

I thought the UK had some good special forces pilots, but the way the French Puma team plucked us out of the danger zone was a testament to their bravery and professionalism. The flight from Gorazde to Sarajevo, conducted at impossibly low altitude, had been exciting, though danger-free – or so I thought.

While we waited for the helicopter ride to Split, the SAS and I were shown around the Puma by its crew. To our surprise, the tail boom and fuselage had been peppered with small-arms fire and we'd not even noticed – possibly owing to all the celebrating that had been going on inside the cabin at the time. We were lucky, the French pilot told us, as he sucked casually on a Gauloise, not to have been shot down.

Soon afterwards, we boarded a Royal Navy Sea King Commando bound for Split, accompanied by Fergie's coffin. Adrian Lloyd Jones and co. were headed back that evening to Hereford to bury their mate, the only member of the patrol not to have made it out. In the sombre mood that prevailed as we parted company, there were no smiles or self-congratulatory words. We simply shook hands and turned towards where our respective aircraft were waiting.

On the 820 Squadron ASW Sea King that had been sent from the *Ark* to fetch me was a familiar face: Oz Phillips. Since he'd pissed off and left me in-theatre, he told me with a grin, it seemed only right that he should be the one who came and got me out. We marked my return to ship with a radio message to Flyco using my old call sign, Vixen Two-Three. About fucking time; what kept you, came the response.

After I'd called home and celebrated with the boys in the ward-room long into the night, I awoke the next morning to the doubts that had first tugged at me on touchdown in Sarajevo. Why had I gone round so many times over the target? How had I allowed myself to deviate so much from the rule book that forbids such practice?

Fortunately, the Navy doesn't allow you too much time for self-analysis. I got back on to the ship on Monday night and by Wednesday, I was in the air again with Oz, the pair of us flying as Vixens Two-Three and Two-Four on a CAS mission. The only difference this time was that it was Mostar, not Gorazde, below us – and neither of us managed to get shot down.

As I looked down on the Balkan hinterland, I wondered how I would react if I were called upon to bomb a couple of Serb T-55s all over again. Being in Gorazde had allowed me to see at first hand what conflict on the ground is like – a perspective that is rare for the modern combat pilot, sitting at heights in excess of 10,000ft and armed as he is with increasingly smart stand-off weapons.

I had seen the effects of high explosive close-up and had known the terror of a relentless artillery bombardment. I knew what it was like to be on the receiving end. With all the ordnance the enemy is throwing at you in the combat zone, it is easy to forget the effects of your own weapons as they hit the ground. Modern air warfare is about placing the cross-hairs of an electro-optical sighting system over the target and holding it there while a smart weapon flies unerringly down a beam and detonates at the centre of your TV screen. It doesn't seem real, but it is. I know that now. All too well.

Part of me was glad that I hadn't released my bombs that day. As a member of a fighting alliance, I knew that what I had been asked to do that day was right. But as a human being, I'm glad that my scorecard is still a clean sheet.

A week later, a very special delegation was flown on to *Ark Royal* from Bari in Italy. After returning Fergie's body to Hereford, Adrian Lloyd Jones' SAS patrol repaired to the Balkans again. Before they got there, Terry Loughran, the *Ark's* captain, intercepted them and invited them on to the ship for a meal and a drink or two to express the Navy's thanks for getting me home. It turned out, of course, to be quite a night. Everyone who had been in Gorazde had their own story to tell.

It was while listening to Simon the FAC's quiet, understated account of my attack on the T-55s that I understood why I had conducted myself in the way I had. It doesn't matter what the rule book says; how you're supposed to fly over a target quickly and either bomb it on the first pass or get out of there. When it's your troops who are on the ground, when there's someone there crying out for help in your own language, the rule book goes out of the window. If I'd been asked to do it again, I wouldn't have acted differently. Ask any pilot in the same situation and I expect he'll say much the same thing. In a world of push-button warfare, I find that strangely reassuring.

Fortunately, all Sea Harrier FRS1s have been upgraded since 1994 to FA2 standard. The Sea Harrier is now a very different machine, with a superb radar, and the glitch that stopped me getting an ASB3 lock on that T-55 has never recurred. With the FA2, the Royal Navy can at last compete with the best of the best – including the very latest versions of the MiG-29.

The morning after the shindig with the SAS on *Ark Royal*, I got up, feeling very much the worse for wear, and wandered into the dining room for breakfast. All the SAS patrol members had already had their fill of bacon, eggs and coffee and were up on deck awaiting the departure of the Sea King that would take them back to Split and into the uncertain crucible of Bosnian operations. All, that is, except Sean, whom I happened to bump into on his way out of the feeder.

I asked him how he and his mates were able to function after benders like the one we'd been on the night before and he responded with an answer that I'm still pondering to this day.

'Hey, Nick, you know what they say. First up, best dressed.'

It was an enigmatic end to a surreal encounter. There are days still, when I have to pinch myself and ask whether it happened at all.

I remain in touch with a couple of the lads and occasionally we get together to shoot the shit. Most of them are either still in the SAS or back with their parent regiments. Situation normal, as they say in Hereford. Since then, there has been another war in the Balkans and I would be gobsmacked if some of the guys who made the trek out of Gorazde with me hadn't been involved in Kosovo or its aftermath. They don't talk about it, so I don't ask. But if I were a Serbian war criminal, knowing what I know now, I'd be shitting myself.

As for the guys on the squadron, almost all of them are still flying fast jets in some capacity or another. The exception is Mel Robinson, the boss, who, having been awarded an MBE for his stewardship of 801 Naval Air Squadron, and after gaining promotion to commander, did a short stint at the MoD and then left to join the airlines.

It's from here on in that the postscript becomes a little vague. In spite of the Serbs' final push, ten days after we made our break for it, the inhabitants of Gorazde were rewarded for their epic defence of their town by the Serbs' agreement to meet a UN deadline for the withdrawal of their heavy guns from the surrounding hills. Shortly after that, the first UN relief convoys rolled in and the killing finally ended. But it would be another year and a half before peace came to Bosnia as a whole.

Some time after my return to England, I was watching the TV and happened to see Mary being interviewed in Sarajevo's sports stadium on the BBC News. It was a good moment. I figured if she'd made it out, then the other UNMOs and medics had too, and there was every hope that Misha and his family had survived.

As for Ahmed, I never did hear what happened to him. I hope he's still out there somewhere.

When I wake in the small hours and think about my time on the ground behind enemy lines, my thoughts always drift to Oskar, Admira and their young son. I'm afraid to ask about Beric, their village, for fear of what the truth may hold. But I know I am only putting off the inevitable. One day I'll go back and find out for myself. I feel after everything that happened there, it is the very least I can do.